Sexology in Culture

Sexology in Culture

Labelling Bodies and Desires

Edited by Lucy Bland and Laura Doan

The University of Chicago Press

LUCY BLAND is senior lecturer in Women' Studies, University of North London. She publishes extensively on the history of sexuality. Her most recent book, *Banishing the Beast: English Feminism and Sexual Morality, 1885–1915*, was published in 1994.

LAURA DOAN is professor of English at the State University of New York, Geneseo. She is the editor of *The Lesbian Postmodern* (1994) and *Old Maids to Radical Spinsters* (1991).

The University of Chicago Press, Chicago 60637
Polity Press, Cambridge CB2 1UR, UK
First published in 1998 by Polity Press in association with
Blackwell Publishers Ltd.
© Polity Press 1998
All rights reserved. Published 1998
Chapter 4 © 1994 The University of Chicago. First published as "Scientific Racism and the Emergence of the Homosexual Body" in the *Journal of the History of Sexuality* 5.2 (October 1994): 254–66, The University of Chicago

07 06 05 04 03 02 01 00 99 98   1 2 3 4 5 6

ISBN: 0-226-05665-1 (cloth)
ISBN: 0-226-05667-8 (paper)

Library of Congress Cataloging-in-Publication Data

Sexology in culture : labelling bodies and desires / Lucy Bland and
    Laura Doan, co-editors.
        p.   cm.
    Companion volume to: Sexology uncensored.
    Includes index.
    ISBN 0-226-05665-1 (cloth : alk. paper). — ISBN 0-226-05667-8
(pbk. : alk. paper)
    1. Sexology—History.   I. Bland, Lucy.   II. Doan, Laura L., 1951– .

HQ60.S496   1998
306.7'09—dc21   98-16625
                                                           CIP

This book is printed on acid-free paper.

Contents

Contributors

Lucy Bland is Senior Lecturer in Women's Studies at the University of North London. She is author of *Banishing the Beast* (Penguin and New Press, 1995). She is co-editor, with Laura Doan, of *Sexology Uncensored: The Documents of Sexual Science* (Polity Press, 1998), a companion volume to this present collection. She is currently working on sexuality and race in interwar Britain.

Joseph Bristow is Professor of English at the University of California, Los Angeles. His recent books include *Effeminate England: Homoerotic Writing after 1885* (Open University Press, 1995) and *Sexuality* (Routledge, 1997). At present, he is completing a full-length study, provisionally titled 'The Sex of Victorian Poetry', and a collection of essays on Englishness and perversity.

Carolyn Burdett is Senior Lecturer in the School of Literary and Media Studies at the University of North London. She teaches in the field of nineteenth-century literature, culture and science, and feminist theory. Her book *Olive Schreiner and the Progress of Feminism: Evolution, Sexuality and the Nation* is forthcoming from Macmillan.

Jane Caplan is Marjorie Walter Goodhart Professor of European History at Bryn Mawr College. Her article '"Speaking Scars": The Tattoo in Popular Practice and Medico-Legal Debate in 19th-century Europe' appeared in *History Workshop Journal* (Autumn 1997). She is currently editing two books of essays, on the history of the tattoo in the West since antiquity, and (with John Torpey) on the history of identity documents.

Laura Doan is Professor of English at the State University of New York, Geneseo. She has edited *The Lesbian Postmodern* (Columbia University Press, 1994), and co-edited with Lucy Bland *Sexology Uncensored: The Documents of Sexual Science* (Polity Press, 1998). She is currently working on *Fashioning Sapphism: The Origins of a Modern English Lesbian Culture*.

Rita Felski is Professor of English at the University of Virginia. She is the author of *Beyond Feminist Aesthetics* (1989) and *The Gender of Modernity*, (1995), both published by Harvard University Press, and of a forthcoming collection of essays entitled *Doing Time*.

Judy Greenway is Senior Lecturer in the Cultural Studies Department at the University of East London, where her teaching includes utopian studies and lesbian and gay cultures. She is currently researching and writing on anarchism, gender and sexuality in Britain from 1880, and working towards a book on practical utopianism.

Lesley A. Hall is Senior Assistant Archivist at the Contemporary Medical Archives Centre, Wellcome Institute for the History of Medicine, London. Her publications include *Hidden Anxieties: Male Sexuality 1900–1950* (Polity Press, 1991), and (with Roy Porter) *The Facts of Life: The Creation of Sexual Knowledge in Britain, 1650–1950* (Yale University Press, 1995), and numerous articles and reviews. She is currently co-editing two volumes on sexual cultures in Europe, and working on a biography of Stella Browne.

Alison Oram is Principal Lecturer in Women's Studies at Nene University College, Northampton. A historian, she has published works on women's politicization, citizenship and sexuality in the context of twentieth-century feminism, and on lesbian history. Recent publications include *Women Teachers and Feminist Politics 1900-39* (Manchester University Press, 1996). She is currently working on a sourcebook of British lesbian history in the nineteenth and twentieth centuries for Routledge (forthcoming).

Jay Prosser is Lecturer in English and American Studies at the University of Leicester. His book, *Second Skins: The Body Narratives of Transsexuality*, is published by Columbia University Press (1998).

Suzanne Raitt is Associate Professor of English and Women's Studies at the University of Michigan. She is author of *Vita and Virginia: The Work and Friendship of V. Sackville-West and Virginia Woolf* (Oxford University Press, 1993) and a number of articles on modernist women writers. She is currently working on a book on May Sinclair.

Siobhan B. Somerville is Assistant Professor of English and Women's Studies at Purdue University. Her forthcoming book, to be published by Duke University Press, explores the intersections of racial and sexual discourses in fiction, film and sexology in late nineteenth- and early twentieth-century American culture. Her work has also appeared in journals such as *American Literature* and the *Journal of the History of Sexuality*.

Merl Storr lectures in Sociology at the University of East London. She has published a number of articles on sexuality and sexual identity. She is co-editor of *The Bisexual Imaginary* (Cassell, 1997) and editor of a *Bisexuality Reader* (Routledge, forthcoming). Her current research is on the interface between sexuality and economics.

Chris Waters is Associate Professor of History at Williams College. He is author of *British Socialists and the Politics of Popular Culture, 1884–1914* (Manchester University Press and Stanford University Press, 1990) and co-editor of *Moments of Modernity: Reconstructing Britain 1945–1964* (forthcoming). He is currently at work on a book-length study of the development of Freudian thought pertaining to homosexuality in twentieth-century Britain.

Editors' Note

Many of the writings of individual sexologists or other primary materials which are referred to in the following chapters appear in a companion volume, *Sexology Uncensored: The Documents of Sexual Science* edited by Lucy Bland and Laura Doan (Cambridge: Polity Press, 1998).

Introduction

Rita Felski

To speak of sexology is surely to invoke an obsolete science and a vanished world. The term brings to mind sepia-tinted images of earnest Victorian scholars labouring over lists of sexual perversions with the taxonomical zeal of an entomologist examining insects. Who would claim to be a sexologist nowadays? One of the effects of the Freudian revolution was to erect a seemingly impenetrable barrier between the modern view of sexuality as an enigmatic and often labile psychic field rooted in unconscious desires, and the work of nineteenth-century sexologists such as Richard von Krafft-Ebing and Havelock Ellis, with its emphasis on the physiological and congenital roots of human erotic preferences. The awkward circumlocutions, the passages of dry Latin prose, the strange, defunct, neologisms – 'invert', 'Urning,' 'eonism' – all seem to confirm the anachronism of sexology, its remoteness from our current interests and concerns.

One of the achievements of Michel Foucault was to dissolve this barrier between a Victorian and a post-Freudian culture by revealing the essential continuity between them. We share with the Victorians, Foucault argues, the conviction that sexuality holds the key to our identity. While the nineteenth century was punitive of many forms of sexual expression and our own time prides itself on its more permissive and tolerant attitudes, the two eras are united in the belief that sexual identity constitutes the truth of the self. The Victorians, in spite of their famous *pudeur*, were in fact constantly talking about sex. In Foucault's powerful revision of cultural history, sexuality was redefined as a central category of modernity, a key to understanding the way in which individuals have come to view themselves as modern subjects.[1]

In one sense, the point may seem obvious. Sexuality has long served as a touchstone for individuals anxious to diagnose the decadent or progressive nature of the modern age. From flappers to women in mini-skirts, from moral panic about female cyclists to moral panic about teenage sexuality, from images of inverts to images of people with AIDS, hopes, anxieties and fantasies about sex have informed cultural attitudes towards the pleasures and dangers of modern life. Indeed, sex has often been identified as a distinctively modern problem by those harbouring nostalgic fantasies of an earlier, more innocent era. Yet paradoxically, sex has also been seen as a primitive, atavistic need, fundamentally at odds with the necessary constraints and deferred gratifications of modernity. This view was to receive powerful support from Freud's conception of an eternal, tragic struggle between our innermost drives and the requirements of civilization, between the opposed demands of the pleasure principle and the reality principle. Thus while sexual desires could be unnaturally stimulated by such modern inventions as the cinema, or new forms of transportation, or the dangerous proximity of bodies in modern cities, sexuality itself was deemed ahistorical and asocial, an archaic impulse welling up from the dark realms of the unconscious.

For Foucault, however, this way of thinking about sex is itself distinctively modern. The Freudian view of sex was to be understood not as an explanation but rather as a symptom, yet another example of modern society's preoccupation with the sexual and its compulsive creation of discourses about sex. Viewed in this light, Freud's status as a pioneering genius in the field of psychoanalysis suffered a significant setback. Rather than the founding father of a radical new field, Freud became simply one more contributor, albeit a highly influential one, to a long history of scientific discourses about sex that had begun with the sexologists. It was they, in fact, who had coined many of the analytical terms – homosexuality, heterosexuality, sadism, masochism – still in use today. Nineteenth-century theories of bodies, emotions and desires came to acquire new importance in understanding modernity's preoccupation with the sexual.

Foucault's history of the rise of sexual science, however, is intentionally a history without agents. New discourses of sexuality emerged in nineteenth-century Europe, creating such types as the hysterical woman, the masturbating child, the homosexual and the Malthusian couple. In turn, we are led to believe, new identities were created by these discourses; individuals recognized themselves in the impersonal, medical descriptions of the sexologists and took on these sexual identities as their own. What is missing from Foucault's version is any substantive account of the messy and complicated interaction, conflict and negotiation between the discourses of sexual science, other aspects of nineteenth-century culture and the experiential realities of human subjects. How influential or marginal a field was sexology and how much power did sexologists wield? Did they simply impose forms of sexual classification on their patients, or were their findings significantly altered by their interactions with these patients? How much impact did the often inaccessible works of sexology actually have on popular attitudes to sex in the nineteenth and early twentieth centuries? To what extent were the findings of sexology accepted or rejected in other areas such as art, journalism or the law?

These and other questions are taken up in the chapters that follow, which contribute to the current debate on sexology a much-needed density of historical and cultural detail. This historical richness in turn militates against any hasty conclusions about the social and political meanings of sexology, which could be used to support a variety of different social and ideological agendas. It is surely as unwise to reduce sexology to a repressive disciplinary apparatus for the administration of psyches as it is to underwrite the self-description of sexologists as heroic pioneers aiding the cause of human progress. While the nineteenth century has often been targeted by scholars eager to show their radical credentials by engaging in generalized denunciations of a repressive Western modernity (in turn counterposed to a supposedly more enlightened postmodernism), there is a growing sense of the profound complexities and internal contradictions within the modern era. Undoubtedly, the power and privilege accorded to ideas such as science, reason and progress shaped the parameters of what could be thought at given historical moments, but the interpretation and use of such ideas followed varied and sometimes surprising paths. Nowhere is this more evident than in the field of sexology and its reception.

Thus the focus of the present volume is not simply the work of famous sexologists but the cultural context and impact of such work. The distinction is important: ideas are not transmitted smoothly and seamlessly from the printed page to the social domain, but are often profoundly altered in the process. As Roy Porter and Lesley Hall note, 'the relationship between sexual advice literature and the uses made of it is not self-evident but requires to be historically reconstructed'.[2] Several chapters in this volume engage in such processes of reconstruction. Lucy Bland and Laura Doan, for example, examine the recourse to sexological ideas about lesbianism in the dual contexts of parliamentary legal debate and a famous libel trial. Judy Greenway considers the reception of Otto Weininger in England, as exemplified in the contradictory responses to his notorious *Sex and Character*. And Chris Waters looks at the uses of sexology in criminological and psychiatric discourses and institutions in interwar Britain. The rationale underlying this volume's British focus brings a much-needed specificity to the discussion of the cultural impact of sexology; a science whose prestige and influence varied markedly in different countries.

While *Sexology in Culture* concentrates on a particular historical period (1890–1940) and national context, it includes a broad range of analytical perspectives. Readers will find examples of most of the approaches associated with the current renaissance of interest in sexology. The most visible of these include feminist and gay and lesbian scholarship, but there is also exciting work being done on the racial dimensions of sexology and on its relevance to contemporary debates about transsexuality and transgenderism. It may be helpful, then, to present a brief overview of the central issues addressed in this recent research.

The rediscovery of sexology is largely due to the emergence of the gay rights movements of the 1960s and 1970s and a growing interest in constructing a history and tradition of same-sex desire. The late nineteenth century was clearly a crucial period in the creation of a homosexual identity, as the legal and medical discourses of the period sought to redefine the homosexual as a distinctive kind of person. Sexuality was no longer simply a question of particular acts, but was expressed in appearance, personality and even bodily structure. Sexologists such as Karl Heinrich Ulrichs, Krafft-Ebing and Ellis were to play an important role in developing new conceptions of same-sex desire. The vocabulary of morality and religion ceded ground to the discourse of science; homosexuality was redefined as an inborn condition, a medical aberration rather than a form of sin.[3]

The social and political ramifications of the medical model of homosexuality were varied; while it could encourage a pathologization of same-sex desire, it was also used to justify pleas for greater social tolerance towards 'inverts' and campaigns for legal reform. Ellis, furthermore, differed from many of his European counterparts in explicitly rejecting the vocabulary of degeneration, insisting that homosexuality should be seen as a harmless physiological variation rather than a neuropathic taint. *Sexual Inversion* sought to normalize male homosexuality by rendering it acceptable to a wider audience, downplaying its association with effeminacy and anxiously stressing the rarity of anal intercourse as a sexual practice. In his detailed analysis of this work and its collaborative origins, Joseph Bristow's chapter explores the tensions between John Addington Symonds's historical and cultural approach to homosexuality and Ellis's own emphasis on the primacy of heredity and biology.

Of course, the same political and cultural movements that inspired a resurgence of interest in sexology have also brought into being a very different sexual politics. The whole project of normalizing homosexuality has been called into question by several waves of gay, lesbian and queer theory. The case against liberal toleration is perhaps most vehemently made by Leo Bersani in his account of the transgressive, profoundly antisocial implications of male same-sex desire. Furthermore, the sexological belief that heterosexuality is the unproblematic biological norm against which deviations are to be measured has been called into question by recent accounts of heterosexuality as a historical and cultural invention.[4]

In this regard, some gay theorists have found in the work of Freud a potentially more radical theory of sexuality, as embodied in the idea of polymorphous perversity and Freud's recognition of the social factors shaping the development of human sexuality. Yet, as Chris Waters suggests in this volume, the popular dissemination of Freudian ideas was not necessarily beneficial; against sexology's insistence on the innateness of inversion, Freudianism encouraged a view of the homosexual as a victim of arrested development and hence as potentially amenable to treatment. Suzanne Raitt also compares the legacy of Freud and the sexologists at the former's expense. In spite of their *risqué* reputations, writers such as Ellis and Edward Carpenter emphasized love rather than sex in their descriptions of inversion, presenting an often idealized account of the power of the emotions. By contrast, Freudian theory was to pave the way for a much more reductive account of romantic love as little more than a quasi-pathological symptom.

Feminist responses to sexology have been shaped by feminism's more general critique of male-defined forms of sexuality and the policing of women's bodies and psyches by male medical experts. Questioning the view that discourses of sexual freedom necessarily serve women's interests, female scholars have pointed to the dubious and often misogynistic portrayals of female sexuality in the work of male sexologists. This work in turn fed into a larger nineteenth-century field of 'sexual science' premised upon evolutionary arguments about women's distinctive and inferior biological nature, their sexual passivity and the inescapability of their maternal destiny. Thus the birth of sexology has been identified by scholars such as Sheila Jeffreys as part of the backlash against women's growing autonomy and independence, as exemplified in suffragette campaigns for social and sexual purity.[5]

Lesbian scholars, in particular, have noted the detrimental influence of sexology on attitudes to female same-sex love. Whereas intimacy between women was long held to be a natural expression of female friendship, sexology encouraged a new perception of such relations as morbid and perverse. As lesbianism had never been declared illegal in England, there was no legal advantage for women in the new stress on congenital abnormality. Female sexual pathology, moreover, was almost invariably linked to gender pathology. While Ellis challenged the stereotype of the effeminate homosexual, he concurred with other sexologists in portraying the lesbian as a gruff, often grotesque, mannish figure. Yet this image of the mannish lesbian was also to take on new resonances in the 1920s and 1930s, as it was appropriated and redeployed by women to express their own discomfort with conventional sexual categories.[6]

Recent feminist research has further complicated the politics of sexology. Without denying sexology's male-dominated structure, scholars note that figures such as Havelock Ellis and Edward Carpenter held relatively progressive views on women's rights and that sexologists were often marginal figures rather than representatives of an all-powerful medical establishment. Questioning the claim that the interests of suffragettes and sexologists were invariably in conflict, they have examined the various social and political interrelations between these two groups. 'All kinds of feminists in this period,' notes Lucy Bland, 'including those highly critical of male sexuality, drew on sexology. They did so selectively as part of their *own* project: the exploration of what sex meant and could mean for women and men.'[7] In this volume Lesley Hall provides one example of such selective usage, showing how two well-known women, Marie Stopes and Stella Browne, made different, by no means uncritical appropriations of sexology to articulate what they considered to be women's experiences and concerns. Alison Oram describes an alternative tradition of radical sexual theory associated with the feminist journal *Urania*, whose critiques of gender duality and interest in cross-dressing uncannily foreshadow many contemporary concerns.

Lesbian and gay scholars have frequently assumed that sexual inversion, a key concept of sexology, is more or less synonymous with homosexuality. References to masculine women and to female souls trapped in male bodies have been read as stumbling if inaccurate attempts to talk about same-sex desire at a time when desire was invariably interpreted through the prism of gender, so that women who desired women were presumed to be necessarily masculine and male homosexuals feminine. Such an interpretation, Jay Prosser argues in this volume and in more detail in his book *Second Skins*, is inaccurate and misleading. While the sexological concept of the invert clearly included some types of homosexuality, the term embraced a much wider range of transgender identifications, including clearly recognizable instances of a powerful and ineradicable desire to 'change sex'. The discourse of sexology was to play an important historical role in the recognition of the transsexual subject and the consequent development of medical and surgical aids to gender reassignment. Against social constructionist views of gender as simply an effect of discourse, Prosser's account of transsexuality suggests that at least some forms of gender identification may have a biological and material dimension and a stubborn intractability that contemporary theory has yet to acknowledge.[8]

Finally, there is growing interest amongst cultural critics in the complex interactions between attitudes to gender and sexuality and the new importance accorded to the influential if indeterminate notion of race in the nineteenth century.[9] Several of the following chapters explore this issue by examining the connections between discourses of sexual pathology and conceptions of race, nation and the primitive. Siobhan Somerville examines the relations between scientific discourses of race and emerging models of homosexuality in the *fin de siècle*. Both, she argues, drew upon similar interpretative techniques, seeking to transform the body into a legible text by isolating and classifying physiological markers of difference. Carolyn Burdett considers the ways in which the ostensibly empirical, rational discourse of sexual science, specifically eugenics, was powerfully imbricated with a Romantic discourse of the nation indebted to the tradition of German idealism. Finally, Jane Caplan's investigation of the history of the tattooed woman reveals the importance of conceptions of the primitive and exotic to the emerging disciplines of criminology and sexual science.

Part of the fascination of sexology undoubtedly lies in its ambition to provide a comprehensive classification of sexual behaviour. Inevitably, such an attempt could hardly hope to succeed. 'Subjects are never simply coterminous with categories', as Merl Storr reminds us in her investigation of sexology's difficulty in coming to terms with what we would now call bisexuality. Yet our own preoccupation with such investigative projects has intensified rather than decreased, as ever more media attention is devoted to sexual surveys, sexual confessions and other documentary sources of what people do, want to do, or refuse to do in bed. While the domain once covered by sexology has now splintered into various, largely unconnected fields – reproductive biology, psychoanalysis and psychotherapy, manuals of sexual advice and sexual techniques – our culture still largely endorses Havelock Ellis's conviction that sex is 'the central problem of life'.[10] *Sexology in Culture* provides an illuminating introduction to some of the major historical sources of that view.

Notes

1 Michel Foucault, *The History of Sexuality, vol. 1: An Introduction* (Harmondsworth: Penguin, 1978).
2 Roy Porter and Lesley Hall, *The Facts of Life: The Creation of Sexual Knowledge in Britain, 1650–1950* (New Haven: Yale University Press, 1995), p. 6.
3 Jeffrey Weeks, *Coming Out: Homosexual Politics in Britain, from the Nineteenth Century to the Present* (London: Quartet, 1977).
4 Leo Bersani, *Homos* (Cambridge, MA: Harvard University Press, 1995); Jonathan Ned Katz, *The Invention of Heterosexuality* (New York: Dutton, 1995).
5 Sheila Jeffreys, *The Spinster and her Enemies: Feminism and Sexuality 1880–1930* (London: Pandora, 1985); Cynthia Eagle Russett, *Sexual Science: The*

Victorian Construction of Womanhood (Cambridge, MA: Harvard University Press, 1989).

6 Lillian Faderman, *Surpassing the Love of Men: Romantic Friendship and Love between Women from the Renaissance to the Present* (New York: William Morrow, 1981); Carroll Smith-Rosenberg, *Disorderly Conduct: Visions of Gender in Victorian America* (New York: Knopf, 1985)

7 Lucy Bland, *Banishing the Beast: Sexuality and the Early Feminists* (New York: New Press, 1995), p. 278.

8 Jay Prosser, *Second Skins: The Body Narratives of Transsexuality* (New York: Columbia University Press, 1998).

9 See, e.g., Sander Gilman, *Difference and Pathology: Stereotypes of Sexuality, Race and Madness* (Ithaca, NY: Cornell University Press, 1985).

10 Havelock Ellis and John Addington Symonds, *Sexual Inversion* (London: Wilson and Macmillan, 1897), p. x.

Part I

A Dangerous New Science

1 Transformations: Subjects, Categories and Cures in Krafft-Ebing's Sexology

Merl Storr

The scene is resonant: a dead father's handwriting, a jolting self-discovery.

> Then she noticed that on a shelf near the bottom was a row of books standing behind the others; the next moment she had one of these in her hand, and was looking at the name of the author: Krafft Ebing – she had never heard of that author before. All the same she opened the battered old book, then she looked more closely, for there on its margins were notes in her father's small, scholarly hand and she saw her own name appeared in those notes – She began to read, sitting down rather abruptly.[1]

The book that Radclyffe Hall's long-suffering heroine Stephen Gordon holds in her hand is almost certainly Richard von Krafft-Ebing's *Psychopathia Sexualis*, which ran to twelve editions between 1886 and 1903 and was by far the most widely read of his works.[2] No doubt many of my readers will already have known the book's title despite its omission from Hall's text, particularly those readers who are at least a little familiar with recent work on the history of sexuality. The importance of sexology for the history of sexuality in general, and for the historical emergence of homosexual identities in particular, has become something of a truism for work in this field.[3] Indeed Hall's *The Well of Loneliness* is perhaps the most celebrated case in point: as is well known, not only did Hall draw extensively on Krafft-Ebing's portrait of the 'mythic mannish lesbian' in both her art and her life,[4] she also called upon the British sexologist Havelock Ellis to give his written blessing to the novel.[5]

Amid all this familiarity it is easy now for us to overlook what is *not* known so clearly. *Psychopathia Sexualis* is compendious, containing commentary on not just homosexuality but sadism, masochism, fetishism, bestiality, necrophilia and more: Hall does not actually tell us which chapter Stephen is reading. Even that section of chapter 4 which pertains particularly to homosexuality or 'inversion' is full of diverse possibilities, with differences of both degree and kind between the various cases found there. If we know that Stephen discovers herself in its pages, we still do not know for sure what it is that she has discovered. History is always written from the present, and it is arguable that the body of scholarship known as 'lesbian and gay studies' has produced a 'lesbian and gay' history of sexuality – including sexology – which has unwittingly flattened out some of that history's contours. Lesbian and gay scholarship has arguably produced a version of sexology which, like the readers of *The Well of Loneliness*, takes for granted a knowledge of texts which may in fact be more – or less – than they seem. In particular, as I shall argue, the category of 'inversion' is both more and less unstable than it has tended to appear in much recent lesbian and gay historical scholarship. Genealogical enquiries into other sexualities, and/or from other vantage points, may light on different features of hitherto familiar terrain.

Bisexuality and categorization

One such vantage point which has become particularly visible in recent years is that of bisexuality. Neither interest in nor political activism around bisexuality is new, but they have been newly prominent since the early 1990s.[6] It is hard to know why bisexuality should have become significant at this historical moment, although it is tempting to extrapolate from Plummer's work on sexual narratives to suggest that narratives of bisexual identity are of the kind whose 'time has come' in late modernity. Whereas 'modernist' narratives of lesbian and gay identity tell 'coming-out' tales of crisis and resolution, late modern narratives, Ken Plummer suggests, are articulated around fragmentation, indeterminacy, excess and resignification.[7] Although Plummer himself does not mention bisexuality in this context, it is possible to see such traits in at least some recent bisexual literature which presents bisexuality as incomplete, fluid and hybridized: the narratives themselves may not always be new, but perhaps they are newly legible in today's late modern climate.[8] Be that as it may, bisexuality presents something of a problem for historians of sexuality.[9] Stephen Gordon's bisexual cousin (or lover, for that matter)[10] might or might not have been able to discover herself so abruptly in Krafft-Ebing's pages, but in any case the 'self' so discovered would not have been called a 'bisexual', nor would it necessarily be recognized as such by self-identified bisexuals today. Nevertheless, tracing the genealogy of contemporary bisexual subjects – or at least of subjects who desire both women and men – in Krafft-Ebing's well-thumbed pages throws some of the details of this dangerous new science into relief.

Subjects who desire both men and women appear in profusion in *Psychopathia Sexualis*, particularly in the discussion of same-sex love, which Krafft-Ebing variously calls 'sexual inversion' or 'antipathic sexual instinct'. Such subjects are not 'bisexual' for Krafft-Ebing: 'bisexuality' is not in fact a subject position at all, but rather a (primarily physiological) predisposition or point of origin from which sexual subjects will later develop.[11] Thus, for example, Krafft-Ebing writes of 'the original bisexual predisposition of the [human] foetus', which is the point of departure for both 'normal' and 'inverted' forms of sexuality after birth.[12] Even in 'normal' adults this predisposition leaves physical 'residua' (such as male nipples) which Krafft-Ebing regards as left-overs of an earlier stage of development, analogous to the appendix.[13] The original bisexuality can produce 'intermediary gradations between the pure type of man and woman':[14] since the 'pure type' of man is heterosexually masculine, and the 'pure type' of woman heterosexually feminine, such gradations are, quite explicitly, gradations of sexual inversion. It is something like this notion of the 'intermediary' that Stephen Gordon's governess calls on when she tells her that she 'may write with a curious double insight – write both men and women from a personal knowledge'.[15] Thus adult bisexuality in Krafft-Ebing's sense is, if anything, an attribute of homosexuals rather than a discrete category of sexual beings. Those who desire both women and men appear, rather, as members of various grades *within* the 'intermediary gradations' of inversion. Two categories in particular are presented as locations of such subjects: psychical hermaphrodites, who are congenitally inverted but who nevertheless continue to desire heterosexually, although their heterosexual impulses are generally the weaker; and those whose inversion is acquired rather than congenital, and who may desire or engage sexually with both women and men either concurrently or sequentially. Nevertheless, subjects who desire both women and men easily overspill the boundaries of these categories and, as we shall see, the transformations they bring – from masculine to feminine, from heterosexual to homosexual, from curable to incurable – play havoc with Krafft-Ebing's theory.

At this point a few words of clarification are necessary in relation to the kinds of transformation bisexuality can and cannot effect. The recent wave of interest in bisexuality has brought with it some interesting work, but also some inflated claims for bisexuality's radical and disruptive potential. By far the most sophisticated of these claims is made by Marjorie

Garber, whose enormous study of bisexuality in 'Western' culture presents bisexuality as 'a category that defies and defeats categorization'.[16] Far from endorsing such a claim here, I would suggest that, on the contrary, 'bisexuality' as a category often appears in profoundly conservative guise and serves to shore up otherwise unstable categorizations rather than to defeat them.[17] Indeed the role of 'bisexuality' in Krafft-Ebing's text is an illustration of this. As Rudi C. Bleys has pointed out, sexologists and sexual reformers of the day were faced with a dilemma on the role of perverse sexuality in relation to 'race' and 'civilization': 'during the period 1860–1918 there emerged an ambiguous image, representing "homosexual deviance" as both a degenerate syndrome *away from* an original, heterosexual drive, and a regression *into* an original, "polymorph" sexuality'.[18] On the one hand, perverse sexuality could be seen as a 'primitive' phenomenon which 'civilized' people had left behind; on the other, it could be seen as an outcome of industrial modernity's ill effects upon natural sexuality, and hence as something to which 'civilized' people were particularly prone. Clearly the categories of the 'civilized' and the 'primitive' are very much at stake here, and Victorian racial thinking insists that the dilemma be resolved in favour of whites' 'natural superiority' without sacrificing either the superiority or the naturalness. It is precisely the category of bisexuality that allows Krafft-Ebing to reach such a resolution. All humans share 'the original onto- and phylogenetic bisexuality' according to Krafft-Ebing,[19] and strongly developed sexual dimorphism is a sign of advanced evolution: 'the higher the anthropological development of the race, the stronger the contrasts between man and woman, and vice versa'.[20] Krafft-Ebing is therefore able to claim both that certain 'primitive' peoples such as native Americans, who are closer to their original bisexuality, are prone to perverse manifestations such as sexual inversion,[21] *and* that those 'civilized' individuals whose constitutions are weakened by what he calls 'an inherited diseased condition of the central nervous system'[22] can lapse into less evolved sexual states, and hence into perversion, when faced with the extraordinary strains of modern life.[23] Thus, confronted with a potentially unstable distinction between what is 'primitive' and what is 'civilized' in sexual life, Krafft-Ebing deploys the category of bisexuality not to defeat racial categorization, but to preserve it.[24]

Gradations and acquisitions

For Krafft-Ebing, sexual transformations are *ipso facto* of pathological significance:

> If the original constitution is favourable and normal, and factors injurious to the psycho-sexual personality exercise no adverse influ-

ence, then a psycho-sexual personality is developed which is un-
changeable and corresponds so completely and harmoniously with
the sex of the individual in question, that subsequent loss of the
generative organs (as by castration) or the *climacterium* [menopause]
or senility, cannot essentially alter it.[25]

The twin factors of 'personality' (or 'character') and 'instinct' are crucial
to Krafft-Ebing's view of the 'normal' and the 'pathological', and their
stability or otherwise is the key to his characterization of sexual inversion. These twin factors have a complex relation both to each other and
to the individual's physical sex, and although their relation as such does
not receive any substantive discussion it is instructive to tease out its
implications. Krafft-Ebing begins his discussion of sexual inversion with
the observation that 'among the most important elements of self-consciousness in the individual are the knowledge of representing a definite sexual
personality and the consciousness of desire [. . .] to perform sexual acts
corresponding with that sexual personality'.[26] In cases where the psychosexual personality does not correspond with the desire or 'instinct' (the
terms are used interchangeably) – where, for example, a man feels and
behaves sexually like a woman or vice versa[27] – this is a sign of an 'abnormal psycho-sexual constitution'.[28] In extreme cases this disturbance can
extend to physical effects, such that men become feminized or women
masculinized in both appearance and feeling.

Abnormal manifestations such as inversion may appear either sponta-
neously during the individual's sexual development, or as a disturbance in
the otherwise normal development of an individual who has suffered damaging influences of some kind. The former may be regarded as cases of
congenital inversion; the latter as acquired. But even in 'acquired' cases, it
is probable that a congenital latent predisposition to inversion is already
present and is merely activated by external causes. This apparently peculiar proviso – that even 'acquired' cases must have a congenital basis –
may make more sense in the light of Krafft-Ebing's subsequent discussion
of the distinction between perversity and perversion: '*The determining
factor here is the demonstration of perverse feeling for the same sex; not
the proof of sexual acts with the same sex*. These two phenomena must
not be confounded with each other; perversity must not be taken for perversion' (italics original).[29] Perversity as vice may be indulged in by liber-
tines with jaded appetites or by those who merely lack opportunity for
'normal' sexual outlet, but this is not true perversion – in other words,
not really inversion – unless the sexual *feeling* is perverse: to paraphrase
Michel Foucault's famous claim, it is not perverse acts but perverse identities which are the issue here.[30] Thus some lovers of both women and
men are doing it not because of a true inner compulsion, but just for the

sake of it: the difference between them is that the inner compulsion is based on a real, congenitally predisposed constitution.

Those who can be said actually to acquire a perversion rather than merely to indulge a perversity begin, according to Krafft-Ebing, by feeling sexual excitement in the presence of members of their own sex: 'This decidedly degenerate reaction is the beginning of a process of physical and mental transformation [. . .] This metamorphosis presents quite different stages, or degrees.'[31] The metamorphosis is given a four-stage typology:

1   the subject has sexual feelings towards his (the paradigm is male throughout) own sex, but the sexual personality and instinct remain basically normal – in other words, the man will continue to take the active role during sex;
2   the subject's personality is transformed, so that he becomes passive and feels like a woman during sex: this stage is known as 'eviration' ('defemination' in women) and resembles congenital inversion;
3   the subject is in a state of transition to a full delusion of having changed sex altogether, with not just psychical feelings but physical sensation now being affected;
4   the subject, at last believing that he has changed sex completely, falls into paranoia – these cases, Krafft-Ebing assures us, are very rare.[32]

These intriguing stages of inversion offer genealogical possibilities not just to present-day bisexuals and homosexuals, but also to transsexuals and other transgendered people. Of particular interest for my present argument however is the fact that the case histories presented as examples of each stage of 'inversion' always include subjects who have desired members of the 'opposite' sex, even in stages 3 and 4. Indeed, one of the case histories presented in stage 3, the autobiography of a doctor who undergoes a sudden sexual transformation after years of marriage, gives a highly complex portrayal of a feminine male subject. After his transformation, the doctor's sexual relations with his wife feel to him like acts of lesbianism; eventually he falls in love with a woman who is anatomically female but has undergone a sexual transformation into masculinity complementary to his own transformation, and who thus acts as a masculine – and hence heterosexual – object of his feminine desire.[33] All three of the (male) cases presented in stage 4 similarly begin their sexual careers heterosexually, and while two of the three begin to desire men *after* their sexual transformations, none of them acts upon it.[34] These cases of 'inversion', then, are far from straightforward examples of exclusive love for one's own sex.

What I want to focus on is the relation between personality and instinct as it is played out in this uneven four-stage continuum. The relative importance of personality and instinct is steadily reversed as subjects move along the continuum, with increasing tension between Krafft-Ebing's clinical outlines and the case histories themselves. The first stage consists in same-sex attraction, and case histories show subjects who desire both women and men either concurrently or sequentially: clearly here it is the instinct (or 'desire') which is the determinant of the subject's inverted status. The second stage is described by Krafft-Ebing as 'deep and lasting transformations of the *psychical* personality',[35] but the case histories tend to reveal a shift in *instinct* which is only later followed by more gradual changes in personality: for example, one man's autobiography shows him first becoming sexually interested in male school-fellows, then becoming impotent with women, then having sexual encounters with adult men and only eventually, during adulthood, becoming feminine and playing the 'wife' in his same-sex relationships.[36] Thus in this case the personality seems to have followed instinct rather than vice versa. In stages 3 and 4 the relation is dramatically reversed: here there is clearly a pronounced change of personality but, as already indicated, this change tends to be followed by little or even no evidence of any change in instinct, which may continue (as with the doctor) in a more or less heterosexual, if convoluted, direction, or indeed disappear altogether. In terms of relative importance, then, instinct seems to be the determining factor at the beginning of the continuum, but character supersedes it at the end.

Once again, Krafft-Ebing here is using a concept which, to contemporary eyes, may appear to harbour the potential to disrupt conservative sexual categories – the concept of 'continuum' – to shore up rather than to dissolve his categorization. Krafft-Ebing's characterization of sexual inversion, as we have seen, insists that sexual inversion is not merely a desire for members of one's own sex, but such a transformation of one's entire sexual being that the latter no longer corresponds 'completely and harmoniously' with one's physical sex. This characterization, of which Stephen Gordon is of course the ideal type, so straitens the parameters of 'normality' that *any* deviation – from active, masculine heterosexuality for men or from passive, feminine heterosexuality for women – constitutes inversion and should be policed as such: hence the inclusion of those who desire both women *and* men under its terms. The case histories, however, are more diverse than this concept of 'inversion' allows: some are feminine but do not desire men; some are masculine but do not desire women; some desire both, and some neither; some, like the doctor, present a picture so much more complex than Krafft-Ebing's analysis can deal with that the terms 'inversion' and 'normality' fall into disarray. By invoking the model of 'gradation' or continuum, Krafft-Ebing is able to contain the disruptive potential of all this diversity: what would otherwise be extremely troublesome disjunctions between 'personality' and 'instinct' are smoothed over as merely endpoints of a single scale.

Imperfect inverts

Just as with acquired inversion, Krafft-Ebing presents congenital sexual inversion in four gradations:

1   psychical hermaphroditism, where subjects are mainly homosexual but traces of heterosexuality remain;
2   homosexuality, where there is inclination towards members of the same sex only;
3   effemination (in men) or viraginity (in women), where there is an inverted psychical character corresponding completely with the inverted sexual instinct;
4   hermaphroditism or pseudo-hermaphroditism, where the subject's physical form begins to correspond to the inverted sexual instinct so that men's bodies become feminized and women's bodies masculinized, although Krafft-Ebing stresses that this never extends to actual physical hermaphroditism.[37]

These gradations appear as a relatively straightforward continuum, from the early gradations where only instinct is inverted to the later where both instinct and personality are inverted: 'the whole character, in cases of the complete development of the anomaly, correspond[s] with the peculiar sexual instinct, but not with the sex which the individual presents anatomically and physiologically.'[38]

Once again, however, there is a tension between Krafft-Ebing's clinical characterization of the perversion and the evidence of the case histories. Krafft-Ebing begins with a definition of congenital inversion: 'The essential feature of this strange manifestation of sexual life is the want of sexual sensibility for the opposite sex, even to the extent of horror, while sexual inclination and impulse toward the same sex are present'.[39] Clearly this definition of congenital inversion's 'essential feature' contradicts Krafft-Ebing's own description of psychical hermaphroditism as the first grade, whose 'characteristic mark [. . .] is that, by the side of the pronounced sexual instinct and desire for the same sex, a desire toward the opposite sex is present', albeit only secondarily to the homosexual instinct.[40] But each of the next three gradations also includes at least one case history of a subject who continues not just to engage in but even in some measure to enjoy heterosexual encounters. Thus the second gradation includes a young man who, while clearly preferring men, regards sex with women as 'a coarsely sensual enjoyment';[41] the third includes a man who – again, while nevertheless preferring men – pays weekly visits to a brothel where he dresses as a woman and gets a female prostitute to masturbate him;[42] the fourth includes a man who, while of a markedly feminine personality since childhood and being definitely attracted to his own sex, engages in sex with women during a short period of his youth and 'is able to perform the act of coitus normally', although he gives this up later.[43] In a subsequent discussion Krafft-Ebing explains exceptions to the alleged 'want of sensibility' or even 'horror' of inverts for women by claiming that in such cases 'the heterosexual instinct [. . .] is still but an episodical phenomenon which has no root in the mental constitution, and is essentially but a means to satisfaction of sexual desire'.[44] However, even here he persists with the view, quite unsupported by his own evidence, that this occurs only in cases of the first grade (i.e., psychical hermaphroditism). He also claims that diagnosis of sexual inversion can be absolutely certain:

> when absolute proof is at hand that a homosexual person is permanently attracted by a person of the same sex and led to a sexual act with that person, the act granting full satisfaction to the sexual instinct, whilst similar attractions do not exist in persons of the opposite sex, and if the disgust for persons of the opposite sex is insuperable,[45]

a set of criteria which only a minority of Krafft-Ebing's own case histories manage to fulfil. Again, Krafft-Ebing is deploying a category – 'congenital inversion' – which covers a multitude of perversions and reduces the diversity of desires and practices to a single clinical entity.

Distinctions and diagnoses

Although Krafft-Ebing rigorously separates acquired inversion from congenital, he repeatedly acknowledges the points of similarity, and even of convergence, between them. For example, he acknowledges that it may be difficult to distinguish congenital psychical hermaphroditism from acquired inversion, 'for, in such cases, so long as the vestiges of a normal sexual instinct are not absolutely lost, the actual symptoms are the same'.[46] In fact the two anomalies share not just symptoms but often immediate, if not ultimate, causes (particularly masturbation, the dangers of which are a constant theme for Krafft-Ebing), making the distinction even more difficult.

The picture is yet more complicated with congenital inversion in women. Krafft-Ebing acknowledges the paucity of data on inversion in women, but insists that despite the relative invisibility of female homosexuality, as many women as men are congenitally inverted. However, women are more likely to have been led into heterosexual relations: women's education stifles their sexuality; mutual masturbation among schoolgirls is far less common than it is among boys; and girls' sexual instinct does not begin to develop until puberty, which is also the age at which they are introduced into mixed society for the first time and so are directed towards heterosexuality. While Krafft-Ebing ascribes many cases of frigidity in married women to underlying sexual inversion, overall women are so strongly steered towards heterosexuality and marriage that few congenitally inverted women ever actually deviate. But some such women, whose constitutions are especially degenerate or who are seduced by other women, do begin to acknowledge and even act upon their inversion: 'In these cases we find situations analogous to those which have been described as existing in men afflicted with "acquired" antipathic sexual instinct'.[47] In other words, *congenital* inversion in women manifests itself in the same way as *acquired* inversion in men. How, this being so, one may distinguish congenital female inverts from women whose inversion is acquired is not explained.

Here again we find Krafft-Ebing applying distinct categories to material which exceeds their boundaries. Not only are the gradations which constitute congenital and acquired inversion woefully inadequate to the case histories they present as evidence, particularly when faced with subjects who doggedly desire and engage sexually with both women and men, but the very distinction between the congenital and the acquired itself is thoroughly unstable. To us late modern readers, there is an obvious temptation at this point to deconstruct Krafft-Ebing's argument: to declare, for example, in Garberian style that the contents of the various categories disrupt or subvert the categories as such, that the category of 'inversion' – and, by extension, of 'normality' – is revealed to be not just a fiction but an internally inconsistent one. Indeed all of this might be taken as an illustration of the category-busting properties that Garber ascribes to what we today call 'bisexuality': subjects who desire both women and men continually exceed the categories mapped out for them, and in doing so make those categories conceptually unviable. This move is tempting, and at a certain conceptual level would be something like a happy ending.

However, there are two problems with this happy ending. First, as I have already suggested, concepts such as 'bisexuality' or 'continuum' which appear to offer possibilities of flux, instability and even subversion can also just as easily be used to maintain fixity, rigidity and conservatism, precisely because their openness and flexibility allow them to incorporate what might otherwise be incompatible, or at least divergent, features. This capacity of concepts such as 'bisexuality' for conservatism as well as radicalism makes the task of serious enquiry into their historical and contemporary effects all the more urgent. Second, the conceptual happy ending fails to deal with the historical fact that sexology, the dangerous new science of the nineteenth century, is not just a conceptual edifice, but a clinical practice. As Jonathan Dollimore has pointed out, it is too easy just to point to 'a repressive dominant always allegedly on the edge of its own ruin' because it is 'rendered unstable by contradictions intrinsic to it', discussed in abstraction from its real historical conditions – especially those historical conditions which may have prevented it from actually being ruined.[48] Too exclusive a focus on textual instabilities tends to lose sight of the material and sometimes violent practices in which texts are embedded, and of the material and sometimes violent means by which textual ambivalence and internal contradiction or subversion are erased. The instability and internal contradictions of Krafft-Ebing's categorizations do not, by any means, prevent him from invoking those categorizations when dealing with his patients.

Indeed it is precisely the gravity and import of sexology as a clinical practice which impels Krafft-Ebing to insist on the distinction of sexual categories even when he himself is aware of the difficulty of the enterprise. He knows full well how difficult it is to distinguish perversity from perversion, or congenital inversion from acquired, but he insists on the importance of doing so not just for theoretical reasons but for clinical and therapeutic ones: one must know to which category one's patient belongs so as to be able to reach a prognosis and, if the patient falls into one of the categories which is potentially 'curable', to prescribe a course of treatment to combat the abnormal instinct.[49] It is here that the gradations of inversion operate in full force, no matter how inadequate they have been to the material hitherto: only certain types or grades of inversion are amenable to treatment. Treatment may include the prevention of masturbation and the removal of other damaging influences; cure of the patient's underlying neurosis or neurasthenia; and general encouragement of the patient to give up homosexual relations in favour of heterosexual ones. Such methods only rarely succeed, however, and a more favourable course of action is hypnosis, by means of which one may sometimes be able to treat those categories of inversion deemed curable, 'remov[ing] the impulse to masturbation and homosexual feelings, and [. . .] encourag[ing] heterosexual emotions with a sense of virility'.[50] The distinction between congenital and acquired comes into its own here, and it is primarily the latter category of inversion which can be treated in this way. However, congenital inversion may be treatable in its less developed forms, and 'the most favourable cases are those of *psychosexual hermaphroditism* in which at least rudimentary heterosexual feelings may be strengthened by suggestion and brought into active practice':[51] Krafft-Ebing goes on to outline briefly a handful of successfully treated cases of various kinds of inversion. While acknowledging that it is often difficult to place such patients under hypnosis, he makes it quite plain that submission to this treatment need not be voluntary: 'By reason of the great benefit that can be given to such unfortunates, [. . .] in all such cases, everything should be done to *force* hypnosis – the only means of salvation' (my italics).[52]

Transformations?

A chilling example of what the forced treatment of patients can mean is the case of Ilma S., who appears in *Psychopathia Sexualis* as a female invert. At the age of 18, Ilma falls 'passionately' in love with a male cousin, and her relationship with him is 'not platonic'.[53] She then spends some time disguised as a man 'in order to earn a living', and while so disguised is obliged to socialize with her workmates and to observe men – including, by chance, her cousin – behaving in ways that she finds distasteful. Thereafter she dislikes men, and finds herself, as she puts it, 'more and more powerfully drawn towards intelligent women and girls who were in sympathy with me'.[54] At the age of 29 she is arrested for theft, discovered to be suffering from 'severe hystero-epilepsy' and so sent to hospital, where her sexual inversion 'expressed itself in a stormy and decidedly sensual way.'[55]

The distinction between congenital and acquired inversion is enforced in this case: in hospital Ilma's inversion is 'considered congenital', but Krafft-Ebing regards it as 'clearly acquired'.[56] As such it is, of course, eligible for treatment, and Ilma in fact becomes one of Krafft-Ebing's most celebrated patients. A detailed account of her treatment appears in his *Experimental Study in the Domain of Hypnotism*, first published in 1888. Here he records how he demonstrates her susceptibility to post-hypnotic suggestion at meetings of the medical societies of Graz and Steiermark, as well as using her to conduct daily experiments in the power of hypnosis. These experiments include not just trying to prevent her from kissing her (female) nurses and fellow patients – and from trying to leave the clinic – but also inducing her to perform strange antics (some in public places) such as singing and acting out various emotions, and suggesting that she has been branded with hot irons or cut in certain ways so that real blisters and scars appear on her skin. He also records that Ilma repeatedly complains that she dislikes the hypnosis, resists it increasingly effectively, and takes measures such as placing pieces of paper in her waistband so that she can check later to see whether the doctors undo her clothes while she is under hypnosis (which they do). Consent is neither asked nor given for these experiments; when a fellow patient shows Ilma a newspaper account of one of her medical society appearances, she is 'very angry and amazed'.[57] She attempts suicide while at the clinic.

Contemporaries noted of Krafft-Ebing after his death that he was kind to his patients, walking with them in the garden and playing the piano for them.[58] Indeed he presents his desire to 'cure' inverted patients as a desire to relieve them of an affliction which 'means nothing more or less than a hopeless existence, a life without love, an undignified comedy before human society, [. . .] loss of social position, civic honour and liberty'.[59] Moreover he makes it plain that the 'health and welfare of the patient must ever be paramount to that of society at large' – in other words, that he is not imposing social conformity merely for its own sake.[60] There is thus no reason to suppose that his treatment of Ilma is malicious or wilfully cruel – or, on the other hand, that it is particularly unusual, although her remarkable susceptibility to hypnosis probably means that her treatment is more intense than many of her fellow patients'. The instability of Krafft-Ebing's categories offers her no consolation, and the only kind of happy ending on offer here is that, after moving to another clinic for further treatment, she is eventually 'entirely freed of her neurosis and sexual inversion, and discharged cured'.[61]

But *is* she cured? Discussing the hypnotic treatment of inverts, Krafft-Ebing notes that even 'decided and lasting results [. . .] after all, are nothing more than suggestive training, not a real cure. They are marvellous artefacts of hypnotic science practiced on abnormal beings, but by no means "*transformations*" [. . .] of a psychosexual existence' (italics original).[62] Krafft-Ebing's own typology means that, since inversion (or, at the least, a predisposition to it) is congenital, it is also permanent. Abnormal subjects remain steadfastly abnormal, even when their behaviour is reformed.

They also remain *subjects*. Even as Krafft-Ebing records his power over Ilma, he records her resistance too. The intensity of his treatment of her is, at least in part, a response to the intensity of her refusal: he must repeatedly rehypnotize Ilma because she repeatedly has attacks of hysteria and auto-hypnosis which erase all his post-hypnotic suggestions.[63] Indeed all of the case histories in *Psychopathia Sexualis* reveal their subjects to be not just material, unruly or otherwise, for Krafft-Ebing's categories, but complex sites of negotiation – even, or perhaps especially, those cases of inversion who willingly adopt the sexological categories as subject positions from which to combat a sense of themselves as, as one subject puts it, 'monsters'.[64] Subjects are never simply coterminous with categories, and the fact that the former always exceed the boundaries of the latter should neither surprise us nor lead us to issue premature obituaries for categorization as such. The perfectly formed inversion of Stephen Gordon is a fiction: not even Hall herself could live up to it.[65] For all her martyred heroism, Stephen – in my eyes, at least – is no match for the tempestuous Ilma, who lacked Stephen's advantages of class, wealth and fictional status, but whose refusal to be transformed by sexology, if not an unqualified success, was at any rate – while it lasted – categorical.

Notes

I would like to thank Lucy Bland, Laura Doan, Jo Eadie and Clare Hemmings for their comments on earlier drafts.

1 Radclyffe Hall, *The Well of Loneliness* (Virago, London, 1982), p. 207.
2 My discussion focuses on a translation of the final edition of 1903.
3 See, e.g., Lillian Faderman, *Odd Girls and Twilight Lovers: A History of Lesbian Life in Twentieth-Century America* (Penguin, New York, etc., 1991), esp. pp. 37–61; Jeffrey Weeks, *Coming Out: Homosexual Politics in Britain, from the Nineteenth Century to the Present* (Quartet, London, 1977), esp. pp. 23–32.
4 See Esther Newton's seminal discussion of Hall and Krafft-Ebing in 'The mythic mannish lesbian: Radclyffe Hall and the New Woman', in *Hidden from History: Reclaiming the Gay and Lesbian Past*, eds. Martin Bauml Duberman, Martha Vicinus and George Chauncey, Jr (Penguin, London, etc., 1991), pp. 281–93; cf. Michael Baker, *Our Three Selves: A Life of Radclyffe Hall* (GMP Publishers, London, 1985), pp. 216–20.
5 See Baker, *Our Three Selves*, pp. 202–6.
6 See, e.g., *Plural Desires: Writing Bisexual Women's Realities*, ed. Bisexual Anthology Collective (Sistervision: Black Women and Women of Colour Press, Toronto, 1995); *Closer to Home: Bisexuality and Feminism*, ed. Elizabeth Reba Weise (Seal Press, Boston, 1992).
7 Ken Plummer, *Telling Sexual Stories: Power, Change and Social Worlds* (Routledge, London and New York, 1995), pp. 113–43.
8 See, e.g., Jo Eadie, 'Being who we are (and anyone else we want to be)', in *Bisexual Horizons: Politics, Histories, Lives*, eds Sharon Rose, Cris Stevens et al./Off Pink Collective (Lawrence and Wishart, London, 1996), pp. 16–20; Ann Kaloski, 'Bisexuals making out with cyborgs: politics, pleasure, con/fusion', *Journal of Gay, Lesbian, and Bisexual Identity*, 2:1 (1997), pp. 47–64.
9 See, e.g., Donald E. Hall, 'Graphic sexuality and the erasure of a polymorphous perversity', in *Representing Bisexualities: Subjects and Cultures of Fluid Desire*, eds Donald E. Hall and Maria Pramaggiore (New York University Press, New York and London, 1996), pp. 99–123.
10 For a discussion of Stephen's lovers and their importance in the history of bisexual femme subjectivity, see Clare Hemmings, 'Waiting for no man: bisexual femme subjectivity and cultural repudiation', in *Butch/Femme: Inside Lesbian Gender*, ed. Sally R. Munt (Cassell, London, 1998), pp. 90–100; Frann Michel, 'Do bats eat cats? Reading what bisexuality does', in *Representing Bisexualities*, pp. 55–69.
11 See Merl Storr, 'The sexual reproduction of "race": bisexuality, history and racialization', in *The Bisexual Imaginary: Representation, Identity and Desire*, ed. Bi Academic Intervention (Cassell, London, 1997), pp. 63–78, esp. pp.69–71.
12 Richard von Krafft-Ebing, *Psychopathia Sexualis, with Especial Reference to the Antipathic Sexual Instinct*, tr. Franklin S. Klaf (Staples Press, London, 1965), p. 30.

13 Ibid., p. 227.
14 Ibid., p. 30.
15 Hall, *The Well of Loneliness*, p. 208.
16 Marjorie Garber, *Vice Versa: Bisexuality and the Eroticism of Everyday Life* (Penguin, London, etc., 1996), p. 70.
17 Cf. Sue Wilkinson, 'Bisexuality as backlash', in *All the Rage: Reasserting Radical Lesbian Feminism*, eds Lynne Harne and Elaine Miller (Women's Press, London, 1996), pp. 75–89, for a discussion of bisexuality's conservative role in sexual politics, albeit one written from a perspective very different from my own.
18 Rudi C. Bleys, *The Geography of Perversion: Male-to-Male Sexual Behaviour Outside the West and the Ethnographic Imagination 1750–1918* (Cassell, London, 1996), p. 189.
19 Krafft-Ebing, *Psychopathia Sexualis*, p. 227.
20 Ibid., p. 28.
21 See, e.g., ibid., pp. 199–200; cf. Bleys, *The Geography of Perversion*, esp. pp. 145–206, on the differential attribution of perversion to 'inferior races' by European observers.
22 See, e.g., Krafft-Ebing, *Psychopathia Sexualis*, p. 32.
23 Cf. Richard von Krafft-Ebing, *Textbook on Insanity: Based on Clinical Observations, for Practitioners and Students of Medicine*, tr. Charles Gilbert Chaddock (F. A. Davis Co., Philadelphia, 1904), pp. 136–96.
24 This is not to suggest that bisexuality can never be radical or disruptive: merely that it is not necessarily or inherently so. For further discussion of this question see the editors' roundtable discussion in *The Bisexual Imaginary*, pp. 189–202.
25 Krafft-Ebing, *Psychopathia Sexualis*, p. 187.
26 Ibid., p. 186.
27 Sexology's tendency to heterosexualize homosexual desire by presenting it as feminine (where men desire men) or masculine (where women desire women) is well known and has received exhaustive commentary elsewhere. See, e.g., Gert Hekma, '"A female soul in a male body": sexual inversion as gender inversion in nineteenth-century sexology', in *Third Sex, Third Gender: Beyond Sexual Dimorphism in Culture and History*, ed. Gilbert Herdt (Zone Books, New York, 1994), pp. 213–39.
28 Krafft-Ebing, *Psychopathia Sexualis*, p. 187.
29 Ibid., p. 188.
30 See Michel Foucault, *The History of Sexuality: An Introduction*, tr. Robert Hurley (Penguin, London, etc., 1984), pp. 42–4.
31 Krafft-Ebing, *Psychopathia Sexualis*, p. 190.
32 Ibid., pp. 188–221.
33 Ibid., pp. 200–14.
34 Ibid., pp. 216–20.
35 Ibid., p. 195.
36 Ibid., pp. 196–9.
37 Ibid., pp. 230–61.
38 Ibid., p. 221.

39 Ibid.
40 Ibid., p. 231.
41 Ibid., p. 246.
42 Ibid., p. 257.
43 Ibid., pp. 258–61.
44 Ibid., p. 294.
45 Ibid., p. 298.
46 Ibid., p. 232.
47 Ibid., p. 263.
48 Jonathan Dollimore, 'Bisexuality, heterosexuality and wishful theory', *Textual Practice*, 10:3 (1996), pp. 523–39, 532.
49 Krafft-Ebing, *Psychopathia Sexualis*, pp. 295–7.
50 Ibid., p. 299.
51 Ibid., pp. 302–3.
52 Ibid., p. 300.
53 Ibid., p. 193.
54 Ibid., p. 194.
55 Ibid.
56 Ibid.
57 Richard von Krafft-Ebing, *An Experimental Study in the Domain of Hypnotism*, tr. Charles G. Chaddock (G.P. Putnam's Sons/Knickerbocker Press, New York and London, 1889), p. 60.
58 Frederick Peterson, introduction to Krafft-Ebing, *Textbook on Insanity*, pp. xiii–xvi, xv.
59 Krafft-Ebing, *Psychopathia Sexualis*, p. 306.
60 Ibid., p. 307.
61 Ibid., p. 194.
62 Ibid., p. 306.
63 On hysteria as a medium of resistance, see, e.g., Elaine Showalter, *The Female Malady: Women, Madness and English Culture, 1830–1980* (Virago, London, 1987), esp. pp. 145–64.
64 Krafft-Ebing, *Psychopathia Sexualis*, pp. 212–13. Cf. Harry Oosterhuis, 'Richard von Krafft-Ebing's "Step-Children of Nature": Psychiatry and the Making of Homosexual Identity', in *Science and Homosexualities*, ed. Vernon A. Rosario (Routledge, New York and London, 1997), pp. 67–88.
65 On Hall's conventionally feminine childhood (and her subsequent attempts to erase it), see Baker, *Our Three Selves*, pp. 14–22.

2 It's What You Do With It That Counts: Interpretations of Otto Weininger

Judy Greenway

Vienna, 1903: a 23 year-old Jew, Otto Weininger, shoots himself through the heart. His book, *Geschlect und Charakter* (*Sex and Character*),[1] published four months previously, immediately goes into a second edition, becoming a best-seller in Austria and Germany; fourteen editions by 1914.[2] The 1906 English translation is still being reprinted in the 1920s.[3] The notoriety of the book is inseparably entwined with the scandal of the suicide; though little is known about Weininger himself, *Sex and Character* becomes a major source of speculation and analysis. Misogynist, anti-semitic, anti-sexual, the book's themes highlight the anxieties of the age. Weininger was one of the examples used to develop Theodor Lessing's theory of Jewish self-hatred. Feminists indignantly repudiated this 'horrible book',[4] and even many anti-feminists found it necessary to distance themselves from it in public.

Knowing this I was surprised to find *Sex and Character* excerpted and seriously discussed in the English anarchist-feminist paper the *Freewoman* in 1912. Why did it give him space? A liking for polemic, perhaps – the editor points out that English anti-feminists are much less interesting than Germans (*sic*)[5] – but maybe there was more to it. I began noticing frequent references to Weininger's work in early twentieth-century debates about homosexuality. It seemed that Weininger's contemporaries took him seriously, and some campaigners for women's and homosexual liberation were able to find something valuable in his work. My initial attempt to find out more about Weininger in relation to these seemingly contradictory images eventually led me into a wider investigation of some of the complexities of early twentieth-century feminism and sexual radicalism.

Sexology at that time was part of a wider debate about gender and sexuality, but its role and influence cannot be understood simply from an analysis of sexological texts. *Sex and Character* was published in England at a time of intense feminist activity. Although the book can be seen as an example of anti-feminist backlash, it is important to look at how such works were actually used by their readers. Aspects of Weininger's theories were taken up by Edward Carpenter, whose extensive writings on sexuality had already given him a key role among those who were trying to think about the relationship between sexual and social change in their own lives. Selective use and combination of Carpenter's and Weininger's ideas enabled some readers, including feminists, to rethink sexual and gender categorization.

Weininger was born in Vienna in 1880 and attended university there, studying mainly philosophy and psychology, but also taking courses in medicine, experimental zoology and biology. He was one of a group of young men who discussed new theories in all these areas, as well as the works of such writers as Ibsen, Strindberg and Zola.[6] He read Freud and Breuer on hysteria, and showed some of his early work to Freud.[7] In 1902, Weininger's doctoral thesis, which forms the first part of *Sex and Character*, was accepted. Shortly afterwards he converted to Protestantism. During the next few months he wrote the second part of his book, and it was published in June 1903. That October, he killed himself.

Fin-de-siècle Vienna in the last years of the Austro-Hungarian empire has been characterized as both a 'city of dreams' and 'the proving ground for world destruction'.[8] Intellectuals pondered the fate of the individual as old certainties were challenged by new scientific ideas, modernist aesthetics, feminism and mass nationalist movements. The city fermented with new movements in art, music, architecture, law, politics and psychology, and Jews played a prominent part in most of these.[9] Numbering about 10 per cent of the population, many Viennese Jews were highly assimilated. However, the emerging Germanic nationalist movement cast them as outsiders, or enemies within; Vienna was the nursery for rapidly growing anti-semitism, as well as the Zionism which responded to it.[10]

Misogyny was intellectually commonplace and institutionalized, taking on new modernist forms. Prostitution was legally regulated in Vienna, though it was alleged at the turn of the century that only about one in twenty prostitutes was registered with the police. Behind this claim lay a notion of so-called 'hidden prostitution': any woman, however respectable she seemed, could be secretly a 'prostitute' (that is, engaging in illicit sex), and the police operated a system of informers and *agents provocateurs* to discover such women and force them to register.[11] This suggests that notions of the sexualized woman were widespread; the 'hidden prostitute' idea is particularly relevant to Weininger's work.

Viennese feminists criticized prostitution for reducing women to sex objects, and campaigned for economic and social reforms, as well as sex education and a modernization of sexual morality. Like their opponents they drew on new ideas from psychology and sociology about the nature of men, women and sexuality.[12] Both male and female homosexuality were illegal, and there seems to have been no organized homosexual movement in Vienna before 1911, though the active campaigns for women's and homosexual rights in Germany would certainly have been influential.[13] Weininger himself says that agitation for women's rights seems to coincide with what he calls the effeminacy and Jewishness of the age, an increase in homosexuality and masculinized women.[14]

Sex and Character is Weininger's answer to the 'Woman Question'. In it he attempts 'to place the relations of Sex in a new and decisive light [. . .] to refer to a single principle the whole contrast between man and woman [. . .] it is a gradual approach to the heart of psychology.'[15] The book sets out to provide a new rationale for the relations between men and women, based on the ethics of the transcendent individual.

Part One, 'Sexual Complexity', draws extensively on biological and psychological evidence to demonstrate that all organisms are fundamentally bisexual; that the categories 'male' and 'female' are no longer adequate. In the case of humans, Weininger argues that there is no such thing in reality as a man or a woman. Man and Woman, he says, are ideal types; anatomically and psychologically, actual men and women contain elements of both. In principle the amounts of masculinity and femininity in us could be represented mathematically, our destiny in love worked out in the form of an equation. (We are attracted to those, of whichever biological sex, who will together with us add up to the ideal sum total 1M[an] + 1W[oman]). In practice, our constitution is not fixed; we all oscillate between the masculine and the feminine within ourselves, over time and in relation to our environment.[16] He also says that 'In my view all actual organisms have both homo-sexuality and hetero-sexuality',[17] and therefore rejects both legal penalties and attempts at 'curing' homosexuality.

He argues that all individuals should be able to develop their fullest potential, so women should not be excluded from education or particular occupations. On the same grounds, he criticizes the movement for women's emancipation – emancipation should be based on the individual, not on membership of a category. Throughout this section Weininger follows tradition in characterizing masculinity and femininity as polar opposites, with masculinity representing a higher degree of development. He derives from this, however, the unexpected conclusion that the highest type of woman is the masculine lesbian.[18]

Part Two, 'The Sexual Types', sets out a typology of Man and Woman in social context. 'The ideas "man" and "woman" cannot be investigated separately; their significance can be found out only by placing them side by side and contrasting them.' Although he repeats that he is not talking about actual men and women, this is not a distinction he maintains clearly. Woman, he says, 'is devoted wholly to sexual matters [. . .] to the sphere of begetting and of reproduction', while 'the male is something more than sexual'. He mentions the possibility that this, 'the most significant difference between the sexes', could be historically produced, but does not develop the point.[19]

There are, moreover, two types of Woman, the Mother and the Prostitute. Again, any actual woman will have varying amounts of these (as will men). Both types devote their lives to promoting (hetero)sexual intercourse, simply engaging in different types of matchmaking. The Mother represents the false morality of the bourgeois family. Motherhood is merely animal, non-moral, a means to reproducing the race; prostitution, though, is human, anti-moral, a more authentic expression of sexuality.[20] However, 'to put it bluntly, man possesses sexual organs; her sexual organs possess woman.' Man, in other words, can transcend sexuality, 'can know about his sexuality, whilst a woman is unconscious of it and can in all good faith deny it, because she is [. . .] sexuality itself'. Women are incapable of self-knowledge. They have no boundaries: 'as there is no such thing as one-ness for her there can be no plurality, only an indistinct state of fusion with others'.[21] They lack the prerequisites for a transcendental morality. Only men can be separate individuals, recognizing and respecting the boundaries of others like themselves.

Jewishness is presented in an analogous way. Judaism is sexual, feminine, family-centred, lacking in individuality, slavish. However, 'I mean by Judaism [. . .] neither a race nor a people nor a recognised creed. I think of it as a tendency of the mind, as a psychological constitution which is a possibility for all mankind, but which has become actual in the most conspicuous fashion only among the Jews.' Again he mentions, then drops, the possibility of historical rather than innate causes for this. He attacks the persecution of Jews. Every individual, man or woman, Jew or Christian, deserves equal justice, equal freedom. '[W] hoever detests the Jewish disposition detests it first of all in himself [. . .] Hatred, like love, is a projected phenomenon; that person alone is hated who reminds one unpleasantly of oneself.'[22] Anti-semitism is a form of self-hatred. In passages like these, Weininger could be analysing himself.

Jewishness and femaleness, he says, are the enemies within our own souls, to be transcended if we are to become authentic moral individuals. '[W] oman, as woman, must disappear [. . .] not the emancipation of woman from man, but rather the emancipation of woman from herself.'

Can a woman cease to be 'Woman'? Yes, but 'only if [she] can place her-self in relation to the moral idea, the idea of humanity'.[23] The only way in which this can happen is by men and women refusing sexual intercourse with one another: women because they must reject the sexuality which enslaves them; men because it goes against the categorical imperative which says human beings must not use one another as means to an end. In the present state of society, he says, men and women are unable to encounter one another as free and equal individuals.[24]

What I find most remarkable about Weininger is the clarity of his in-sight into his own intense misogyny. A few feminists of the time recog-nized the value of this:

> [M]any women [. . .] feel instinctively that, as Weininger expresses it, the man does despise them and hold them in contempt, and they despise themselves.[25]

> The real importance of this book lies in its so fully concentrating and carrying to its logical conclusion the andro-centric view of hu-manity.[26]

> What Englishman has the courage and clarity to speak his inmost thoughts like that?[27]

His attempts to explain male subjectivity, his perception of the connec-tions between misogyny and self-hatred, and his critique of femininity as destructive to women are rare among feminists or anti-feminists of his time. (Weininger cites no feminist author in his 132 pages of bibliogra-phy.)[28] However, his characterization of Woman's diffuse physical and psychological selves involves a deeply confused and confusing slippage between Woman and women. Like Freud and many others he concludes that Woman is a mystery, unknowable. But he explains why:

> The highest form of eroticism, as much as the lowest form of sexu-ality, uses the woman not for herself but as a means to an end – to preserve the individuality of the artist. The artist has used the woman merely as the screen on which to project his own idea [. . .]
> Woman is nothing but man's expression and projection of his own sexuality. Every man creates himself a woman, in which he embodies himself and his own guilt. [. . .] She is only a part of man, his other, ineradicable, his lower part. [29]

He could hardly express more clearly the basis for men's hatred for women as a form of self-hatred. Elsewhere he says, 'The hatred of the woman is always an unsuccessfully overcome hate of one's own sexuality.'[30] In the end, then, it is the enemy within who has to be killed. 'Love is a phenom-enon of projection just as hate is, not a phenomenon of equation as friend-

ship is [. . .] [S]exual union, considered ethically, psychologically, and bio-
logically, is allied to murder; it is the negation of the woman and the man
[. . .] Love is murder', because it destroys the reality of the woman.[31]
Although in theory this leaves open the possibility of love between men,
Weininger's all-important logic implies that such a love would have to be
non-sexual.

Discussing the reception of Weininger's book, author Ford Madox Ford
writes:

> . . . it had an immense international vogue. It was towards the mid-
> dle of '06 (when the English translation came out) that one began
> to hear in the men's clubs of England and in the cafés of France and
> Germany [. . .] singular mutterings amongst men [. . .] Even in the
> United States where men never talk about women, certain whispers
> might be heard. The idea was that a new gospel had appeared. I
> remember sitting with a table full of overbearing intellectuals in that
> year, and they at once began to talk about Weininger [. . .] under
> their breaths.[32]

The year of first publication, 1903, also saw a new wave of agitation for
women's suffrage in England, initiated by the Women's Social and Political Union (WSPU). By 1906 militant campaigns were well under way, and
politicians could no longer speak in public without being interrupted by
cries of 'Votes for Women'. According to Ford, advanced young men,
'serious, improving, ethical, [. . .] careless about dress and without exception Young Liberals', discussed Weininger in relation to these unruly suffragettes, and their tones 'contained a mixture of relief, of thanksgiving,
of chastened jubilations, of regret and of obscenity. [. . .] For [he] had
proved to them that women were inferior animals [. . .] And they were
[. . .] unfeignedly thankful.' No longer need they 'live up to the idea that
women should have justice [. . .] In this respect they would at least be able
to be at one with the ordinary male man. It made them very happy.' [33]
   Ford depicts Weininger being used to validate misogyny, or rather to
reconstruct it in a new form. His account substantiates the theories of
those feminists, in particular Sheila Jeffreys, who see sexology as part of
an anti-feminist backlash.[34] The editor of the *Individualist* wrote that the
worst aspects of men's character had been roused by the advance of the
women's revolution, and that Weininger's 'abominable' book could not
have sold so well 'were not the demand for expression of foul hatred of
woman prevalent in a certain quarter'.[35] But although Weininger's work
was openly welcomed by some German anti-feminists, their English counterparts, whatever they said in low voices among themselves, in public
repudiated his work for its sexualized account of womanhood. An anony-

mous reviewer in the *Times Literary Supplement* wrote:

> Underneath all this verbiage there is little more than an assertion in
> technological phraseology of the Mahomedan or Mormon view that
> woman is merely an unintellectual and non-moral organism for the
> perpetuation of the race [. . .] the discussion of matters which [. . .]
> are commonly excluded from conversation [. . .] seems to have been
> well received [. . .] in Germany.[36]

The majority of English readers, the writer continues, can confidently be
expected to reject it. Misogyny, it seems, conforms to national character.
A similar comment in an American context is made by feminist Charlotte
Perkins Gilman, who in her review of the book accuses Weininger of taking the 'oriental' position that women have no souls.[37] In fact, in his own
twist of orientalist rhetoric, Weininger explicitly repudiates what he calls
the 'Asiatic system' of women's sexual oppression which he sees operating in his own society.[38]

A more complex response to Weininger came from influential German
sexologist Iwan Bloch, whose book *The Sexual Life of Our Time* was published in English in 1908. Bloch, denying that male homosexuals are necessarily women haters, labels misogynists such as Weininger a 'fourth sex'.
He calls Weininger 'the apostle of *asexuality*' (emphasis in original), 'whose
views are unquestionably strongly pathological [. . .] the work of a luna-
tic'.[39] Despite these comments, elsewhere in his book Bloch treats Weininger's
theories critically but seriously, rather than as the ravings of a madman.

Already we can see that there is no one simple way in which Weininger's
work was being understood. His repudiation of sexual intercourse between men and women, which Bloch takes as a sign both of misogyny and
of madness, could be seen in a quite different light. Revolutionary celibacy was a call being heard from some strange bedfellows at this period.
Tolstoy, for instance (cited by Weininger),[40] advocated celibacy as a means
to greater spirituality, and his writings on the relations of the sexes were
debated in England by Christian socialists and anarchists, among whom
the 'sex question' was at the forefront of debates about how to live a new
life.[41] Many feminists and their male supporters responded to the sexual
double standard with a call for chastity for men. A few went further,
claiming that until women were fully emancipated, equal sexual relations
were impossible. Jeffreys points out that for many women such arguments
led to a conscious political choice of spinsterhood.[42] Some men were also
putting forward similar arguments. For example, 20-year-old anarchist-
communist Guy Aldred argued in *The Religion and Economics of Sex
Oppression* that marriage is a licence to rape, that as long as women are
economically, legally and socially unfree they are oppressed by sexual intercourse in or outside marriage, and that men and women should ideally

relate as non-sexual friends and companions.[43]

Some homosexual men, most notably Edward Carpenter, used evolutionary theory to argue that humans were evolving towards a spiritual stage beyond gender and sexuality, and that uranians were in the vanguard of this process.('Uranian', 'urning' or, after 1908, 'intermediate' were preferred to 'homosexual' as terms of self-identification by both men and women in the early years of the century.) Theoretically, for them asexuality was not a transitional demand, but a desired end. Since expression of their own sexuality was illegal, this could be seen as merely an expedient position, although the idea appears in private correspondence as well, suggesting genuine belief. Similar notions were shared by some lesbians, for instance those involved with the Aëthnic Union, which hoped for an androgynous, asexual future.

Carpenter himself, however, was not prepared to renounce sex publicly or privately, and as I will show, chose to focus on other aspects of Weininger's work. Carpenter holds an uneasy place in the pantheon of sexology, and is often omitted altogether. There are several possible reasons for this, not least the propensity of writers on the subject to construct theoretical lineages which lend support to those perspectives and methodologies they themselves favour. Carpenter did not write as a scientist, although qualified to do so, and he prefigured modern radical critiques of science, claiming that it often embodied the prejudices of the day. His methodology was eclectic; his writings draw on socialist utopianism, feminism, Hindu mysticism, anthropology and evolutionary theory with equal enthusiasm. Unlike other sexological writings of the period, all his work was intended for a general readership. Sexology was to have a long and never entirely successful struggle to establish itself as a reputable discipline, and Carpenter, with his anarchist and socialist connections and his unconcealed homosexuality, could hardly be claimed as an objective scholar. (Heterosexuality is rarely seen as a disqualification for writing on the subject.)

As his writings show, for him the personal – including the sexual – and the political were inseparable. Havelock Ellis was to call him 'a pioneer in living almost openly a homosexual life, which needs a rare combination of skill and courage [. . .] He succeeded where Oscar Wilde miserably failed.'[44] Ellis solicited Carpenter's advice, information, and life experiences when writing his own book *Sexual Inversion*, declared an obscene libel after its English publication in 1897. It was many years before Ellis was again able or willing to publish in England on sexuality, or to associate himself publicly with radical causes. In the early years of this century, then, Carpenter stands in England as a lone figure writing in positive terms about homosexuality and arguing for sexual and women's liberation as an integral part of progress towards a good society. He could perhaps be called an intermediate sexologist, his work bridging those purportedly objective writings aimed at an elite audience of experts and professionals, and the private speculations of individuals uncertain how to understand their feelings and experiences. Well known as a lecturer and writer, his works dealing with sexuality brought him letters and pilgrims from all over the world; he was seen as someone who lived his politics and could help others do likewise.

Early in 1895 Carpenter published, for private circulation only, the pamphlet *Homogenic Love: and its Place in a Free Society*, in which he argued that same-sex love was natural, had a positive part to play in social progress, and should not be persecuted. Later that year, amidst huge publicity, Oscar Wilde was tried and imprisoned for homosexual acts; Carpenter was one of his few public supporters. At the time, Carpenter was preparing to publish *Love's Coming of Age*, incorporating revisions of earlier pamphlets on sex, marriage and women, but although at this stage he was not proposing to include *Homogenic Love*, his publisher took fright, cancelling the contract. 'The Wilde trial had done its work; and silence must henceforth reign on sex-subjects', comments Carpenter.[45] He eventually managed to get the book published in 1896 by the Labour Press in Manchester, and it sold so well that by 1902 it was taken up by Swan Sonnenschein in London, who also that year published Carpenter's *Iolaus: An Anthology of Friendship*, celebrating same-sex friendships (mainly male) through the ages. By 1906 *Love's Coming of Age* was in its fifth edition and included a new chapter called 'The Intermediate Sex', based on an 1897 article 'An Unknown People'. It was in a 1905 revision of that article that Carpenter first used the term 'intermediate' – a concept he was to develop most fully in his book *The Intermediate Sex*, published in 1908.[46]

Carpenter, a feminist and supporter of the suffrage movement, believed that uranians – not just intermediates but intermediaries – could help heterosexual men and women towards a better understanding of one another, and that male uranians were more naturally sympathetic to women and their fight for freedom. When *Sex and Character* appeared in English, one of his women friends hoped that he would 'publish a counter blast'.[47] Instead, when *The Intermediate Sex* appeared two years later, Carpenter took its epigraph from Weininger. In part, it reads: 'The improbability may [. . .] be taken for granted of finding in Nature a sharp cleavage between all that is masculine [. . .] and all that is feminine [. . .] or that any living being is so simple in this respect that it can be put wholly on one side, or wholly on the other, of the line.'[48]

Ignoring Weininger's misogyny, Carpenter chooses quotations first to strengthen his own arguments for the naturalness of different forms of sexuality, and second to suggest tentatively that perhaps all men and women, not just uranians, have both male and female characteristics. Carpenter's concept of the intermediate sex thus has more flexibility than other current concepts like sexual inversion or the third sex, which depend on notions of fixed gender characteristics and identifiably different subgroups. Weininger himself writes: 'So long as there are two sexes, there will always be a woman question, just as there will be the problem of mankind. [. . .] truth will not prevail until the two become one, until from man and woman a third self, neither man nor woman, is evolved'.[49] Unlike third-sex theories, which leave unchallenged the dualism of Man and Woman, Weininger's 'third self' is not an additional category but may be interpreted as transcending category altogether. Both Carpenter and Weininger argued that homosexuality was natural and rejected the prevalent pathological models and the multiplication of sexual categories produced by contemporary sexologies. While Carpenter suggests that it may be the case that there is some degree of intermediacy in most people, Weininger claims that all humans are both heterosexual and homosexual, masculine and feminine. This claim that all men and women are to a greater or lesser degree intermediate was taken up with particular enthusiasm by some readers, who interpreted the idea variously in their struggle to formulate ways of thinking about their feelings and experiences. The combination of Weininger's universalism with Carpenter's high valuation of intermediacy produced a self-affirming context in which to discuss their own lives.

This creative interpretation and appropriation of Weininger, Carpenter and other sexologists can be seen among members of the friendship and political networks around the *Freewoman*.[50] Its editor, individualist anarchist Dora Marsden, was a former suffragette organizer. The paper's open editorial policy meant its readers and contributors came from a wide range of occupations and political perspectives, and it became notorious for its open discussion of sexual matters. Carpenter, a subscriber and contributor, gave public support for its 'broadminded and courageous' contribution to 'the cause of free and rational discussion of human problems'.[51] The *Freewoman*'s readiness to discuss political and sexual revolution meant that it was denounced in *The Times*, banned by W.H. Smith, and subject to harassment by the police. More than just a paper, it seeded spin-off groups, and its Discussion Circle meetings attracted large numbers to hear talks on such subjects as sex oppression, eugenics and prostitution.

In 1911, Marsden was intending to write a philosophical work incorporating a critique of Weininger;[52] her friend Mary Gawthorpe urged her to allow herself the time properly to 'set the balance to the Weininger–Nietzsche–Freud excesses'.[53] The closest Marsden came to this was to publish long selections from *Sex and Character*, commenting on them in an editorial in which she both praises and criticizes Weininger. His genius, she says, was to recognize the two great oppositions, personality and amorphousness; his 'boyish misstatement' to locate these respectively in men, and in Jews and women. If 'femaleness' is not co-extensive with the term 'women', but refers to a loss of personality, then it is, she agrees, 'the Great Denial – the thing to be overcome' in women and men.[54] Some subsequent contributors attacked the decision to publish Weininger's 'poison',[55] but his influence is evident in a number of articles on sexuality, particularly those debating homosexuality.

The subject is first broached in the *Freewoman* by Harry Birnstingl in the article 'Uranians'. Birnstingl, an architect, was a supporter of women's suffrage; his aunts, Kate and Ethel Birnstingl were WSPU members and early subscribers to the *Freewoman*. Ethel and her long-time companion Alice Pollard ran a feminist bookshop in London.[56] Harry, a friend of Marsden and her companion Grace Jardine, wrote frequently for the paper and gave talks to the Discussion Circle. In 'Uranians', perhaps drawing on the experience of his friends and relatives, he points out that many women in the women's movement, far from being sexless spinsters, form romantic, passionate relationships with one another based on their common struggle. 'It is splendid that these women [. . .] should suddenly find their destiny in thus working together for the freedom of their sex.' He cites Carpenter's positive comments on uranians and in language clearly drawn from Weininger says: 'The atoms which go to compose the normal male and the normal female are capable of infinite combinations.'[57]

Before publishing this article Dora Marsden had approached Dr Charles Whitby as 'a medical man' for advice.[58] Whitby, a socialist who had previously worked at a dispensary in Liverpool, recommended publication, followed by a reply by himself. (He was paid ten shillings and sixpence for this. Since contributors were normally unpaid, the transaction suggests particular anxiety about the 'Uranians' article.)[59] Preferring 'homosexual' to 'uranian', using the language of inversion and perversion, abnormality and aberration, drawing on the spectre of child abuse, Whitby at least concedes that the paper is right to 'let the light of day into these dark and dusty corners'.[60]

In reply, Birnstingl uses Whitby's own arguments to claim, echoing Weininger and Carpenter, that 'all men and women are in a greater or lesser degree Intermediates', and criticizes Whitby's views on masculinity and femininity as well as uranianism.[61] Whitby's response concedes that 'Every human being is in some sense an incarnate contradiction', but draws on biological and racial discourses of evolution and degeneration as well as stereotypes of pathologically (but not constitutionally) effeminate men. 'There are men, as Mr Birnstingl must know, with whom it is more compromising for another man to be seen in the street than with a prostitute', he writes.[62] A similar note of heterosexual panic can be seen in another contributor, Fabian lawyer E.S.P. Haynes, who (despite the fact that he likes and agrees with Birnstingl) is so anxious about appearing in the same journal – never mind the street – with him, that he asks to be published only as E.S.P.H. To use his full name would be 'like walking through Lincoln's Inn in pyjamas'.[63]

Birnstingl particularly wanted his full name used. Other contributors used pseudonyms. In a letter drawing directly upon Weininger's sexual equations, 'Scython' writes about his real, inner self, '80F + 20M' (80 per cent female plus 20 per cent male), concealed from all but a few friends 'who know me as I am'. [64] Weininger's attempt to provide mathematical formulae for an individual's precise quantities of masculinity and femininity may seem rigid and scientistic, if not quaint, but in practice it allows the scope to enunciate individual variability and to elude the crude classifications of the sexologists, as well as providing an adaptable way of thinking through personal experience of gender dissonance.

Another contribution, 'The Intellectual Limitations of the "Normal"', came from Albert Löwy, a trainee solicitor who was a friend of Birnstingl and Mary Gawthorpe. It was published shortly after he returned from a life-changing visit to Carpenter. ('In the marvel of your touch I learned the magic secrets of love [. . .] I know now [. . .] a life-course [. . .] a hope-force.')[65] In his letter to the paper, Löwy argues that the vast majority of people are intermediates, neither inverts nor monosexuals.[66] Related ideas can be seen in the letters of David Thompson, a close friend of Carpenter's from 1890s' Sheffield socialist circles. On reading The Intermediate Sex Thompson, now married and working at the Library of Congress in Washington, wrote, 'I feel more and more that I am somewhat in that category.'[67] Later, a widower visiting England, he wooed Ruth Slate, a socialist feminist member of the Freewoman Discussion Circle and fellow Carpenter fan. 'Psychically I think I am much nearer to women than to other men', he wrote to her, 'but combined with this intermediate temperament are most unruly masculine bodily desires [i.e. for women].' Later he speaks of 'the woman part of me'.[68] Other friends also drew on the fruitful ambiguities of the concept of intermediacy. A married man wrote secretly to his lover Jessie (who lived with another woman), calling her a 'child of Uranus', and 'my dear, healthy, gay, philosopher, wife, my boy and comrade'.[69] Minna Simmons, who had a passionate physical relationship with Eva Slawson, as well as with men, is lent a copy of The Intermediate Sex and identifies herself as 'an eaning [sic]'.[70] For all of them, the concept of intermediacy opens up rather than forecloses ways of thinking about gender and sexuality.

Lucy Bland argues that the Freewoman generated a space for the public discussion of new ideas about gender and sexuality, with women contributors in particular making selective use of sexological ideas in an attempt to reconfigure heterosexuality for themselves.[71] If heterosexuality is reconfigured, so also is homosexuality. Though Dora Marsden called in the *Freewoman* for the voice of direct experience,[72] she and other women involved in passionate relationships with one another generally kept public silence on these issues. However, private letters show women as well as men were drawing on sexology as part of the process of formulating an identity.[73] As Bland says, the language of sexuality was by no means fixed during this period.[74] Marsden calls Weininger a poet, and although she had earlier argued for the importance of precise definitions in order to discuss sex 'scientifically, cleanly, and openly', she says elsewhere 'the "Sex-psychologist" should be a poet, not a physical scientist'.[75] The *Freewoman* articles and correspondence and the private letters and diaries all show their writers using terms interchangeably from quite different conceptual frameworks, referring for example to intermediates, urnings, homosexual and homogenic feelings, sapphists, inverts, the third sex and bisexuality, without seeming to be troubled by theoretical incompatibility. Far more important than choice of terminology to those who were trying to develop new ways of thinking about and understanding themselves and their friends were the values and attitudes of a particular writer, and the respect shown (or not) to those who fell outside the framework of 'normality'.

'There is wanted', writes Weininger, in a quotation cited by Carpenter, 'an "orthopaedic" treatment of the soul, instead of the torture caused by the application of ready-made conventional shapes.'[76] This desire to escape classification is echoed in criticisms of sexology by those who did not fit conventional sexual categories:

> Intermediates are a 'disturbing factor' in the understanding of the human race; hence the scientist, intent on classification and 'practical purposes' is concerned with eliminating those examples which obstinately refuse to be labelled. Complete Inverts he puts in prison or a madhouse, and he 'explains away' [. . .] those who do not conform to his rigid categories.[77]

> Nature [. . .] abhors rules and regulations.[78]

> [H]ow can one classify and label the different kinds of love![79]

> [F]or the classifier, the maker of laws, and other similar guardians of the public morals, these persons form a serious obstruction, seeing that they refuse to be 'pigeon-holed' [. . .] the best of all remedies would be to abolish the pigeon-holes altogether.[80]

Most accounts of sexology, whether presenting it as stepping stone, obstacle, or something to be negotiated, are embedded within a narrative of progress towards contemporary sexual enlightenment, and tend to focus only on those figures who can be seen as on the right track. Perhaps this is inevitable – as Carpenter cogently argued, there are limits to how far we can escape the presuppositions of our own time[81] – but a more careful attention to the uses and users of sexology gives us a more complex version of how particular sexologies affected and were affected by lived experiences. In spaces they carved out for themselves, we can see women and gay men becoming the authors rather than the objects of discussion, and can begin to understand something of how they negotiated their identities and understood their deepest feelings. The search for truth, says Marsden, is the search for a diversity of voices, all with their own tales to tell.[82] What matters above all is what tales a text makes possible. Eclecticism, seen as a weakness by the theoretically inclined, can also be seen as a strength. Those readers who ignored the unpalatable aspects of Weininger's work were not endorsing them; they were taking what they needed in order to construct their own versions of the world.

Notes

1 '*Geschlect*', as well as carrying the ambiguities of the English word 'sex', also means race, species, family, generation. This linguistic overloading adds to the complexity of the symbolic connections rehearsed in the book.

2 Jaques le Rider, *Le Cas Otto Weininger: Racines De L'Antifeminisme Et De L'Antisemitisme* (Presses Universitaires de France, Paris, 1982).

3 Thanks to Jean Rose for this information.

4 Grace Freud to Carpenter, 20 October 1906, Carpenter Collection, Sheffield.

5 Dora Marsden, 'The Emancipation of Man', *Freewoman*, 1:20, 4 April 1912, pp. 381–2.

6 David Abrahamsen, *The Mind and Death of a Genius* (Columbia University Press, New York, 1946).

7 Vincent Brome, *Freud and his Early Circle* (Heinemann, London, 1967); Le Rider, *Le Cas Otto Weininger*.

8 Robert Musil and Karl Kraus quoted in Allen Janik and Stephen Toulmin, *Wittgenstein's Vienna* (Weidenfeld and Nicolson, London, 1973), pp. 33, 67.

9 Ibid.; Carl E. Schorske, *Fin-de-Siècle Vienna* (Knopf, New York 1980).

10 Josef Fraenkel, ed., *The Jews of Austria* (Vallentine, Mitchell and Co., London, 1967); Le Rider, *Le Cas Otto Weininger*.

11 Karin J. Jušek, 'Sexual morality and the meaning of prostitution in fin-de-siècle Vienna', in *From Sappho to de Sade: Moments in the History of Sexuality*, ed. Jan Bremmer (Routledge, London, 1991), pp. 123–42.

12 Harriet Anderson, *Utopian Feminism: Women's Movements in fin-de-siècle Vienna* (Yale University Press, London, 1992).

13 Charlotte Wolff, *Magnus Hirschfeld* (Quartet, London, 1986).

14 Weininger, *Sex and Character* (Heinemann, London, 1906), pp. 72–3, 329.
15 Ibid., p. ix.
16 Ibid., pp. 54–5.
17 Ibid., p. 48.
18 Ibid., pp. 66, 75.
19 Ibid., pp. 292, 88–89.
20 Ibid., Part Two, Ch. 10.
21 Ibid., pp. 92, 287.
22 Ibid., pp. 303–4.
23 Ibid., pp. 348–9.
24 Ibid., pp. 343–9.
25 A Grateful Reader, *Freewoman*, 1:25, 9 May 1912, p. 497.
26 Charlotte Perkins Gilman, 'Dr. Weininger's "Sex and Character"', *Critic*, 5:48, May 1906, pp. 414–17.
27 Marsden, 'The Emancipation of Man'.
28 Otto Weininger, *Geschlecht und Charakter: Eine Prinzipielle Untersuchung* (Braumüller, Vienna and Leipzig, 1903).
29 Weininger, *Sex and Character*, pp. 248, 300.
30 Weininger, *Taschenbuch*, cited in Sander L. Gilman, *Jewish Self Hatred: Anti-Semitism and the Hidden Language of the Jews* (Johns Hopkins, London, 1986), p. 247.
31 Weininger, *Sex and Character*, pp. 245, 248–9.
32 Ford Madox Ford, *Women and Men* (Contact Editions, Paris, 1923), p. 30.
33 Ibid., pp. 30–2.
34 Sheila Jeffreys, *The Spinster and her Enemies* (Pandora, London, 1985).
35 'Notes and Comments', *Individualist*, NS25:318, March–April 1912, p. 18.
36 *Times Literary Supplement*, 16 February 1906, 54c.
37 Gilman, 'Dr. Weininger's "Sex and Character"'.
38 Weininger, *Sex and Character*, p. 343.
39 Iwan Bloch, *The Sexual Life of Our Time*, tr. Eden Paul (Heinemann, London, 1908), pp. 481, 95, 117–18.
40 Weininger, *Geschlecht und Charakter*, p. 596.
41 Leo Tolstoy, *The Relations of the Sexes* (Free Age Press, C.W. Daniel, London, n.d.), is probably the pamphlet cited by Weininger and read by Ruth Slate and Eva Slawson. Slate to Slawson, 24 February 1908; Slawson's diary, 15 April 1913, Slate Collection, London. See also Tierl Thompson, ed., *Dear Girl: The Diaries and Letters of Two Working Women 1897–1917* (Women's Press, London, 1987); Dennis Hardy, *Alternative Communities in Nineteenth Century England* (Longman, London, 1979).
42 Jeffreys, *The Spinster and her Enemies*.
43 Guy Aldred, *The Religion and Economics of Sex Oppression* (Bakunin Press, London, 1907).
44 Havelock Ellis, cited in Stephen Winsten, *Salt and his Circle* (Hutchinson, London, 1951), p.162.
45 Edward Carpenter, *My Days and Dreams*, 3rd edn (George Allen and Unwin, London, 1918), p. 196.
46 Edward Carpenter, *An Unknown People* (A. and H.B. Bonner, London, 1897,

1905); *The Intermediate Sex: A Study of Some Transitional Types of Men and Women* (Swan Sonnenschein, London, 1908).

47 Grace Freud to Carpenter, 20 October 1906, Carpenter Collection.

48 Carpenter, *The Intermediate Sex,* epigraph.

49 Weininger, *Sex and Character*, p. 345.

50 It became the *New Freewoman*, 'An Individualist Review', in 1913, before finally metamorphosing into a non-feminist literary journal, the *Egoist*, in 1914.

51 Edward Carpenter, *New Freewoman*, 1:2, 1 July 1913, p. 40.

52 Les Garner, *A Brave and Beautiful Spirit: Dora Marsden 1882–1960* (Avebury, Aldershot, 1990), p. 144.

53 Mary Gawthorpe to Marsden, 29 September 1912; 20 August 1913, Marsden Collection, Princeton.

54 Dora Marsden, 'Sex and Character', *Freewoman*, 2:30, 13 June 1912, pp. 61–3.

55 'True Womanhood', *Freewoman*, 2:28, 30 May 1912, p. 38.

56 WSPU Annual Reports 1908–13 (WSPU, London); further information thanks to Martin Birnstingl.

57 Harry J. Birnstingl, 'Uranians', *Freewoman*, 1:7, 4 January 1912, pp. 127–8. This is probably the piece which led Robert Ross (friend and sometime lover of Oscar Wilde) to enquire about him. E.S.P. Haynes to Marsden, 1 February 1912, Marsden Collection.

58 Charles J. Whitby, 'Tertium Quid', *Freewoman*, 1:9, 18 January 1912, pp. 167–9.

59 Whitby to Marsden, 29 December 1911, 26 February 1912, Marsden Collection.

60 Whitby, 'Tertium Quid'.

61 Birnstingl, 'The Human Minority', *Freewoman*, 1:12, 8 February 1912, p. 235.

62 Charles J. Whitby, 'A Matter of Taste', *Freewoman*, 1:11, 1 February 1912, pp. 215–6.

63 E.S.P. Haynes to Marsden, 7 November 1911, 29 March 1912, Marsden Collection.

64 'Scython', *Freewoman*, 1:14, 22 February 1912, p. 274. 'Scython' may have been A.(?) Samuel or Harold Picton. See letters from Samuel, 12 November 1912, and Picton, 24 October 1913, Marsden Collection.

65 Albert Löwy to Carpenter, 9 October 1911, Carpenter Collection. Mr and Mrs H. Löwy, subscribers, and friends of Mary Gawthorpe, were probably his parents. See *Freewoman* accounts, n.d.; letter to Marsden, 4 May 1911, Marsden Collection.

66 Albert E. Löwy, 'The Intellectual Limitations of the "Normal"', *Freewoman*, 1:11, 1 February 1912, p. 212.

67 David Thompson to Carpenter, 2 September 1909, Carpenter Collection.

68 Thompson to Slate, 10 December 1913, 30 March 1916, Slate Collection.

69 Poul Mittler to Jessie Marsh, 10 June 1921, 8 November 1921, Slate Collection.

70 Minna Simmons to Slate, January 1917, Slate Collection.

71 Lucy Bland, *Banishing the Beast: English Feminism and Sexual Morality 1885–*

1914 (Penguin, Harmondsworth, 1995*)*, Ch. 7.

72 Dora Marsden, 'On Affirmations', *Freewoman*, 1:13, 15 February 1912, pp. 243–4; 'Views and Comments', *New Freewoman*, 1:9 , 15 October 1913, p. 166.

73 See Bland, *Banishing the Beast*, Ch. 7; Liz Stanley, 'Epistemological Issues in Researching Lesbian History: The Case of Romantic Friendship', in Hilary Hinds, Ann Phoenix and Jackie Stacey, eds, *Working Out: New Directions for Women's Studies* (Falmer Press, London, 1992), pp. 161–72.

74 Bland, *Banishing the Beast*, Ch. 7.

75 Dora Marsden, 'The New Morality', *Freewoman*, 1:6, 28 December 1911, pp. 101–2; 'More Plain Speaking', 1:17, 14 March 1912, p. 332; 'Views and Comments', p.166.

76 Carpenter, *The Intermediate Sex*, p. 164.

77 Löwy, 'The Intellectual Limitations of the "Normal"'.

78 Birnstingl, 'Uranians'.

79 Kate Salt to Carpenter, 22 October 1909, Carpenter Collection.

80 Birnstingl, 'The Human Minority'.

81 Edward Carpenter, 'Modern Science: A Criticism', in Carpenter, *Civilisation: Its Cause and Cure* (Allen and Unwin, London, 1921), pp. 79–119.

82 Marsden, 'On Affirmations'; 'Views and Comments'.

3 The Hidden Romance of Sexual Science: Eugenics, the Nation and the Making of Modern Feminism

Carolyn Burdett

In the late nineteenth century sexual science was, on the one hand, a language of detail and delineation, creating ever more particularized classificatory systems by which new identities emerged to be, in turn, scrutinized as the perverse objects of medical knowledge. On the other hand, sexual science took the population *en masse* as its object of enquiry – not as a model of normality, but as a great body needing regulation at the point of its most intimate sexual affairs. Biological heredity made sex the court at which the future would be decided, a future which would be one of improvement and progress or one of degeneration and decay. As Foucault puts it, in *The History of Sexuality*, 'sex and its fertility had to be administered. The medicine of perversions and the programmes of eugenics were the two great innovations in the technology of sex of the second half of the nineteenth century.'[1]

The end of the nineteenth century was, too, the very moment that middle-class women were finding their way into the educational, professional and political spaces which a rhetoric of modernization and individualism promised to make available to all those with the wit to help themselves. Our contemporary feminism has – unsurprisingly – been hostile to much of the sexual science of the nineteenth century, particularly to those medical discourses whose objective was the sexual physiology of women. Femaleness *per se* tended to be seen as pathological in medicine and thus akin to the perversions, the first of Foucault's 'two great innovations in the technology of sex'. Modern feminism has seen such medical discourses as powerful, naturalizing languages which served to reinforce gender stereotypes and to block the making of more equitable relations between men and women. By contrast, heredity and eugenics have been given less attention in relation to the emergence of feminism in the late nineteenth century. Eugenics has been, in the twentieth century, far more closely associated both with a rhetoric of class superiority and with colonialism and imperialism (eugenic ideas began to be established in the popular imagination in England during the Anglo–Boer war of 1899–1902) and, finally, in the 1930s and 1940s, with the terrible spectre of a state using the language of science to justify the mass and efficient killing of its own people.

I want to argue, however, that the relation between an emerging middle-class feminism and eugenics, in the late nineteenth and early twentieth centuries, is indeed an important one. To do so, I will look at the work of the eugenist, Karl Pearson, and the South African novelist and feminist, Olive Schreiner. Pearson, as I will describe below, saw himself as a crusader establishing the scientific credentials of eugenics; Schreiner came to prominence in England after the appearance of her first novel, *The Story of an African Farm*, and published, in 1911, an influential feminist work, *Woman and Labour*. The work of both writers is idiosyncratic in some ways – Pearson was resolutely opposed to the major eugenic body in the twentieth century, the Eugenics Education Society, for example, and Schreiner was a colonial – but, I will argue, both nevertheless make for a revealing case study of the difficult inheritances with which a distinctively modern feminism, which emerged at the end of the nineteenth century, had to struggle. In particular, Pearson's eugenics, and Schreiner's response to it, reveal just how intimately an imagining of women's emancipation and transformed relations between the sexes was bound up with the concept of the nation and racial identity.

Francis Galton's New Religion

The idea of *biological* inheritance belongs to a secularized and democratizing social world. If different qualities and capacities of human beings were no longer ordained by God, they had to be made elsewhere, either by humans themselves or by some other force. In the nineteenth century, biology was increasingly seen as the arbiter of human difference and, with it, heredity began to be conceived as a natural law by which like begets like, as well as a law governing the distribution of property. Francis Galton first began to try to establish this idea on a systematic basis, after his studies had persuaded him that the concentration of eminence in a relatively small number of families proved that ability was inherited, rather than randomly distributed. The method he used was statistical – counting, recording and correlating numbers – and he published his initial findings as a two-part article for *Macmillan's Magazine*, which was subsequently developed into his influential *Hereditary Genius*.[2] Through this statistical method, Galton set about formulating the bases of a new science, a science he later called 'eugenics'. This was:

> the science of improving stock, which is by no means confined to questions of judicious mating, but which, especially in the case of man, takes cognisance of all influences that tend in however remote a degree to give to the suitable races or strains of blood a better chance of prevailing speedily over the less suitable than they otherwise would have had.[3]

Born into a commercially successful and intellectually renowned family (his mother was the daughter of Erasmus Darwin), Galton was adamant that progress and improvement lay neither with a decaying landed gentry, nor with a vulgar and self-interested entrepreneuralism, but with the aristocracy of intellect found in the professional classes. Inheritance, in the modern world, meant the passing on of a healthy physique and a good brain, rather than property and land. Eugenics was this world's new religion, in which the scientist had a priestly duty toward 'the health and well-being of the nation in its broadest sense'.[4]

Galton acknowledged that his work had been facilitated by the publication in 1859 of *Origin of Species* by his cousin, Charles Darwin. The seething, fecund world of nature imagined by Darwin, however, was very different to Galton's eugenically oriented future. In the mid-nineteenth century, social theory was influenced by Herbert Spencer's ideas about social competition as much as by Darwin's biological theory, and evolutionary struggle thus appeared the perfect mirror, in the natural world, to the laissez-faire liberal individualism which partnered the development of capitalist economy.[5] In contrast, the political implications of eugenics were largely antagonistic to laissez-faire because the individual – even in its most apparently private matters – was subordinated to a *larger* body. Eugenics shifted the emphasis from economic struggle to focus directly on *sexual* selection. But eugenic sexual selection is not driven by the brutal and wasteful mechanisms Darwin described, or by the traditional, aristocratic aim of managing land and property, and even less by individual desire and serendipity. Rather sexuality – in so far as it is connected to procreation (and some eugenists came to argue that the two should be separated)[6] – had to be brought under the aegis of a greater, controlling body. Unlike the instinctual, passionate, individual body, this greater body is one motivated by rationality and oriented towards the greater good – namely the state.

Karl Pearson and the Calculable World

Galton's acknowledged protégé was Karl Pearson. Pearson trained as a mathematician and, in 1884, became professor of applied mathematics at University College, London. By the 1890s, working with another colleague, and inspired by Galton's work, he set about 'making biology a mathematical science'. He developed and honed statistical tools and methodologies in order to produce data about heredity and evolution.[7] With enormous commitment, and what Phyllis Grosskurth describes as an 'immense, humourless, self-important rectitude',[8] he argued the case for biometric study – the measurement of biological life – in the service of eugenics. In the mid-1890s, he set up the Biometric Laboratory and, in 1902, founded a journal, *Biometrika*. After Galton's death, Pearson was established at the head of the Galton Laboratory for National Eugenics, where he presided until his retirement in 1933. The laboratory was the country's primary eugenic eugenic's primary research institution, 'the scientific benchmark of all eugenic discussion in England',[9] and Pearson was zealous in keeping it free of unscientific influences, such as he believed were promulgated by the popularizing Eugenics Education Society. He was, at all times, antagonistic to arguments he felt were not scientifically grounded. For Pearson, 'the strife of parties, [. . .] the conflict of creeds, [. . .] false notions of charity, or the unbalanced impulses of sentiment' were not simply antipathetic to truth, but dangerous impediments to social life and national progress.[10]

Pearson described his eugenic work as the 'discovery of a new calculus' by which differentiated groups of humans could be measured 'to ascertain which of these differentiated groups is, according to its characteristics, the most effective for this or that purpose, to determine not only its rate of increase, but the extent to which its qualities are transmitted to its offspring and modified by environment'.[11] It is precisely this new calculus – the new statistical methods of dealing with large numbers that Pearson was developing – that made eugenics possible. Bourgeois society privatized the family but its privatization depended upon the breakdown of traditional, religious forms of regulating sexual and familial life. The statistical work pioneered by Pearson promised a new means of knowing about families and the consequences of human sexuality: through measuring and categorizing the populace in terms of different physical and mental characteristics, and correlating them between parents and offspring, 'fitness' and 'unfitness' could be identified and traced back through family lines of heredity.

Eugenic research thus opened up the working-class family to the scrutiny of the professional and the expert, but it also targeted the middle-class family – especially its women. As a young man, Pearson was fascinated by debates about women's emancipation. In 1885 he set up a discussion group, the Men and Women's Club, which aimed to foster a free and frank exchange of ideas about all matters concerning relations between the sexes. However, Pearson was concerned only to establish what *science* had to say about sexuality; other forms of knowledge were strictly off-limits at the club's discussions.[12] While he did not yet espouse explicitly eugenic views, the major features of Pearson's eugenics were there: an unwearying and even bullying defence of science as the only true knowledge and a firm belief in the nation as the basis of social progress.

It is the latter – the importance of the nation – which so often gets overlooked when *feminist* responses to eugenics are considered. Feminists like Schreiner who were enthusiasts for the new scientific view of sexuality and sexual relations, who saw science as a force breaking down convention and prejudice, astutely recognized that it could also become dogmatic. Schreiner repeatedly challenged Pearson about his failure to understand that humans were emotional as well as rational creatures, for example.[13] In other words, she understood what romanticism had, in various ways, argued throughout the nineteenth century: namely that there is something about humanness – something which gets called feeling or emotion or sensibility – which escapes calculation. But eugenic discourse is not only – as Pearson's rhetoric often suggests – an attempt to perfect the methods of rational calculation which post-Enlightenment culture saw as the route out of the archaism, privilege and custom left over from a feudal rule of might. Pearson's eugenic ideas are also fuelled by a romantic and idealist vision of the nation-state which, I will argue, was integral to the arguments for women's emancipation being made by feminists like Schreiner at the end of the nineteenth century. When women were addressed, by eugenic discourse, as maternal, they were at the same time interpellated as mothers *for* the nation. When women defined themselves as social and ethical agents, they simultaneously positioned themselves within a national context. Thus, while Schreiner was able to combat an overly deterministic scientific rationalism in her feminism, her own rhetoric depends upon a problematic vision of the nation and its associated language of race.

National Socialism and the Perfectible World

The nation is at the centre of all Pearson's eugenics. He argues, for example, in *The Academic Aspect of the Science of National Eugenics*:

> We have to take our own racial qualities as they are given to us, and study how they are being, or may be improved or impaired. The moment you realize this, you will see that the words '*National* Eu-

genics' have been rightly used. Every nation has in a certain sense its own study of eugenics, and what is true of one nation is not necessarily true of a second.[14]

The nation-state and statistics: they are not surprising companions, given that 'statistics' *means* the state's numbers, numbers which register and record the state's affairs and interests. The emphasis on the nation, in Pearson's eugenics, stems from time he spent as a young man in Germany, where he went in 1879 on a postgraduate fellowship from King's College. There, he was drawn to German folk-lore, to the German Reformation and the influence of the German humanists. He read the idealist philosophers and was intensely attracted to Spinoza.[15] During this intellectually fertile period, Pearson was seduced by the idea of the nation-state. Drawing from the work of the idealist philosopher Johann Fichte, as well as Kant and Hegel, he began to envisage the nation as the place in which the good of the people could be realized in a modern, technological and rational world.

Pearson quickly identified himself as a socialist. In this he was influenced by writers such as Fichte, who, in his 1800 work, *The Closed Commercial State*, imagines the good life in terms of an eventually sealed-off state. This state, in closing itself off to worldly competition, would dispel all conflict and exist in peace and happiness. It would be socialistic in the sense that Marx, later in the century, came to formulate, in that what a citizen has and can expect to have is determined by need; economics functions by 'an absolute balance of value' of resources, overseen by the state, rather than by a drive to profit; and the stability of the whole is guaranteed by the state, which unifies all its disparate elements (the individuals who make it up) by 'a great deal of business and many calculations and inspections in order to keep a stable equilibrium'. This closed state, according to Fichte, will also produce a robust national feeling; in it 'a high degree of national honour and a sharply distinguished national character are bound to arise very quickly'.[16]

Fichte's belief in the development of a German national character shares its themes with the enormously important work, being produced at about the same time, of Johann Herder. Raymond Williams identifies Herder as making the decisive break from a dominant, Enlightenment-inspired account of history-as-civilization. Herder's romantic response to the grand accounts of secular human progress was to pull apart civilization ('external' material progress) and culture, and to use the latter as a term to 'express other kinds of human development, other criteria for human well-being and, crucially, in the plural, "the specific and variable cultures of different nations and periods"'.[17] The nation is the organic repository of a national spirit formed in the past and unfolded from its distant prototype.[18] Furthermore: 'The most natural state [. . .] is *one* nation, with one national character [. . .] a nation is as much a natural plant as a family, only with more branches.'[19] Thus, while Herder on the one hand offered a vision of cultural relativism (different peoples developing differently, depending upon geography, climate and so on), his emphasis on locality as productive of such distinctive human differences fuelled later theories of racial difference that justified racial categorization in terms of superiority and inferiority. His theory also paved the way for asserting – as Herder himself and others after him did – the superiority of German culture.

When he was still in Germany, Pearson embraced a form of romantic anti-colonialism inspired by writers such as Herder[20] but, on his return to London, began to rework the romantic concept of the nation in relation to Darwinian evolution. A widely accepted tenet of evolution provided him with his starting point: struggle is the condition of progress. However cruel it seems – and it 'means suffering, intense suffering' – struggle is 'the fiery crucible out of which comes the finer metal' of human development. The day when all peoples exist side by side in harmony might be the enlightened modern's wish, 'But, believe me, when that day comes, mankind will no longer progress; there will be nothing to check the fertility of inferior stock; the relentless law of heredity will not be controlled and guided by natural selection.'[21] The only scientifically viable response, according to Pearson, is eugenics: '[Man] may consciously undertake what Nature has done for him by her selective death-rate; to prepare him for this function is the true aim of the science of eugenics.'[22] The struggle, in the civilized world is not, however, between individuals but between nations: the ordering of its population's sexual and procreative life to produce the 'fittest' possible human beings is the primary task of any successful nation.

What emerges at the heart of Pearson's eugenics, therefore, is an aggressive advocacy of imperial expansion as the civilized form of the struggle for survival. The older evolutionists, Pearson argues, emphasized only the individual struggle:

> They do not appear to have recognised that many of the characters which gave man his foremost place in the animal kingdom were evoked in the struggle of tribe against tribe, of race against race, and even of man as a whole against other forms of life and against his physical environment [. . .] They forgot that the herd exists owing to its social instincts, and that human sympathy and racial and national feelings are strong natural forces controlling individual conduct.[23]

In other words, they misunderstood the *gregarious* nature of 'man'. A strong nation, according to Pearson, is one in which *social* instinct has been developed. It is this belief which underlines his socialism: 'You must not have class differences and wealth differences and education differences so great within the community that you lose the sense of common interest.'[24] It does not, however, mean that difference as such can, or should, be erased. Rather, for Pearson, it is a matter of understanding which of such differences are natural, and therefore unalterable, and then recognizing that the state's task is to contain them. Thus state policy is a matter of maximizing the coherence and homogeneity of the nation – through eugenic policies – in order best to fit it for the *proper* clash of like and unlike, which is the struggle of nations and races:

> You will see that my view – and I think it may be called the scientific view of a nation – is that of an organized whole, kept up to a high pitch of internal efficiency by insuring that its numbers are substantially recruited from the better stocks, and kept up to a high degree of external efficiency by contest, chiefly by way of war with inferior races, and with equal races by the struggle for trade-routes and for the sources of raw material and of food supply.[25]

Human love and sympathy – all those empathetic sentiments associated with morality – are, Pearson argues, properly understood as social feelings which extend – just as Herder and Fichte argued – to the limits of the nation *and no further*. After that is aggressive commercial or military struggle, up to and including genocide. The romantic concept of the nation-state which gained such popularity in Germany at the beginning of the nineteenth century is offered as a scientific and *socialist* account of national life by Pearson at the beginning of the twentieth. It is anti-capitalist inasmuch as it is fervently anti-individualist and anti-liberal. Pearson was adamantly opposed to the language of rights which characterized the liberal utilitarian tradition exemplified by John Stuart Mill. Capitalism produced a class-divided society, with a disaffected working class; the market-led vicissitudes of laissez-faire economics encouraged the kind of unskilled, cheap, plentiful and easily discardable labour which Pearson identified as the 'unfit', and which would inevitably foster decay rather than forge the united nation.

Like Herder, Pearson makes the purity of national identity essential to its strength and efficacy. The man who professes brotherly love for those of another race 'is probably deceiving himself'; in any case, such sentiment is simply counter to the force of progress, which *is* national struggle, predicated on the existence of a 'national spirit'. Thus Pearson argues that forms of colonization in which the colonizers and colonized live together invariably produce disastrous effects, hampering the processes of natural selection which supposedly reigns amongst 'primitive' peoples and, at worse, mixing the blood of 'superior' and 'inferior' peoples to the detriment of the former. He argues instead for the absolute right – indeed, evolutionary necessity – for 'superior' races to take, if they should so wish, what he calls the 'unutilized lands' of the earth. As he puts it in 'Socialism and Natural Selection': 'No thoughtful socialist, so far as I am aware, would object to cultivate Uganda *at the expense of its present occupiers* if Lancashire were starving.'[26] As far as Pearson is concerned, the socialist understands this because she or he understands that society depends absolutely for its progress on a social instinct or drive which is synonymous with national feeling and which all the members of the nation feel. The socialist also understands that the social system must be based upon labour, rather than wealth. Those who fail to labour effectively – the idle rich in Britain and Europe, or the feckless 'Kaffir and the Negro' who, despite thousands of years undisturbed by white men, 'have not yet produced a civilization in the least comparable with the Aryan' – are simply the 'waste' of both the natural and the rational forces of progress.[27]

The Woman Question

For eugenists like Pearson, women were the key to national progress. While fears about the feckless breeding of the 'improvident' classes were never far from eugenic concerns, Pearson, like many other eugenists, was especially interested in middle-class women. In the 1880s he used the Men and Women's Club to work out ideas about the changing role of women in a changed world. In the club's inaugural paper, 'The Woman's Question', he reflects on what changes might occur if women were to gain access to education, to the professions, and to political representation. In particular, he is concerned about the division between single women and those with children, if the former are able to find rewards in the world of remunerative work, and thus find dependency and motherhood less attractive. If there is to be sexual equality it will, Pearson claims, entail the entire reconstruction of the family, something which could only be achieved through state intervention.

As usual, Pearson insists such issues can only be resolved through scientific knowledge, but he ends his address to his eager young audience – which included Olive Schreiner – with the following 'ray of hope':

> That the past subjection of women has tended largely to expand men's selfish instincts I cannot deny; but may it not be that this very subjection has in itself so chastened woman, so trained her to think rather of others than of herself, that after all it may have acted more as a blessing than a curse to the world? [. . .] She may see more clearly than he the real points at issue, and as she has learnt self-control in the past by subjecting her will to his, so in the future she may be able to submit her liberty to the restraints demanded by social welfare, and to the conditions imposed by race-permanence.[28]

This conclusion might seem surprising in the light of Pearson's hostility to Lamarckianism (the notion, deriving from the work of Jean-Baptiste Lamarck, that an organism can *acquire* characteristics which it can then pass on to its offspring). But if the focus of his argument here is understood to be the issue of self-control and subjection, rather than the mechanisms of inheritance, it is consistent with what I have been arguing is the influence of idealism on his work. In his *Addresses to the German Nation* and other writings on education, Fichte insists upon the importance of compulsion in the training of the child, of the necessity for the child's subjection to the will of its parent. Freedom derives from obedience to authority: the voluntary obedience of the child – its doing without compulsion what its parents command – is not obedience but *insight*.[29] The *voluntary* submission to the needs of the nation – albeit derived from an initial compulsion – is precisely what Pearson wants to replace the individualism of liberalism.

For Pearson, then, it is essential that individual, instinctual, sexual life is subordinated to the state. A whole panoply of ideas about female sexuality – not necessarily consistent ones – tends to make women the focus of this rhetoric of subordination, and it is middle-class women who, in arguing for their own emancipation, become the model for a voluntary submission to a wider social good which is at the heart of the eugenic vision. At the end of the 1860s, John Stuart Mill had voiced the logic of the democratizing movements of the nineteenth century in calling for an end to the subjection of women, justifying his modest proposals for equality in the language of rights. The scientific languages of the last years of the century cracked Mill's calm logic apart, and sent a nascent feminism into crisis. Its crisis was not, as some feminist commentators have argued, *simply* that the culture produced, at the moment women began most effectively to demand the rights a modern society seemed to offer, a powerful new justification for their traditional powerlessness.[30] The new sciences could also offer potent arguments for the necessity – even urgency – of women's access to the public, political spaces of a world in trouble. If women *were* different from men, such difference might be just what the modern world, lost and wandering without God, needed in order to reforge an ethics and make secure a future. The 'truth' that science spoke could be feminist, but only at a cost.

Warrior Maids

Olive Schreiner was born in South Africa to missionary parents (an English mother, a German father), and came to England at the beginning of the 1880s, soon winning a reputation for her ideas about women's emancipation through her acclaimed novel, *The Story of an African Farm*.

Already a devotee of evolutionary theory and committed to science as the new and beneficent truth language, she was invited to join the Men and Women's Club, where she met, and fell unrequitedly in love with, Karl Pearson. Throughout the time of their acquaintance, Schreiner imagined writing a historical and scientific survey of 'the sex question', but it was not until 1911 that she published what is, perhaps, her most significant contribution to the 'Woman Debate', *Woman and Labour*. Together with her short stories and allegorical writings, it made her one of the most influential feminist literary voices of the time. For some, *Woman and Labour* was 'the bible of the Woman's Movement'.[31] It shares its title with an article Pearson published in 1894, some five years after Schreiner had returned to South Africa. By that time, her relationship with Pearson had come to a painful end, but his influence, including his eugenic ideas, pervades her book.

Pearson's 'Woman and Labour' is his most direct and outspoken attack on middle-class feminism as a movement for equality. In it, he castigates the political call of 'equality of opportunity' for failing to acknowledge, and actively hampering, both the natural impulse towards maternity and the eugenic responsibility to bear children, and argues instead for the state protection of motherhood in order to lessen the economic advantages of remaining childless for middle-class women.[32] Schreiner's *Woman and Labour* has a repeated refrain, which seems directly to counter Pearson: she describes it as 'that clamour which has arisen in the modern world [. . .] *Give us labour and the training which fits for labour!*'[33] This is instantly recognizable as the demand of modern feminism for women's access to education and employment, and therefore financial independence and all its corollaries. It is the demand, in other words, for equality.

In fact, *Woman and Labour* is not really an argument for equality at all; it is rather a defence of the feminist demand for education and work on the basis that such a demand is for the wider good. Although it ends with an upbeat, prophetic vision of the future, in which transformed sexual relations will bring men and women together in a new harmony, its keynote is the suffering and renunciation of women. Its refrain, '*Give us labour and the training which fits for labour*', has a sequel: '*We demand this, not for ourselves alone, but for the race.*' What Schreiner tries to do, in effect, is contest Pearson on his own ground, precisely by evoking and making explicit the romantic element of his eugenics. The woman's movement is not characterized by self-interest, or any form of individualism, but is an *organic* movement, driven by 'impersonal' ends. Women must have access to work and, as their traditional spheres of labour shrink in the newly technologized world, they must find new forms of work if they are not to become – as Schreiner puts it, in another organic metaphor –

parasitic. Modern society is threatened by decadence and degeneration; in it, the feminist is the properly moral being, trying to stay such threats:

> It is this consciousness of great impersonal ends [. . .] which gives to many a woman strength for renunciation [. . .] and which enables her often to accept poverty, toil, and sexual isolation (an isolation even more terrible to the woman than to any male) and the renunciation of motherhood, that crowning beatitude of the woman's existence, which, and which alone, fully compensates her for the organic sufferings of womanhood – in the conviction that, by so doing, she makes more possible a fuller and higher attainment of motherhood and wifehood to the women who will follow her.[34]

The 'impersonal end' for which the feminist works is, it becomes clear, the progress of her race; what she is saving the modern world from, is degeneration. Her wish to be educated and to work is, finally, a *means* to transformation – to the new social Eden – and not an end in itself.

Schreiner once told Havelock Ellis that she would write a 'sex book' for his Contemporary Science Series which would be 'a purely scientific collection of facts'.[35] What she published instead, in *Woman and Labour,* was a polemic saturated with romantic motifs – of nature and organicity, of tradition and conservation, of religion and affect. Pearson's eugenics is predicated upon a romantic concept of the nation, and it is precisely this which Schreiner uses to try to contest his conclusions about middle-class women. Thus her historical ideal of femininity is 'that old, old Teutonic womanhood' from which – she argues – modern women descend. The 'New Woman' is not, she insists, new.

What Schreiner does is to evoke a rhetoric of racial health and virility in order to support the central distinction she makes in her book between labouring women and 'parasites' who are the 'passive tools of reproduction'. She employs, in a way that echoes Pearson, a labour theory of value that *includes* child-bearing and child-rearing, but only in so far as it is supplemented by other forms of work: 'For countless ages [. . .] we have laboured [. . .] Within our bodies we bore the race, on our shoulders we carried it; we sought the roots and plants for its food.' In the modern world, however, she argues, 'something that is entirely new has entered into the field of labour, and left nothing as it was'. Modern technology has completely transformed traditional working patterns and, in that transformation, women's work is particularly threatened. The possibility which haunts modern women is that they will become what Schreiner calls '*sex-parasites* '. By this, she means women who are financially dependent and do neither domestic nor remunerative work. Such a woman secures her living through 'the passive exercise of her sex-functions alone'.[36]

Schreiner holds forth the prospect of a capitalism so successful that large sections of women will become 'idle' on the model of the Victorian upper middle-class woman supported by a substantial domestic staff, whose position in turn is likened to a decaying ancient civilization in which passivity, weakness and degeneracy became endemic. The idle woman, the 'human female parasite', is 'the most deadly microbe which can make its appearance on the surface of any social organism'.[37] The parasite woman is sexualized and child-bearing but, without the metonymic support of other kinds of labouring, her maternity is *not* 'labour'. It falls outside the ethic of work, which is presented as the fundamental, human ethic, and it thus becomes a force for degeneration, not progress.

It is the 'New Woman' – the feminist woman – demanding new forms of work, who will prevent this slide into degeneracy. Like the Teutonic woman, she is working *for the race* and in the process, her labour – in all its forms – becomes a force for good. The impetus of this racialized rhetoric produces the following passage, which is an extraordinary one, given that Schreiner wrote *Woman and Labour* during the Boer war, an experience which helped to confirm her as an absolute pacifist. It is extraordinary, too, in the context of a book which contains a chapter called 'Woman and War' which was reprinted as a separate pacifist pamphlet during World War I, and which argues that women are inevitably and uniquely opposed to military conflict, precisely because they are mothers, and therefore know the value of human life:

> We who lead this [woman's] movement to-day are of that old, old Teutonic womanhood, which twenty centuries ago ploughed its march through European forests and morasses beside its male companion; which marched to the Cimbri to Italy, and with the Franks across the Rhine, and with the Varagians into Russia, and the Alamani into Switzerland [. . .] We have in us the blood of a womanhood that was never bought and never sold [. . .] whose realised ideal of marriage was sexual companionship and an equality in duty and labour; who stood side by side with the males they loved in peace and war, and whose children, when they had borne them, sucked manhood from their breasts [. . .]. We are women of a breed whose racial ideal was no Helen of Troy [. . .] but that Brynhild whom Segurd found, clad in helm and byrne, the warrior maid.[38]

Even if Schreiner counters this vision of the warrior maid by explaining that the physical battlefield is no longer the one on which the modern woman has to fight, the feminist New Woman of the modern world is nevertheless modelled here on the language of European supremacy that characterized nineteenth-century philology, history and, eventually, racial science. These are the knowledges which, in the nineteenth century, supported European colonialism and imperialism.

To make her feminist argument then, Schreiner can only move between the exclusivity and inclusivity which her terms inevitably set up. 'Race' blurs with nation, and separates out again; one people – the Teutons – will lead the way for 'all earth's women [. . .] the entire race'.[39] The vision of emancipation hovers between timelessness and universal female values and capacities, and the historical privilege accorded to the women of the modern, capitalist, democratic nation-state. At its most troubling, Schreiner's argument suggests that the 'New Women' arguing for emancipation are at the forefront of progress, precisely because they are able to identify with the state's aggressive aims.[40]

By the time she published *Woman and Labour*, Schreiner had long been an eloquent and passionate critic of British imperialism. The fact that her most important feminist work is pervaded by a rhetoric of racial supremacy is a consequence of the way in which feminism – as a progressive movement – depended upon narratives of progress and improvement which were central to the formation of *national* identities in Europe in the nineteenth century. What makes eugenic discourse so important in relation to feminism is that eugenics uniquely focused attention on the woman's sexual identity in order to answer the question of what mothering is *for*. Its answer was a potent one because of the way in which it was able – while presenting itself as a consummately rational and scientific knowledge – to tap a rich *romantic* language of the nation. Eugenics made procreative sexuality of the first order of importance for the successful nation of the twentieth century and, in doing so, it produced maternity in the modern world as a national and racial imperative, with profound consequences for feminism which have continued to make themselves felt throughout the century.

Notes

1 Michel Foucault, *The History of Sexuality: Vol. 1 An Introduction* (Penguin, Harmondsworth, 1981), p. 118.

2 Francis Galton, 'Hereditary Talent and Character', *Macmillan's Magazine*, 12 (June and August 1865); *Hereditary Genius: An Inquiry into its Laws and Consequences* [1869] (Watts, London, 1892).

3 Francis Galton, *Inquiries into Human Faculty and its Development* (Macmillan, London, 1883), p. 25.

4 Galton, quoted in Donald A. MacKenzie, *Statistics in Britain 1865–1930: The Social Construction of Scientific Knowledge* (Edinburgh University Press, Edinburgh, 1981), p. 55.

5 Herbert Spencer's account of social evolution emphasized that society is made up of a collection of individual wills and that the struggle for survival takes place between individuals. State intervention which attempted to ameliorate

the causes of social hardship therefore ran the risk of hampering the forces of evolutionary progress. See Greta Jones, *Social Darwinism and English Thought: The Interaction Between Biological and Social Theory* (Harvester, Brighton, 1980).

6   See Herbert Brewer, 'Eutelegenesis', in Lucy Bland and Laura Doan (eds), *Sexology Uncensored: The Documents of Sexual Science* (Polity Press, Cambridge 1998).

7   See Daniel J. Kevles, *In the Name of Eugenics: Genetics and the Uses of Human Heredity* (Harvard University Press, Cambridge, MA, and London, 1995), pp. 27–35.

8   Phyllis Grosskurth, *Havelock Ellis: A Biography* (Allen Lane, London, 1980), p. 98.

9   Kevles, *In the Name of Eugenics*, p. 40.

10 Karl Pearson, *The Scope and Importance to the State of the Science of National Eugenics* (Dulau, London, 1909), p. 11.

11 Karl Pearson, *The Groundwork of Eugenics* (Dulau, London, 1909), pp. 9–10.

12 Lucy Bland, *Banishing the Beast: English Feminism and Sexual Morality 1885–1914* (Penguin, Harmondsworth, 1995), pp. 25–7.

13 See, for instance, letters to Karl Pearson of 6 and 8 July 1886, in Richard Rive (ed.), *Olive Schreiner: Letters 1871–1899* (Oxford University Press, Oxford, 1988), pp. 87–95.

14 Karl Pearson, *The Academic Aspect of the Science of National Eugenics* (Dulau, London, 1911), p. 4.

15 See E.S. Pearson, *Karl Pearson: An Appreciation of Some Aspects of his Life and Work* (Cambridge University Press, Cambridge, 1938), p. 5.

16 Johann Fichte, *The Closed Commercial State* [1800], in I.H. Fichte (ed.), *Sämmelte Werke* (Berlin, 1845–6) (this quotation from 'History of Ideas: Nineteenth-Century Studies' dossier, Hatfield Polytechnic).

17 Robert J.C. Young, *Colonial Desire: Hybridity in Theory, Culture and Race* (Routledge, London and New York, 1995), p. 37. Young is quoting Raymond Williams, *Keywords* (Fontana, London, 1976), p. 89. See also, George W. Stocking, Jr, *Victorian Anthropology* (Free Press, New York, 1987), ch. 1.

18 Stocking, *Victorian Anthropology*, p. 20.

19 Johann Gottfried Herder, *Outlines of a Philosophy of the History of Man* [1784–91], quoted in Young, *Colonial Desire*, p. 39.

20 See Kevles, *In the Name of Eugenics*, p. 23.

21 Karl Pearson, *National Life from the Standpoint of Science* (Black, London, 1901), pp. 24–5.

22 Pearson, *Groundwork of Eugenics*, p. 23.

23 Pearson, *National Life*, p. 53.

24 Ibid., p. 48.

25 Ibid., pp. 43–4.

26 Karl Pearson, 'Socialism and Natural Selection', in *The Chances of Death and Other Studies in Evolution*: Vol. 1 (Edward Arnold, London, 1897), p. 111.

27 Pearson, *National Life*, p. 15. The stereotype of the 'lazy African' was well established, of course, not least in Thomas Carlyle's 'The Nigger Question'; Carlyle was also heavily influenced by the German romantics.

28 Karl Pearson, 'The Woman's Question', *The Ethic of Freethought* (Adam & Charles Black, London, 1888), p. 394.

29 Fichte discusses education in his *Addresses to the German Nation* (Open Court, Chicago and London, 1922). I have drawn here from Morton Schatzman, *Soul Murder: Persecution in the Family* (Penguin, Harmondsworth, 1976), an account of Daniel Paul Schreber, about whom Freud wrote his famous account of psychosis. Schreber's father was a leading German physicist and pedagogue, much influenced by Fichte's educational ideas, who believed that the child's human will could only be fashioned through a rigorous control of its body. There is a suggestive parallel here with the way in which eugenics targets the most intimate bodily behaviour of human beings and attempts to regulate it. See pp. 145–6.

30 For this argument, see Flavia Alaya, 'Victorian Science and the "Genius" of Woman', *Journal of the History of Ideas*, 38, 2 (1977), pp. 261–80.

31 Vera Brittain discusses the influence of *Woman and Labour* in *Testament of Youth* (Virago, London, 1978).

32 Karl Pearson, 'Woman and Labour', *Fortnightly Review*, 329 (May 1894), pp. 561–577.

33 Olive Schreiner, *Woman and Labour* (Virago, London, 1978), p. 33.

34 Ibid., p. 127.

35 See S.C. Cronwright-Schreiner, *The Life of Olive Schreiner* (Unwin, London, 1924), pp. 353–9.

36 Schreiner, *Woman and Labour*, pp. 116, 33, 40, 78.

37 Ibid., p. 82.

38 Ibid., pp. 144–5.

39 Ibid., p. 147.

40 Schreiner's image of 'warrior maids' would have found kinship with the wide use made in women's suffrage campaigns of images of militant martyrdom and female heroism. See Lisa Tickner, *The Spectacle of Women: Imagery of the Suffrage Campaign 1907–14* (Chatto & Windus, London, 1987).

4 Scientific Racism and the Invention of the Homosexual Body

Siobhan B. Somerville

One of the most important insights developed in the field of the history of sexuality is the notion that homosexuality and, by extension, heterosexuality are relatively recent inventions in Western culture, rather than transhistorical or "natural" categories of human beings. As Michel Foucault and other historians of sexuality have argued, sexual acts between two people of the same sex had been punishable through legal and religious sanctions well before the late nineteenth century, but these acts did not necessarily define individuals as homosexual *per se*.[1] Only in the late nineteenth century did a new understanding of sexuality emerge, in which sexual acts and desires became constitutive of identity. Homosexuality as the condition, and therefore identity, of particular bodies is thus a production of that historical moment.

Medical literature, broadly defined to include the writings of physicians, sexologists and psychiatrists, has been integral to this argument. Although medical discourse was by no means the only – or necessarily the most powerful – site of the emergence of new sexual identities, it does nevertheless offer rich sources for at least partially understanding the complex development of these categories in the late nineteenth and early twentieth centuries. Medical and sexological literature not only became one of the few sites of explicit engagement with questions of sexuality during this period, but also held substantial definitional power within a culture that sanctioned science to discover and tell the truth about bodies.

As historians and theorists of sexuality have refined a notion of the late nineteenth-century "invention" of the homosexual, their discussions have drawn primarily upon theories and histories of gender. George Chauncey, in particular, has provided an invaluable discussion of the ways in which paradigms of sexuality shifted according to changing ideologies of gender during this period. He notes a gradual change in medical models of sexual deviance, from a notion of sexual inversion, understood as a reversal of one's sex role, to a model of homosexuality, defined as deviant sexual object choice. These categories and their transformations, argues Chauncey, reflected concurrent shifts in the cultural organization of sex/gender roles and participated in prescribing acceptable behavior, especially within a context of white, middle-class, gender ideologies.[2]

While gender insubordination offers a powerful explanatory model for the "invention" of homosexuality, ideologies of gender also, of course, shaped and were shaped by dominant constructions of race. Indeed, although it has received little acknowledgment, it is striking that the "invention" of the homosexual occurred at roughly the same time as racial questions were being reformulated, particularly in the United States. This was the moment, for instance, of *Plessy* v. *Ferguson*, the 1896 US Supreme Court ruling that insisted that "black" and "white" races were "separate but equal." Both a product of and a stimulus to a nationwide and brutal era of racial segregation, this ruling had profound and lasting effects in legitimating an apartheid structure that remained legally sanctioned for more than half of the twentieth century. The *Plessy* case distilled in legal form many widespread contemporary fears about race and racial difference at the time. A deluge of "Jim Crow" and anti-miscegenation laws, combined with unprecedented levels of racial violence, most visibly manifested in widespread lynching, reflected an aggressive attempt to classify and separate bodies as either "black" or "white."

Is it merely a historical coincidence that the classification of bodies as either "homosexual" or "heterosexual" emerged at the same time as the United States was aggressively policing the imaginary boundary between "black" and "white" bodies? Although some historians of sexuality have included brief discussions of nineteenth-century discourses of racial difference, the particular relationship and potentially mutual effects of discourses of homosexuality and race remain largely unexplored.[3] This silence around race may be due in part to the relative lack of explicit attention to race in medical and sexological literature of the period. These writers did not often self-consciously interrogate race, nor did they regularly identify by race those whose gender insubordination and/or sexual transgression brought them under the medical gaze in these accounts. Yet the lack of explicit attention to race in these texts does not mean that it was irrelevant to sexologists' endeavors. Given the upheavals surrounding racial definition during this period, it is reasonable to imagine that these texts were as embedded within contemporary racial ideologies as they were within ideologies of gender.

Take, for instance, the words of Havelock Ellis, whose massive *Studies in the Psychology of Sex* was one of the most important texts of the late nineteenth-century medical and scientific discourse on sexuality in the United States and Europe. "I regard sex as the central problem of life," wrote Ellis in the general preface to the first volume. Justifying such unprecedented boldness toward the study of sex, Ellis explained,

> And now that the problem of religion has practically been settled, and that the problem of labour has at least been placed on a practical foundation, the question of sex – *with the racial questions that rest on it* – stands before the coming generations as the chief problem for solution.[4]

Despite Ellis's oddly breezy dismissal of the problems of labor and religion, which were far from settled at the time, this passage points suggestively to a link between sexual and racial anxieties. Yet what exactly did Ellis mean by "racial questions"? More significantly, what was his sense of the relationship between racial questions and the "question of sex"? Although Ellis himself left these issues unresolved, his elliptical declaration nevertheless suggested that a discourse of race – however elusively – somehow hovered around or within the study of sexuality.

In this chapter, I offer speculations on how late nineteenth- and early twentieth-century discourses of race and sexuality might be not merely juxtaposed but also brought together in ways that illuminate both. I suggest that the concurrent bifurcations of categories of race and sexuality were not only historically coincident but in fact structurally interdependent and mutually productive. My goal, however, is not to garner and display unequivocal evidence of the direct influence of racial categories on those who were developing scientific models of homosexuality. Nor am I interested in identifying individual writers and thinkers as racist or not. Rather, my focus here is on racial ideologies, the cultural assumptions and systems of representation about race through which individuals understood their relationships within the world.[5] My emphasis lies in understanding the relationships between the medical/scientific discourse on sexuality and the dominant scientific discourse on race during this period, that is, scientific racism.

My approach combines literary and historical methods of reading, particularly those that have been so crucial to lesbian and gay studies–the technique of reading to hear "the inexplicable presence of the thing not named,"[6] of being attuned to the queer presences and implications in texts that do not otherwise name them. Without this collective project to see, hear and confirm queer inflections where others would deny their existence, it is arguable that our understanding of the historical and cultural meanings of sexuality, particularly same-sex desire, would be considerably impoverished, if not altogether obscured. I use the techniques of queer reading, but modulate my analysis from a focus on sexuality and gender to one alert to racial resonances as well. My aim is not to replace a focus on gender and sexuality with one on race but, rather, to understand how discourses of race and gender buttressed one another, often competing, often overlapping, in shaping emerging models of homosexuality.

Visible Differences: Sexology and Comparative Anatomy

Ellis's *Sexual Inversion*, the first volume of *Studies in the Psychology of Sex* to be published, became a definitive text in late nineteenth-century investigations of homosexuality.[7] Despite the series' titular focus on the psychology of sex, *Sexual Inversion* was a hybrid text, poised in methodology between the earlier field of comparative anatomy, with its procedures of bodily measurement, and the nascent techniques of psychology, with its focus on mental development. In *Sexual Inversion* Ellis hoped to provide scientific authority for the position that homosexuality should be considered not a crime but, rather, a congenital (and thus involuntary) physiological abnormality. Writing *Sexual Inversion* in the wake of England's 1885 Labouchère Amendment, which prohibited "any act of gross indecency" between men, Ellis intended in large part to defend homosexuality from "law and public opinion," which, in his view, combined "to place a heavy penal burden and a severe social stigma on the manifestations of an instinct which to those persons who possess it frequently appears natural and normal."[8]

Like other sexologists, Ellis assumed that the "invert" might be visually distinguishable from the "normal" body through anatomical markers, just as the differences between the sexes had traditionally been mapped upon the body. Yet the study of sexual difference was not the only methodological precedent for the study of the homosexual body. In its assumptions about somatic differences, *Sexual Inversion*, I suggest, also drew upon and participated in a history of the scientific investigation of race.

Race, in fact, became an explicit, though ambiguous, structural element in Ellis's *Sexual Inversion*. In chapter 5, titled "The Nature of Sexual Inversion," Ellis attempted to collate the evidence contained in his collection of case studies, dividing his general conclusions into various analytic categories. Significantly, "Race" was the first category he listed, under which he wrote, "All my cases, 80 in number, are British and American, 20 living in the United States and the rest being British. Ancestry, from the point of view of race, was not made a matter of special investigation" (p. 264). He then listed the ancestries of the individuals whose case studies he included, which he identified as "English [. . .] Scotch [. . .] Irish [. . .]

German [. . .] French [. . .] Portuguese [. . .] [and] more or less Jewish" (p. 264). He concluded that "except in the apparently frequent presence of the German element, there is nothing remarkable in this ancestry" (p. 264). Ellis used the term "race" in this passage interchangeably with national origin, with the possible exception of Jewish identity. These national identities were perceived to be at least partially biological and certainly hereditary in Ellis's account, though subordinate to the categories "British" and "American." Although he dismissed "ancestry, from the point of view of race," as a significant category, its place as the first topic within the chapter suggested its importance to the structure of Ellis's analysis.

Ellis's ambiguous use of the term "race" was not unusual among scientific and medical studies from this period, during which it might refer to groupings based variously on geography, religion, class or color.[9] The use of the term to mean a division of people based on physical (rather than genealogical or national) differences had originated in the late eighteenth century, when Carl von Linnaeus and Johann Friedrich Blumenbach first classified human beings into distinct racial groups.[10] Blumenbach's work in turn became a model for the nineteenth-century fascination with anthropometry, the measurement of the human body. Behind these anatomical measurements lay the assumption that the body was a legible text, with various keys or languages available for reading its symbolic codes. In the logic of biological determinism, the surface and interior of the individual body rather than its social characteristics, such as language, behavior or clothing, became the primary sites of its meaning. Although scientists debated which particular anatomical features carried racial meanings – skin, facial angle, pelvis, skull, brain mass, genitalia – nevertheless the theory that anatomy predicted intelligence and behavior remained remarkably constant. As Nancy Stepan and Sander Gilman have noted, "The concepts within racial science were so congruent with social and political life (with power relations, that is) as to be virtually uncontested from inside the mainstream of science."[11]

Supported by the cultural authority of an ostensibly objective scientific method, these readings of the body became a powerful instrument for those seeking to justify the economic and political disenfranchisement of various racial groups within systems of slavery and colonialism. As Barbara Fields has noted, however, "Try as they would, the scientific racists of the past failed to discover any objective criterion upon which to classify people; to their chagrin, every criterion they tried varied more within so-called races than between them."[12] Although the methods of science were considered to be outside the political and economic realm, in fact, as we know, these anatomical investigations, however professedly innocent their intentions, were driven by racial ideologies already firmly in place.[13]

In exploring the influence of scientific studies of race on the emerging discourse of sexuality, it is useful to look closely at a study from the genre of comparative anatomy. In 1867, W.H. Flower and James Murie published an "Account of the Dissection of a Bushwoman," which carefully catalogued the "more perishable soft structures of the body" of a young Bushwoman.[14] They placed their study in a line of enquiry concerning the African woman's body that had begun at least a half-century earlier with French naturalist Georges Cuvier's description of the woman popularly known as the "Hottentot Venus," or Saartje Baartman, who was displayed to European audiences fascinated by her "steatopygia" (protruding buttocks).[15] As a number of medical journals from this period demonstrate, comparative anatomists repeatedly located racial difference through the sexual characteristics of the female body.[16] Starting with Cuvier, this tradition of comparative anatomy located the boundaries of race through the sexual and reproductive anatomy of the African female body, ignoring altogether the problematic absence of male bodies from these studies.[17]

Flower and Murie's account lingered on two specific sites of difference: the "protuberance of the buttocks, so peculiar to the Bushman race" and "the remarkable development of the labia minora," which were "sufficiently well marked to distinguish these parts from those of any ordinary varieties of the human species" (p. 208). The racial difference of the African body, implied Flower and Murie, was located in its literal excess, a specifically sexual excess that placed her body outside the boundaries of the "normal" female. To support their conclusion, Flower and Murie included corroborating "evidence" in the final part of their account. They quoted a second-hand report, "received from a scientific friend residing at the Cape of Good Hope," describing the anatomy of "two pure bred Hottentots, mother and daughter" (p. 208). This account also focused on the women's genitalia, which they referred to as "appendages" (p. 208). Although their account ostensibly foregrounded boundaries of race, their portrayal of the sexual characteristics of the Bushwoman betrayed Flower and Murie's anxieties about gender boundaries. The characteristics singled out as "peculiar" to this race – the (double) "appendages" – fluttered between genders, at one moment masculine, at the next moment exaggeratedly feminine. Flower and Murie constructed the site of *racial* difference by marking the sexual and reproductive anatomy of the African woman as "peculiar"; in their characterization, sexual ambiguity delineated the boundaries of race.

The techniques and logic of late nineteenth-century sexologists, who also routinely included physical examinations in their accounts, reproduced the methodologies employed by comparative anatomists like Flower and Murie. In Ellis's *Sexual Inversion*, case studies often focused more intensely on the bodies of female "inverts" than on those of their male counterparts.[18] Although the specific sites of anatomical inspection (hymen, clitoris, labia, vagina) differed in various sexological texts, the underlying theory remained constant: women's genitalia and reproductive anatomy held a valuable and presumably visual key to ranking bodies according to norms of sexuality.

The case histories in Ellis's *Sexual Inversion* differed markedly according to gender in the amount and degree of attention given to the examination of anatomical details. "As regards the sexual organs it seems possible," Ellis wrote, "so far as my observations go, to speak more definitely of inverted women than of inverted men" (p. 256). Ellis justified his greater scrutiny of women's bodies in part by invoking the ambiguity surrounding women's sexuality in general: "we are accustomed to a much greater familiarity and intimacy between women than between men, and we are less apt to suspect the existence of any abnormal passion" (p. 204). To Ellis, the seemingly imperceptible differences between "normal" and "abnormal" intimacies between women called for greater scrutiny into the subtleties of their anatomy. He included the following detailed account as potential evidence for understanding the fine line between the lesbian and the "normal" woman:

> *Sexual Organs.* – (a) Internal: Uterus and ovaries appear normal. (b) External: Small clitoris, with this irregularity, that the lower folds of the labia minora, instead of uniting one with the other and forming the frenum, are extended upward along the sides of the clitoris, while the upper folds are poorly developed, furnishing the clitoris with a scant hood. The labia majora depart from normal conformation in being fuller in their posterior half than in their anterior part, so that when the subject is in the supine position they sag, as it were, presenting a slight resemblance to fleshy sacs, but in substance and structure they feel normal. (p. 136)

This extraordinary taxonomy, performed for Ellis by an unnamed "obstetric physician of high standing," echoed earlier anatomical catalogues of African women. The exacting eye (and hand) of the investigating physician highlighted every possible detail as meaningful evidence. Through the triple repetition of "normal" and the use of evaluative language like "irregularity" and "poorly developed," the physician reinforced his position of judgment. Without providing criteria for what constituted "normal" anatomy, the physician simply proclaimed irregularity based on his own powers of sight and touch. Moreover, his characterization of what he perceived as abnormal echoed the anxious account by Flower and Murie. Although the description of the clitoris in this account is a notable exception to the tendency to exaggerate its size in descriptions of the anatomy of lesbians, the account nevertheless scrutinized another site of genital excess. The "fleshy sacs" of this woman, like the "appendages" fetishized in the earlier account, invoked the anatomy of a phantom male body inhabiting the lesbian's anatomical features.

Ellis's and Flower and Murie's taxonomies of the lesbian and the African woman cannot be understood as separate from the larger context of scientific assumptions during this period, which one historian has characterized as "the full triumph of Darwinism in American thought."[19] One of the basic assumptions within the Darwinian model was the belief that, as organisms evolved through a process of natural selection, they also showed greater signs of differentiation between the (two) sexes. Following this logic, various writers used sexual characteristics as indicators of evolutionary progress toward civilization. In *Man and Woman*, for instance, Ellis himself cautiously suggested that since the "beginnings of industrialism," "more marked sexual differences in physical development seem (we cannot speak definitely) to have developed than are usually to be found in savage societies."[20] In this passage, Ellis drew from theories developed by biologists like Patrick Geddes and J. Arthur Thomson, who stated in their important work *The Evolution of Sex* that "hermaphroditism is primitive; the unisexual state is a subsequent differentiation. The present cases of normal hermaphroditism imply either persistence or reversion."[21] In characterizing either lesbians' or African women's bodies as less sexually differentiated than the norm (always posited as white heterosexual women's bodies), anatomists and sexologists drew upon notions of natural selection to dismiss these bodies as anomalous "throwbacks" within a scheme of cultural and anatomical progress.

The Mixed Body

The emergence of evolutionary theory in the late nineteenth century foregrounded a view of continuity between the "savage" and "civilized" races, in contrast to earlier scientific thinking about race, which had focused on debates about the origins of different racial groups. Proponents of monogeny argued that all races derived from a single origin. Those who argued for polygeny (which was referred to as the "American school" of anthropology) believed that different races descended from separate biological and geographical sources, a view, not coincidentally, that supported segregationist impulses.[22] With Darwin's publication of *Origin of Species* in 1859, the debate between polygeny and monogeny was superseded by evolutionary theory, which was appropriated as a powerful scientific model for understanding race. Its controversial innovation was its emphasis on the continuity between animals and human beings. Evolutionary theory held out the possibility that the physical, mental and moral characteristics of human beings had evolved gradually over time from apelike ancestors.[23] Although the idea of continuity depended logically on the blurring of boundaries within hierarchies, it did not necessarily invalidate the methods or assumptions of comparative anatomy. On the contrary, notions of visible differences and racial hierarchies were deployed to corroborate Darwinian theory.

The concept of continuity was harnessed to the growing attention to miscegenation, or "amalgamation," in social science writing during the first decades of the twentieth century in the United States.[24] Miscegenation was, of course, not only a question of race but also one of sex and sexuality. Ellis recognized this intersection implicitly, if not explicitly. His sense of the "racial questions" inherent in sex was surely informed by his involvement with eugenics, the movement in Europe and the United States that, to greater or lesser degrees, advocated selective reproduction and "race hygiene." In the United States, eugenics was both a political and scientific response to the growth of a population beginning to challenge the dominance of white political interests. The widespread scientific and social interest in eugenics was fueled by anxieties expressed through the popularized notion of (white) "race suicide," a phrase that summed up nativist fears about a perceived decline in reproduction among white Americans. The new field of eugenics worked hand in hand with growing anti-miscegenation sentiment and policy, provoked not only by attempts for political representation among African-Americans but also by the influx of large populations of immigrants. As Mark Haller has pointed out, "Racists and [immigration] restrictionists [. . .] found in eugenics the scientific reassurances they needed that heredity shaped man's personality and that their assumptions rested on biological facts."[25] Ellis himself wrote several essays concerning eugenics, including *The Problem of Race Regeneration*, a pamphlet advocating "voluntary" sterilization of the unfit as a policy in the best interest of "the race."[26] Further, in a letter to Francis Galton in 1907, Ellis wrote, "In the concluding volume of my 'Sex Studies' I shall do what I can to insinuate the eugenic attitude."[27]

The beginnings of sexology, then, were related to and perhaps even dependent on a pervasive climate of eugenicist and anti-miscegenation sentiment and legislation. Even at the level of nomenclature, anxieties about miscegenation shaped sexologists' attempts to find an appropriate and scientific name for the newly visible object of their study. Introduced into English through the 1892 English translation of Richard von Krafft-Ebing's *Psychopathia Sexualis*, the term "homosexuality" itself stimulated a great deal of uneasiness. In the 1915 edition of *Sexual Inversion*, Ellis reported that "most investigators have been much puzzled in coming to a conclusion as to the best, most exact, and at the same time most colorless names [for same-sex desire]." (p. 2). Giving an account of the various names proposed, such as Karl Ulrichs's "Uranian" and Karl Westphal's "contrary sexual feeling," Ellis admitted that "homosexuality" was the most widely used term. Far from the ideal "colorless" term, however, "homosexuality" evoked Ellis's distaste for its mixed origins; in a regretful aside, he noted that "it has, philologically, the awkward disadvantage of being a bastard term compounded of Greek and Latin elements" (p. 2). In the first edition of *Sexual Inversion*, Ellis stated his alarm more directly: "'Homosexual' is a barbarously hybrid word."[28] A similar view was expressed by Edward Carpenter, an important socialist writer in England and an outspoken advocate of homosexual and women's emancipation at the time. Like Ellis, Carpenter winced at the connotations of illegitimacy in the word: "'Homosexual,' generally used in scientific works, is of course a bastard word. 'Homogenic' has been suggested, as being from two roots, both Greek, i.e., 'homos,' same, and 'genos,' sex."[29] Carpenter's suggestion of course, resonated both against and within the vocabularies of eugenics and miscegenation. Performing these etymological gyrations with almost comic literalism, Ellis and Carpenter expressed pervasive cultural anxieties about questions of racial origins and purity. Concerned above all else with legitimacy, they attempted to remove and rewrite the mixed origins of "homosexuality." Ironically, despite their suggestions for alternatives, the "bastard" term took hold among sexologists, thus yoking together, at least rhetorically, two kinds of mixed bodies – the racial "hybrid" and the invert.

Although Ellis exhibited anxieties about biracial bodies, for others who sought to naturalize and recuperate homosexuality, the evolutionary emphasis on continuity offered potentially useful analogies. Xavier Mayne, for example, one of the earliest American advocates of homosexual rights, wrote, "Between whitest of men and the blackest negro stretches out a vast line of intermediary races as to their colours: brown, olive, red tawny, yellow."[30] He then invoked this model of race to envision a continuous spectrum of gender and sexuality: "Nature abhors the absolute, delights in the fractional. [. . .] Intersexes express the half-steps, the between-beings."[31] In this analogy, Mayne reversed dominant cultural hierarchies that privileged purity over mixture. Drawing upon irrefutable evidence of the "natural" existence of biracial people, Mayne posited a direct analogy to a similarly mixed body, the intersex, which he positioned as a necessary presence within the natural order.

Despite Carpenter's complaint about "bastard" terminology, he, like Mayne, also occasionally appropriated the scientific language of racial mixing in order to resist the association between homosexuality and degeneration. In *The Intermediate Sex*, he attempted to theorize homosexuality outside of the discourse of pathology or abnormality; he too suggested a continuum of genders, with "intermediate types" occupying a place between the poles of exclusively heterosexual male and female. To construct and embody the "intermediate type," Carpenter appropriated dominant scientific models of race through notions of "shades" of gender and sexual "half-breeds."[32] These racial paradigms, along with models of gender, offered Carpenter a coherent vocabulary for understanding and expressing a new vision of sexual bodies.

Sexual "Perversion" and Racialized Desire

By the early twentieth century, medical models of sexuality had begun to shift in emphasis, moving away from a focus on the body and toward psychological theories of desire. This shift took place within a period that also saw a transformation of scientific notions about race: in the early twentieth century, scientific claims for exclusively biological models of racial difference were beginning to be undermined, although these models have persisted in popular understandings of race.[33] One area in which these shifts in scientific understandings of race and sexuality overlapped and perhaps shaped one another was through models of interracial and homosexual desire. Specifically, two cultural taboos – miscegenation and homosexuality – became linked in sexological and psychological discourse through the model of "abnormal" sexual object choice.

The convergence of theories of "perverse" racial and sexual desire shaped the assumptions of psychologists like Margaret Otis, whose analysis of "A Perversion Not Commonly Noted" appeared in a medical journal in 1913. Otis noted that in all-girl institutions, including reform schools and boarding schools, she had observed widespread "love-making between the white and colored girls."[34] Otis's explicit discussion of racial difference and homosexuality was extremely rare amidst the burgeoning social science literature on sexuality in the early twentieth century. Both fascinated and alarmed, Otis remarked that this perversion was "well known in reform schools and institutions for delinquent girls," but that "this particular form of the homosexual relation has perhaps not been brought to the attention of scientists" (p. 113). Performing her ostensible duty to science, Otis carefully described these rituals of interracial romance and the girls' "peculiar moral code." In particular, she noted that the girls incorporated racial difference into courtship rituals self-consciously patterned on traditional gender roles: "One white girl [. . .] admitted that the colored girl she loved seemed the man, and thought it was so in the case of the others" (p. 114). In Otis's account, the actions of the girls clearly threatened the keepers of the institutions, who responded to the perceived danger with efforts to racially segregate their charges (who were, of course, already segregated by gender). Otis, however, left open the motivation for segregation: Did the girls' intimacy trouble the authorities because it was homosexual or because it was interracial? Otis avoided exploring this question and offered a succinct theory instead: "The difference in color, in this case, takes the place of difference in sex" (p. 113).

Otis's account participated in the gradual shift in medical and scientific literature away from a model of inversion as a physiological difference and toward a model of homosexuality as "abnormal" desire. Despite Otis's focus on desire rather than physiology, however, her characterization of the schoolgirls' "system" of romance drew upon and perpetuated stereotypes based on the earlier anatomical models. She used a simple analogy between race and gender in order to understand their desire: black was to white as masculine was to feminine.

Further, racial difference performed an important visual function in Otis's account. In turn-of-the-century American culture, where Jim Crow segregation erected a structure of taboos against any kind of public (non-work-related) interracial relationship, racial difference visually marked the alliances between the schoolgirls as already suspicious. While there may have been sexual relationships among girls of the same race, in Otis's account, the only relationships to be identified as homosexual were those mediated by dichotomies of race. In effect, the institution of racial segregation and its cultural fiction of "black" and "white" produced the girls' interracial romances as "perverse."

It is possible that the discourse of sexual pathology, in turn, began to inform scientific understandings of race. By 1903, a southern physician drew upon the language of sexology to legitimate a particularly racist fear: "A perversion from which most races are exempt, prompts the negro's inclinations towards the white woman, whereas other races incline toward the females of their own."[35] Using the medical language of perversion to naturalize and legitimate the dominant cultural myth of the black rapist, this account characterized interracial desire as a type of congenital abnormal sexual object choice. In the writer's terms, the desire of African-American men for white women (though not the desire of white men for African-American women) could be understood and pathologized by drawing upon emergent models of sexual orientation.

With the movement toward psychoanalytic models of sexuality, sexologists relied less and less upon the methodologies of comparative anatomy and implicitly acknowledged that physical characteristics were inadequate evidence for the "truth" of the body in question. Yet the assumptions of comparative anatomy did not completely disappear; although they seemed to contradict more psychological understandings of sexuality, notions of biological difference continued to shape cultural understandings of sexuality, particularly in popular representations of lesbians and gay men.

Troubling Science

My efforts here have focused on the various ways in which late nine-teenth- and early twentieth-century scientific discourses on race became available to sexologists and physicians as a way to articulate emerging models of homosexuality. Methodologies and iconographies of compara-tive anatomy attempted to locate discrete physiological markers of differ-ence through which to classify and separate types of human being. Sexologists drew upon these techniques to try to position the "homo-sexual" body as anatomically distinguishable from the "normal" body. Likewise, medical discourses on sexuality appear to have been steeped in pervasive cultural anxieties toward "mixed" bodies, particularly the mu-latto, whose symbolic position as a mixture of black and white bodies was literalized in scientific accounts. Sexologists and others writing about homosexuality borrowed the model of the mixed body as a way to make sense of the "invert." Finally, racial and sexual discourses converged in psychological models that understood "unnatural" desire as a marker of perversion; in these cases, interracial and same-sex sexuality became analo-gous.

Although scientific and medical models of both race and sexuality held enormous definitional power at the turn of the century, they were vari-ously and complexly incorporated, revised, resisted or ignored both by the individuals they sought to categorize and within the larger cultural imagination. My speculations are intended to raise questions and to point toward possibilities for further historical and theoretical work. How, for instance, were analogies between race and sexual orientation deployed or not within popular cultural discourses? In religious discourses? In legal discourses? What were the material effects of their convergence or diver-gence? How have these analogies been used to organize bodies in other historical moments and, most urgently, in our own?

In the last few years alone, for example, there has been a proliferation of "speaking perverts" in a range of cultural contexts, including political demonstrations, television, magazines, courts, newspapers and classrooms. Despite the unprecedented opportunities for lesbian, gay, bisexual and queer speech, however, recent scientific research into sexuality has reflected a determination to discover a biological key to the origins of homosexual-ity. Highly publicized studies have purported to locate indicators of sexual orientation in discrete niches of the human body, ranging from a particu-lar gene on the X chromosome to the hypothalamus, a structure of the brain.[36] In an updated and more technologically sophisticated form, com-parative anatomy is being granted a peculiar cultural authority in the study of sexuality.

These studies, of course, have not gone uncontested, arriving as they have within a moment characterized not only by the development of social constructionist theories of sexuality but also, in the face of AIDS, by a profound and aching skepticism toward prevailing scientific methods and institutions. At the same time, some see political efficacy in these new scientific studies, arguing that gay men and lesbians might gain access to greater rights if sexual orientation could be proven an immutable biological difference. Such arguments make an analogy, whether explicit or unspoken, to earlier understandings of race as immutable difference. Reverberating through these arguments are echoes of late nineteenth- and early twentieth-century medical models of sexuality and race, whose earlier interdependence suggests a need to understand the complex relationships between constructions of race and sexuality during our own very different historical moment. How does the current effort to re-biologize sexual orientation and to invoke the vocabulary of immutable difference reflect or influence existing cultural anxieties and desires about racialized bodies? To what extent does the political deployment of these new scientific "facts" about sexuality depend upon reinscribing biologized racial categories? These questions, as I have tried to show for an earlier period, require a shift in the attention and practices of queer reading and lesbian and gay studies, one that locates questions of race as inextricable from the study of sexuality, rather than as a part of our peripheral vision.

Notes

A longer version of this article was published originally as "Scientific Racism and the Emergence of the Homosexual Body," *Journal of the History of Sexuality* 5.2 (October 1994): 243–66. © 1994 by the University of Chicago. All rights reserved.
   Many thanks to those who generously read and commented on earlier versions of this article, especially Hazel Carby, Lisa Cohen, Susan Edmunds, Heather Hendershot, Regina Kunzel, David Rodowick, Michael Rogin, and the anonymous readers for the *Journal of the History of Sexuality*.

1 See, e.g., Michel Foucault, *The History of Sexuality*, vol. 1 (New York, 1980); Jeffrey Weeks, *Sex, Politics, and Society: The Regulation of Sexuality since 1800* (Vintage, New York, 1981); and David Halperin, "Is There a History of Sexuality?," in *The Lesbian and Gay Studies Reader*, eds Henry Abelove, Michèle Aina Barale and David M. Halperin (Routledge, New York, 1993), pp. 416–31.
2 George Chauncey, "From Sexual Inversion to Homosexuality: Medicine and the Changing Conceptualization of Female Deviance," *Salmagundi*, 58–9 (Fall 1982–Winter 1983), pp. 114–46.
3 Exceptions include David Halperin's brief but provocative suggestion that "all

scientific inquiries into the aetiology of sexual orientation, after all, spring from a more or less implicit theory of sexual races" in "Homosexuality: A Cultural Construct," in his *One Hundred Years of Homosexuality: And Other Essays on Greek Love* (Routledge, New York, 1990), p. 50; and Abdul R. JanMohamed, "Sexuality on/of the Racial Border: Foucault, Wright, and the Articulation of 'Racialized Sexuality,'" in *Discourses of Sexuality: From Aristotle to AIDS*, ed. Domna C. Stanton (University of Michigan, Ann Arbor, MI, 1992), pp. 94–116.

4 Havelock Ellis and John Addington Symonds, *Studies in the Psychology of Sex*, vol. 1: *Sexual Inversion* (London, 1897; rpt New York, 1975), p. x, emphasis added. Ellis originally co-authored *Sexual Inversion* with John Addington Symonds. For a discussion of their collaboration and the eventual erasure of Symonds from the text, see Wayne Koestenbaum, *Double Talk: The Erotics of Male Literary Collaboration* (Routledge, New York, 1989), pp. 43–67.

5 My use of the concept of ideology draws upon Barbara Fields, "Slavery, Race, and Ideology in the United States of America," *New Left Review* 181 (1990): 95–118; Louis Althusser, "Ideology and Ideological State Apparatuses (Notes Towards an Investigation)," in his *Lenin and Philosophy and Other Essays*, tr. Ben Brewster (Monthly Review Press, New York, 1971), pp. 121–73; and Teresa de Lauretis, "The Technology of Gender," in her *Technologies of Gender: Essays on Theory, Film, and Fiction* (Indiana University Press, Bloomington, IN, 1987), pp. 1–30.

6 I borrow this phrase from Willa Cather's essay, "The Novel Démeublé," in her *Not Under Forty* (Knopf, New York, 1922), p. 50.

7 Havelock Ellis, *Studies in the Psychology of Sex*, vol. 2: *Sexual Inversion*, 3rd edn revised and enlarged (F. A. Davis, Philadelphia, 1915). Further references to this edition will be noted parenthetically unless otherwise stated. Although *Sexual Inversion* was published originally as vol. 1, Ellis changed its position to vol. 2 in the second and third editions, published in the United States in 1901 and 1915, respectively. In the later editions, vol. 1 became *The Evolution of Modesty*.

8 Ellis, *Sexual Inversion* (1900), p. xi.

9 Classic discussions of the term's history include Peter I. Rose, *The Subject is Race* (Oxford University Press, New York, 1968), pp. 30–43; and Thomas F. Gossett, *Race: The History of an Idea in America* (South Methodist University Press, Dallas, 1963).

10 On Blumenbach, see John S. Haller Jr, *Outcasts from Evolution: Scientific Attitudes of Racial Inferiority, 1859–1900* (University of Illinois Press, Urbana, IL, 1971), p. 4.

11 Nancy Leys Stepan and Sander Gilman, "Appropriating the Idioms of Science: The Rejection of Scientific Racism," in *The Bounds of Race: Perspectives on Hegemony and Resistance*, ed. Dominick LaCapra (Cornell University Press, Ithaca, NY, 1991), p. 74.

12 Fields, "Slavery, Race, and Ideology," p. 97, n. 3.

13 Haller, *Outcasts from Evolution*, p. 48.

14 W.H. Flower and James Murie, "Account of the Dissection of a Bushwoman," *Journal of Anatomy and Physiology*, 1 (1887), p. 208. Subsequent references

will be noted parenthetically within the text. For brief discussions of this account, see Gilman, *Difference and Pathology: Stereotypes of Sexuality, Race, and Madness* (Cornell University Press, Ithaca, NY, 1985), pp. 88–9; and Anita Levy, *Other Women: The Writing of Class, Race, and Gender, 1832–1898* (Princeton University Press, Princeton, NJ, 1991), pp. 70–2.

15 Georges Cuvier, "Extraits d'observations faites sur le cadavre d'une femme connue à Paris et à Londres sous le nom de Vénus Hottentote," *Memoires du Musée d'histoire naturelle*, 3 (1817), pp. 259–74. On Baartman, see Londa Schiebinger, *Nature's Body: Gender in the Making of Modern Science* (Beacon Press, Boston, 1993), pp. 160–72, and Stephen Jay Gould, *The Flamingo's Smile* (Norton, New York, 1985), pp. 291–305.

16 The *American Journal of Obstetrics* (*AJO*) was a frequent forum for these debates, particularly in the 1870s.

17 According to Sander Gilman, "When one turns to autopsies of black males from [the late nineteenth century], what is striking is the absence of any discussion of the male genitalia," *Difference and Pathology*, p. 89.

18 This practice continued well into the twentieth century. See, e.g., Jennifer Terry, "Lesbians under the Medical Gaze: Scientists Search for Remarkable Differences," *Journal of Sex Research*, 27 (August 1990), pp. 317–39.

19 George Fredrickson, *The Black Image in the White Mind: The Debate on Afro-American Character and Destiny, 1817–1914* (Harper and Row, New York, 1971), p. 246.

20 Havelock Ellis, *Man and Woman: A Study of Human Secondary Sexual Characters*, 4th edn (1894; Scribner's, New York, 1911), p. 13.

21 Patrick Geddes and J. Arthur Thomson, *The Evolution of Sex* (London, 1889; New York, 1890), p. 80. Ellis chose this text to inaugurate the Contemporary Science Series, which he edited for the Walter Scott Company. For more on this series, see Phyllis Grosskurth, *Havelock Ellis: A Biography* (Knopf, New York, 1980), pp. 114–17.

22 For a full account of the debates about monogeny and polygeny, see Stephen Jay Gould, *The Mismeasure of Man* (Norton, New York, 1981), pp. 30–72.

23 See Nancy Stepan, *The Idea of Race in Science: Great Britain, 1800–1960* (Archon Books, Hamden, CT, 1982), p. 53.

24 See, for instance, Edward Byron Reuter, *The Mulatto in the United States: Including a Study of the Role of Mixed-Blood Races throughout the World* (Gorham Press, Boston, 1918).

25 Mark H. Haller, *Eugenics: Hereditarian Attitudes in American Thought* (Rutgers University Press, New Brunswick, NJ, 1963), p. 144.

26 Jeffrey Weeks, *Sexuality and its Discontents: Meanings, Myths, and Modern Sexualities* (Routledge and Kegan Paul, Boston, 1985), p. 76; Grosskurth, *Havelock Ellis*, p. 410. See also Havelock Ellis, "The Sterilization of the Unfit," *Eugenics Review* (October 1909), pp. 203–6.

27 Quoted by Grosskurth, *Havelock Ellis*, p. 410.

28 Ellis and Symonds, *Sexual Inversion* (1897), p. 1 n.

29 Edward Carpenter, "The Homogenic Attachment," in his *The Intermediate Sex: A Study of Some Transitional Types of Men and Women*, 5th edn (George Allen and Unwin, London, 1918), p. 40 n.

30 Xavier Mayne [Edward Irenaeus Prime Stevenson], *The Intersexes: A History of Similisexualism As A Problem in Social Life* ([Naples?, *c*.1908]; rpt Arno Press, New York, 1975), p. 14.
31 Ibid., pp. 15, 17.
32 Quoted in Carpenter, *The Intermediate Sex*, pp. 133, 170. Carpenter gives the following citations for these quotations: Dr James Burnet, *Medical Times and Hospital Gazette*, vol. 34, no. 1497 (London, November 10, 1906); and Charles G. Leland, *The Alternate Sex* (William Rider and Son, London, 1904), p. 57.
33 In *New People: Miscegenation and Mulattoes in the United States* (The Free Press, New York, 1980), Joel Williamson suggests that a similar psychologization of race was underway by 1900 (p. 108).
34 Margaret Otis, "A Perversion Not Commonly Noted," *Journal of Abnormal Psychology*, 8 (June–July 1913), p. 113. Subsequent references will be noted parenthetically within the text.
35 W. T. English, "The Negro Problem from the Physician's Point of View," *Atlanta Journal-Record of Medicine*, 5 (October 1903), p. 468.
36 See Simon LeVay, *The Sexual Brain* (MIT Press, Cambridge, MA, 1993); and Dean Hamer, *The Science of Desire: The Search for the Gay Gene and the Biology of Behavior* (Simon and Schuster, New York, 1994).

Part II

Labelling Bodies

5 Symonds's History, Ellis's Heredity: *Sexual Inversion*

Joseph Bristow

I am so glad H. Ellis has told you about our project. I never saw him. But I like his way of corresponding on this subject. And I need somebody of medical importance to collaborate with. Alone, I could make but little effect – the effect of an eccentric.

John Addington Symonds to Edward Carpenter,
29 December 1892

I

Half way through the autobiography on which he laboured intermittently for more than thirty years, Havelock Ellis recalls a troublesome episode that made a decisive impact on his professional life as a sexologist and social reformer. 'It is time', he announces, 'to refer to an event' that had 'far-reaching significance: the prosecution of the first published volumes of my *Sex Studies* for "obscenity".'[1] The controversial work in question was *Sexual Inversion* (1897), the most detailed enquiry into same-sex desire to appear in Britain before 1900. Ellis lays out in some detail the remarkable circumstances that surrounded the banning of this study for obscene libel at the Old Bailey in 1898. That year George Bedborough was taken to court for selling a copy of the offending work to an undercover detective, and much legal wrangling – including pressure from Scotland Yard – led him to plead guilty. A year after the trial, the police raided the warehouse of Ellis's British publisher, seizing copies of both *Sexual Inversion* and its successor *The Evolution of Modesty, The Phenomena of*

Sexual Periodicity, Auto-Erotism (1899). Ellis then decided to transfer the publication of *Studies in the Psychology of Sex* (1897–1928) – one of the most comprehensive accounts of sexual physiology and behaviour from this period – to the United States. From 1900 to 1936, the seven volumes that eventually comprised the *Studies* were brought out in frequently up-dated editions by F.A. Davis in Philadelphia. Thereafter, the copyright went to the American trade publisher Random House, which reissued them 'in a cheaper and more compact form', no longer restricting their sale 'as hitherto, to professional readers'.[2]

Ellis obviously felt vindicated that the first of his *Studies*, despite its condemnation in court, ultimately enjoyed wide circulation beyond the world of medical research. Undoubtedly, by the mid-1930s, he had be-come a household name where the study of sex was concerned, just as he commanded considerable respect within his profession. In 1942, three years after he died, a long critical essay in the *Psychoanalytic Quarterly* surveyed the main theoretical advances made by each of Ellis's enquiries into sex, praising in particular the way the first volume insisted 'sexual inversion was not a disease', and certainly not – as many of Ellis's contem-poraries believed – 'a condition of degeneration'. Ellis's 'assistance in dis-crediting the whole concept of degeneration', we are told, 'was a matter of wider than sexological importance'.[3] Ellis states that sexual inversion, if a congenital abnormality, is 'bound up with the modification of the secondary sexual characters'; the phenomenon, he argues, cannot be ad-equately characterized as 'degenerate', since 'degeneration' – presum-ably in the light of Max Nordau's influential writings – has become 'a mere term of literary and journalistic abuse'.[4] Focused on physiological development, his analysis helped to dissociate homosexuality from pa-thology, and thus made a positive move towards sexual liberation. As a result, modern gay historians such as Jeffrey Weeks have stressed how *Sexual Inversion* 'greatly contributed to the sense of a homosexual self-consciousness that becomes increasingly apparent from the 1890s'.[5]

Yet Ellis's pioneering role in transforming received medical opinion con-tinued to cause him some unease. Not only was Ellis aggrieved that he was not called to defend *Sexual Inversion* in court. (He had already made his position clear in a pamphlet, 'A Note on the Bedborough Trial' (1898), which appeared before the defendant took the stand.) Ellis also, more importantly, remained unsettled because he disputed the views of the man who first suggested a study of this kind, and whose work on homosexual-ity provided the basis upon which Ellis built his profile as an expert in his chosen field. Ellis's collaborator was the established poet, cultural critic and classical scholar John Addington Symonds, whose own analyses of same-sex desire had in the 1880s and early 1890s been discreetly restricted to Symonds's closest friends, not least because he feared the law. This chapter examines why their collaboration on *Sexual Inversion* frustrated the efforts of both men to bring their very different perspectives on homosexuality to light.

In Ellis's autobiography, it is hard not to notice how Symonds's vital role in the making of *Sexual Inversion* is curiously pushed into the background. Recollecting on the eventual success of his *Studies*, Ellis claims that 1898 marked 'the chief-turning-point' he had 'ever encountered' in his career.[6] He observes that this affair occurred when he was on the brink of emerging as a recognized authority on sex. To prove his point, he takes pleasure in recounting that while his professional standing began to rise, those responsible for the legal assault on his work quickly faded from view. 'The creatures who were the puppets in this show', writes Ellis, 'began to fall to pieces when it was scarcely over.' He reports how the judge, Charles Hall, 'died so swiftly after the trial that one might well believe the home truths he could not fail to hear concerning his part in it had struck him to the heart'.[7] Several years later, the same fate befell Roland de Villiers, the untrustworthy publisher of *Sexual Inversion*. De Villiers ran the dubious Watford University Press, which had no connection with any place of learning, even though its printing press was at Watford and issued the monthly *University Magazine and Free Review*. Several years after the trial, when he still remained loyal to de Villiers, Ellis discovered this was one of many bogus companies set up by the fraudulent owner. De Villiers – the assumed identity of Dr George Ferdinand Springmühl von Weissenfeld – turned out to be a German confidence trickster who had been pursued across Europe for the corrupt share issues he made to himself under various fictitious names. Deceitful to the last, de Villiers collapsed of a heart attack when police officers raided his home in Cambridge. (He was found hiding in one of several secret passages built behind the walls.)

Ellis fills in most of these sensational details to illustrate how *Sexual Inversion* came into the hands of a criminal publisher, only to be sold by Bedborough to an undercover police detective. The politically inexperienced Bedborough was honorary secretary of the Legitimation League, a radical group campaigning for sexual unions free from state regulation; and the league's journal – the *Adult* – was also published by de Villiers. Since anarchists attended meetings of the league, Bedborough and his associates had for some time been under state surveillance. Ellis, by all accounts, appears to have known next to nothing about these political connections. But he was aware there might be difficulties bringing a study of this type before his English colleagues. That is why the edition Bedborough unknowingly sold to the police was not the first in which *Sexual Inversion* appeared. Two years earlier, Ellis placed his manuscript with the German scholar Hans Kurella, who had already translated Ellis's preceding scientific studies – *The Criminal* (1890) and *Man and Woman* (1894) – for Wigand in Leipzig. Although Ellis informed fellow socialist, the sex radical Edward Carpenter, that this analysis of homosexuality was hardly 'required in Germany'[8] (given works like *Psychopathia Sexualis* (1886) by Richard von Krafft-Ebing), he believed a first German edition might 'pave the way' for an English one.

In the meantime, Ellis made progress towards this aim by putting out various chapters in respected periodicals such as the *Alienist and Neurologist* and the *Medico-Legal Journal*,[9] and in 1896 he submitted the completed manuscript to a small company, Williams and Norgate. Their reader, Hack Tuke, editor of the *Journal of Mental Science*, advised the publisher not to accept the study. Phyllis Grosskurth reveals that Tuke solemnly told Ellis such a book 'could not be confined to specialists', since there were always 'the compositors!'.[10] Possibly Tuke's reluctance was based on an unfavourable review of the German edition that appeared in his journal. The reviewer felt that *Das Konträre Geschlechtsgefühl* – to give *Sexual Inversion* its German title – stressed the primacy of 'congenital perverted sexual feeling' at the expense of analysing how 'so-called homosexual customs are artificial and not natural, and in other words the products of peculiar social conditions'.[11] But perhaps more to the point was the anxiety among publishers after the trials that sent Oscar Wilde to prison for committing acts of gross indecency in 1895. (On these grounds, T. Fisher Unwin refused to publish Edward Carpenter's *Homogenic Love* that year.) Ellis himself acknowledged to his friend Arthur Symons that Walter Scott, for whom he edited the influential Contemporary Science Series, was right to think there 'was too much at stake' in 'any really risky pioneering experiment'.[12] Only after discussing the matter with fellow scientist F. H. Perry-Coste was Ellis put in touch with the disreputable de Villiers. Even then, further problems ensued. Once the first English edition emerged from another of de Villiers's spurious imprints, Wilson and Macmillan, it was quickly bought up by Symonds's distressed family when they found his name writ large with Ellis's on the title page. It was left to the Watford University Press to issue an edition representing Ellis as sole author.

Little wonder Ellis was pleased with his rapid rise to fame after surmounting these obstacles. 'It was the end of the upward climb in life', he recalls.[13] Yet the more we examine the intricate events before and after the Bedborough trial the clearer it becomes that Ellis felt ambivalent about both the planning and publication of *Sexual Inversion*. In later life, he admitted that the controversy surrounding this study brought him to maturity. But at the same time he suggests it made him old before his time. 'Until then', he adds, 'although I always looked older than my age, I had retained an instinctive feeling of youthfulness.'[14] In 1898, when he was

39, his hair suddenly turned grey. Not only that, within a year he needed glasses. In part, he maintains, these signs of physical decline showed that he had entered his 'most mature period of mental power'.[15] Never before had he truly felt like 'an adult'. Yet he adds that his resolve to work with Symonds was a definite 'mistake'.[16] Exactly why becomes clear in a revealing passage where Ellis puts his collaborator, their shared enquiries, and indeed the subject matter of the whole enterprise at a rather cautious distance:

> Homosexuality was an aspect of sex which up to a few years before had interested me less than any, and I had known very little about it. But during those few years I had become interested in it. Partly I had found that some of my most highly esteemed friends were more or less homosexual (like Edward Carpenter and [Ellis's spouse, the writer and political campaigner] Edith), and partly I had come into touch through correspondence with John Addington Symonds, for whose work I had once had an admiration which somewhat decreased with years. He had already printed privately two small books on the subject, one on Greek paiderastia [desire by an older man for a younger man], and another, more novel, but of less value, on the modern aspects of the question. He was feeling his way towards the open publication of a comprehensive work on the subject. He now proposed to join forces with me.[17]

Ellis states he accordingly 'drew up a scheme of the book' apportioning segments to himself and Symonds. Yet it would seem that Symonds had some reservations about Ellis's manner of proceeding: 'He accepted my scheme, remarking I had assigned the most important chapters to myself, but making no demur.'[18] Once these matters had been settled, the two men set to work, with Symonds offering half of the male case histories. (Ellis would acquire those cases devoted to same-sex desire among women, and his analysis of lesbians has been acknowledged as far more limited than his view of homosexual men.)[19] But their joint efforts stopped abruptly when Symonds's perpetually poor health worsened, leading to his death from influenza in 1893. Left with the unenviable task of steering *Sexual Inversion* through this hazardous course, Ellis discounted much of the work Symonds hoped would eventually reach a larger audience.

In fairness to Ellis, it is important to note that he furnished a preface to clarify which sections of *Sexual Inversion* can be attributed to himself and to Symonds respectively. He states that Symonds's contributions fall under five headings. First, there is the text of *A Problem in Greek Ethics*, which Symonds wrote in 1874 and privately printed – in a severely limited edition of ten copies – in 1883.[20] This fine scholarly work, which amounts to roughly 40,000 words, explores the development of male same-sex desire throughout the post-Homeric era, especially the martial ethic of the Dorians. The essay makes explicit those details about ancient Greek sexual practices occasionally visible in the two compendious volumes comprising *Studies in the Greek Poets* (1873–6) that established Symonds's high reputation as a cultural critic. It forms the first and longest of the six appendices to the first English edition. Second, *Sexual Inversion* includes unspecified sections of *A Problem in Modern Ethics* (1891), the equally notable essay that Symonds, again for reasons of discretion, published privately in a limited edition, this time of fifty copies. Next are the various 'fragments written to form part of such a book as the present'.[21] Last of all, there are scattered 'extracts from letters' between the two men, together with the fifteen or so case histories supplied by – though not openly ascribed to – Symonds.

Although Ellis attempts some thoroughness in compiling this list, he feels under no obligation to explain precisely which sections of the main text originate in Symonds's researches. This matter becomes of greater concern when we encounter Ellis's rather dismissive treatment of the two detailed essays that Symonds wished to incorporate in this collaboration. In his preface, Ellis doubts that *A Problem in Greek Ethics* 'throws any great light on sexual inversion as a congenital psychic abnormality'.[22] But it is Symonds's carefully argued tract – which Ellis's autobiography estimates as 'more novel, but of less value' than its predecessor – that Ellis took some pains to silence. To be sure, a long section of *A Problem of Modern Ethics* devoted to the theoretical work of German homophile campaigner Karl Heinrich Ulrichs appears under Symonds's own name in appendix C. Yet in entrusting Ellis with copies of this powerful essay for editorial 'scissor use',[23] Symonds did not expect that a large portion of it would be cut out of *Sexual Inversion*.

It is not just that Ellis, as Wayne Koestenbaum rightly observes, eagerly snipped away at Symonds's 'fragments', thus performing 'a symbolic castration on his dead collaborator, accusing him of collage, or worse, incoherence'.[24] The more urgent point is that Ellis gave no room for the incisive criticisms Symonds made against a host of European sexological thinkers in *A Problem in Modern Ethics*. Ellis's unwillingness to engage with Symonds's largely historical challenges to sexology doubtless lay in the fact he had begun to make a career out of compiling and describing, in an often uncritical manner, literature addressing matters of criminal and sexual physiology for a British readership. Had Ellis taken Symonds's sedulous critiques of sexology into account, then he would arguably have produced a more advanced discussion of the material, cultural and psychic forces that shape modern understandings of homosexuality. To the end of his days, Ellis believed that he and Symonds were both far too 'individual' to see eye to eye.[25] In many ways, he was right. For they were the bearers of two largely incompatible intellectual traditions that came into their own during the last third of the nineteenth century. By exploring each tradition in turn, my discussion reveals how Symonds's desire to combine forces with a younger man of science was based on the belief that his own critical approach – well versed in classical scholarship and suspicious of the ahistorical tendency of modern sexology – could command far less respect than the psychological and medical methods that Ellis championed at his peril.

II

Symonds's research into homosexuality – a term he infrequently used – dates back to his years as a student at Balliol College, Oxford. There he experienced the rigorous tutorials of Benjamin Jowett, the broad-minded classical scholar. In her erudite enquiry into Jowett's cardinal role in liberalizing the Greats syllabus (which included for the first time Plato's *Republic*), Linda Dowling observes that, since this type of education emphasized the martial culture of the ancients, 'Greek studies became a vehicle for channeling modern progressive thought into the Victorian civic elite'.[26] Such studies – as Jowett recognized and as Dowling explains – would have 'destabilizing effects on the religious faith of Oxford men'. The consequences of such developments, if designed to educate a cadre of future governors exercising authority across a growing empire, led to no uncertain dangers. Not only were students exposed to forms of non-Christian thought that could result in agnosticism, their eyes were also opened to tabooed styles of sexual conduct, notably the ancient Greek models of *paiderastia* that Symonds himself would take care to document in his privately published essay of 1883. From the 1860s to the 1880s (certainly, until college dons could marry in 1884), Oxford Hellenism provided covert support for university men who desired their own sex. But if homosexuality was one indirect but significant outcome of Jowett's spirit of reform, those whose same-sex desires responded to this distinctive ethos did not always treat it with approbation. In 1889, when Symonds was in his late forties, he told his former tutor: 'the study of Plato is injurious to a certain number of predisposed young men'. 'The Lysis, the Charmides, the Phaedrus, the Symposium,' he would add, 'how many varied and unimaginative pictures these dialogues contain of what is only a sweet poison to such minds!'[27]

Such remarks should hardly be mistaken as signs of internalized oppression or homophobia. They are instead the result of the many years Symonds devoted – first as a student, then as a professional writer – to negotiating the conflict between homosexual desires to some degree legitimated by his Oxford education and the enduring hostility to such passions both inside and outside the university. It is not as if Jowett and his supporters actively encouraged homosexuality among the students. Admiration for Socrates' attraction to young men could precipitate attacks by university members against Jowett's transformed Greek studies. The most famous in this regard occurred in 1877 when Symonds and the homophile don and cultural critic, Walter Pater, announced their candidature for the post of professor of poetry. During the election campaign, Symonds suffered an assault on his *Studies of the Greek Poets* by R. St John Tyrwhitt, who objected to various 'suggestive passages' quoted from Plato. Equipping his essay with references to offensive extracts that could be found in both Jowett's scholarly editions and Symonds's research, Tyrwhitt emphasizes that 'it is well known that Greek love of nature and beauty frequently went against nature'. 'The emotions of Socrates at the sight of Charmides' provide Tyrwhitt with one of several instances where Symonds – whom he ironically claims is 'probably the most innocent of men' – promotes a Hellenism that involves 'the total denial of any moral restraint on human impulses'.[28] Such animosity encouraged Symonds – an ostensibly respectable man, married with four daughters – to withdraw from the election.

One of Symonds's favoured vehicles for celebrating homosexual passion was poetry. The author of several undistinguished collections, he repeatedly used this genre to celebrate the homosexual desires he often termed '*l'amour de l'impossible* '. And he was quick to identify any allusion to male same-sex passion in the poetry of his contemporaries. Especially vexed was his enthusiasm for Walt Whitman's effusive works that in his view upheld a model of democratic comradeship between men that revitalized Greek *paiderastia*. Symonds was particularly impressed by the 'Calamus' cluster in the 1860 edition of Whitman's *Leaves of Grass*.[29] In 1893, he sought to persuade the public that these poems – celebrating 'the manly love of comrades'[30] – recalled 'to our minds that fellowship in arms which flourished among the Dorian tribes, and formed the chivalry of pre-historic Hellas'.[31] He had already made the same point in *A Problem in Modern Ethics*, adding that when we read Whitman's lines 'we are carried back to ancient Greece, to Plato's Symposium'.[32] Yet in 1890 this style of interpretation led Symonds into notorious conflict with his 'dear American Master'. He wrote a detailed letter to Whitman to obtain confirmation that 'Calamus' involved 'praising and propagating a passionate affection between men', even though 'objectors' claimed such love 'has a very dangerous side' and might 'bring people into criminality'. Pursuing this point, Symonds referred to the essay on Whitman that Ellis included in *The New Spirit* (1890), where Ellis observed that readers of 'Calamus' were left with 'some perplexity about the doctrine of "manly love"'. Ellis, remarks Symonds, went so far as to use the phrase 'the intimate and physical love of comrades and lovers'.[33] To this enquiry, Whitman made an indignant reply stating that such 'morbid inferences' were 'damnable'.[34] Yet this testy response did not deter Symonds from claiming the American poet as a worthy celebrant of the modern Dorian mood. In fact, Symonds was the first to acknowledge that 'the man who wrote "Calamus", and preached the gospel of comradeship, entertains feelings at least as hostile to sexual inversion as any law-abiding humdrum Anglo-Saxon could desire'. But he none the less stressed that such 'considerations do not [. . .] affect the spiritual nature of that ideal'.[35] Symonds, I would claim, persisted in elevating Whitman in the name of preserving the ancient Dorian ideal because it provided him with a critical perspective on what he believed were the damaging hereditarian explanations of homosexuality propounded by many sexological writings of the 1880s.

The task of *A Problem in Modern Ethics* was to contest practically every major sexologist and scientific theorist who engaged with the vexed topic of homosexuality. Prefaced with a list of the many sources he consulted, Symonds's essay provides a brief account of the early Christian reaction against sexual love between men, noting Edward Gibbon's hostile discussion of how the Roman Empire under Justinian outlawed the 'odious vice' inherited from the Greeks.[36] Thereafter, he shifts attention to contemporary European scientific studies such as J.L. Casper and Carl Liman's 1889 guide to forensic medicine, a work that gives the impression that 'very many pederasts' – a word Symonds detested – 'are addicted to what may be termed Platonic voluptuousness'.[37] Time and again, he shows that these medical writers' ignorance of ancient Greek customs is so deep that they remain unable to see how cultural forces influence the shaping of homosexual desire. Confronted, for example, by the fourth edition of Paul Moreau's *Des aberrations du sense génésique* (1887) – which follows the late nineteenth-century trend for connecting sexual dissidence with hereditary degeneration – Symonds exclaims: 'it is illogical to treat sexual inversion among the modern European races as a malady, when you refer its prevalence among Oriental peoples and the Hellenes to custom'.[38] But his most incisive arguments were reserved for two much better-known writers, the Austrian psychiatrist, Krafft-Ebing, and the Italian criminal anthropologist, Cesare Lombroso. Both figures, if to markedly different degrees, directed the path of Ellis's own thinking on sexual inversion – a point that Symonds perhaps did not fully appreciate.

Krafft-Ebing's *Psychopathia Sexualis*, though reprinted many times in Britain, was not well received by the medical profession, and Symonds and Ellis – for all their differences of viewpoint on this work – counted among a minority of sexual radicals engaging with sexological writings of this kind. (Roy Porter and Lesley Hall reveal that the medical profession's cautious approach to Krafft-Ebing's research in the early 1890s turned to downright hostility after the turn of the century.)[39] Symonds carefully evaluates how this work traces both acquired and congenital types of homosexuality back to a 'form of inherited neuropathy (*Belastung*)'.[40] On Krafft-Ebing's view, any man with a hereditary disposition to nervous weakness should be averted from masturbation, since such 'self-abuse' might well lead to the breakdown of his virility, making him shy of women, and thus directing his desires towards other men. But as Symonds observes: 'It would be absurd to maintain that all the boy-lovers of ancient Greece owed their instincts to hereditary neuropathy complicated by onanism.'[41] In Symonds's eyes, the more consideration that is given to how each culture develops its customs, the more hereditarian theory appears built on shaky foundations:

> The invocation of heredity in problems of this kind is always hazardous. We only throw the difficulty of explanation further back. At what point of the world's history was the morbid taste acquired? If none but tainted individuals are capable of homosexual feelings, how did those feelings first come into existence? On the supposition that neuropathy forms a necessary condition of abnormal instinct, is it generic neuropathy or a specific type of that disorder? If generic, can valid reasons be adduced for regarding the nervous malady in any of its aspects (hysteria in the mother, insanity in the father) as the cause of so peculiarly differentiated an affection of the sexual appetite? If specific, that is if the ancestors of the patient must have been afflicted with sexual inversion, in what way did they acquire it, supposing all untainted individuals to be incapable of the feeling?[42]

This last enquiry prompts Symonds to comment that one of the main shortcomings of hereditarian thought is the way it mistakenly invokes an infinite regress to an unknowable origin from which the pathology must have sprung. Taken to its logical limit, the belief that neuropathic strains are inherited by one generation after another suggests it is not just a select few who will succumb to such pathology but that 'everybody is liable to sexual inversion'. If, he argues, that point is conceded, then 'the principle of heredity becomes purely theoretical',[43] since the whole population must contain the seeds that cause the race to degenerate.

Symonds levels similar charges when identifying even deeper illogicalities in Lombroso's supposedly scientific methods. Ellis's *The Criminal* (1890) was the first English work to popularize Lombroso's enquiries into the physiognomical distinctiveness of lawbreakers. Although Ellis readily admits that 'Lombroso's work is by no means free from fault', he shows no hesitation in recording the 'vigorous and picturesque' portraits that, according to the Italian anthropologist, disclose evidence of the criminal mind: 'Thieves [Lombroso] describes as frequently remarkable for the mobility of their features and their hands; the eyes are small and very restless; the eyebrows thick and close; the nose often crooked; the beard thin; the forehead nearly always narrow and receding; the complexion pale and yellowish, and incapable of blushing.'[44] From Symonds's perspective, Lombroso's elaborate claims upon the criminal's bodily semiotics tended to contradict themselves. Here, too, Symonds identifies an incoherent approach to cultural customs and hereditary influences. He strongly objects to Lombroso's obsessive concern with neuropathy: 'Having started with the natural history of crime, as a prime constituent in nature and humanity, which only becomes crime through the development of social morality, and which survives atavistically in persons ill-adapted to their civilized environment, he suddenly turns round and identifies the crime thus analyzed with morbid nerve-conditions, malformations, and moral insanity.'[45] This was in Symonds's view a wholly untenable argument: 'If crime was not crime but nature in the earlier stages, and only appeared as crime under the conditions of advancing culture, its manifestations as a survival in certain individuals ought to be referred to nature, and cannot be relegated to the category of physical or mental disease.'[46]

In criticizing Krafft-Ebing and Lombroso, however, Symonds had no wish to claim that biology was without a contributory role in the development of sexual inversion. Although he repudiated heredity as the exclusive determining force, he none the less believed that physiological development was fundamental to any analysis of sexual desire. He found a plausible biological explanation for homosexuality from research on the processes of sexual differentiation in early pregnancy. 'The embryo', he writes, 'contains an undetermined element of sex', and from this inchoate stage it 'is gradually worked up into male and female organs of procreation; and these, when the age of puberty arrives, are generally accompanied by corresponding male and female appetites'.[47] He points out that the sexual division of the embryo does not always reach the expected heterosexual outcome because it sometimes leads, through no fault of nature, to 'so-called hermaphrodites', cross-dressers, and persons who desire their own sex.

To elaborate this theory of intermediate sexual types, Symonds turns to the pathbreaking work of Ulrichs, the legal official, homophile campaigner, and distinguished classical and theological scholar who feared that paragraph 143 of the Prussian penal code (which punished homosexual offences for up to four years) would be extended to his native Hanover. (Ulrichs, as James D. Steakley reminds us, 'had every reason to fear' this item of Prussian legislation. In 1869, three years after Bismarck's victory in the Austro-Prussian war, Paragraph 143 entered Hanoverian law).[48] Like Symonds,

Ulrichs had no medical training, and his reflections on homosexuality could not make any professional claim to scientific fact. But his procedures for analysing styles of same-sex desire rested on a model – the case history – that would be taken up by many clinicians. Furthermore, he helped set the trend followed by sexologists like Krafft-Ebing for inventing categories of distinctive sexual types, calling attention to the fact that same-sex desires belonged to specific persons rather than behaviours. Ulrichs's writings held a powerful appeal to Symonds because they presented an affirmative belief in the wholly natural status of homosexual men and women. Such people, Ulrichs contended, constituted a third sex distinct from both male and female. He specified this third sex in the figure of the urning – which he named after Uranos, featured in Plato's *Symposium*. Hubert Kennedy observes that although the 'term "third sex" (*drittes Geschlecht*) had been used earlier, from Plato (*Symposium*) to Théophile Gautier (*Mademoiselle de Maupin*, 1835), with very diverse meanings', all these different uses, including Ulrichs's, hold in common the idea that '"sex" is not viewed solely from the aspect of reproduction'.[49] Having examined the available literature on hermaphroditism, Ulrichs developed the theory that some biological males had a female psychic disposition, thus attracting them to men. Thus the male urning contained, as it were, the soul of a woman. Correspondingly, the female urning embodied the soul of a man. Even though Ulrichs did not himself design the concept of the invert (Ellis claimed the term was first used in Italy),[50] it was closely correlated with the urning as the individual type commonly associated with congenital homosexuality, notably in Krafft-Ebing's *Psychopathia Sexualis*.

Such hypotheses led Ulrichs, in a series of short studies published between 1864 and 1879, to generate a detailed list of names for those persons soon to be labelled by scientists like Ellis as homosexual and heterosexual. Presenting a chart classifying the various subspecies of Ulrichs's male urning – such as urianiaster (man with acquired homosexuality), mannling (masculine homosexual) and weibling (effeminate homosexual) – Symonds declares these 'outlandish names, though seemingly pedantic and superfluous, have their technical value' because they identify recognizable types. But if impressed by Ulrichs's belief that the natural origins of the urning can be returned to the evolution of the embryo, Symonds remains impatient with any account of sexual desire that places an exclusive stress on biology. 'Ulrichs', he writes, 'seems to claim too much for the position he has won. He ignores the frequency of acquired habits. He shuts his eyes to the force of fashion and depravity.'[51] As Symonds himself clarifies in the long memoir he wrote during the last four years of his life, boys' public schools were one such environment where corrupt homosexual practices occurred, too often involving the abuse of pupils by their teachers.[52] Yet as *A Problem in Modern Ethics* makes plain, an ethical practice such as ancient Greek *paiderastia* was equally the product of a particular cultural environment, except this time the acquired habit was in the name of moral health, not vicious injury.

Symonds's sustained critique of heredity and its impact on sexology culminates in the fourteen points he enumerates in the conclusion that argues for the removal of the infamous clause that Henry Labouchere added to the Criminal Law Amendment Act (1885). The Labouchere Amendment – later nicknamed the 'Blackmailer's Charter' – oulawed acts of gross indecency between males in public and in private. Symonds told Ellis he wanted to see 'Labby's inexpansible legislation' brought into line with the Code Napoleon in France and the Penal Code in Italy.[53] At the same time, he contests arguments made by various detractors who, for example, believe that homosexuality can be eliminated through legal punishment, or claim that same-sex desire threatens population growth, or even suggest to the contrary that urnings will multiply at such a rate they will eventually overwhelm the nation. The final point he makes, however, is by far the most provocative. If, Symonds maintains, those in power 'hold that our penal laws are required by the interests of society', then legislators should recognize that 'our higher education is in open contradiction to the spirit of our laws'.[54] How could a society elevate classical knowledge when it introduced 'the best minds of our youth'[55] to desires – though consecrating the highest Platonic ideals – that would only lead to the bitter suffering he endured? English culture, therefore, hypocritically encouraged the development of ethical homosexual virtues, only to condemn all same-sex eroticism as vice.

III

Given Symonds's extensive reservations about sexology, it may come as a surprise that he turned to Ellis in the hope of bringing his own research on homosexual desire to a much wider public. In 1892 he first explored this possibility by approaching a mutual friend, the English poet Symons. At this time, Symonds's plans appear to be plain enough. He asked Symons if Ellis would consider a book on sexual inversion for Ellis's Contemporary Science Series. This prestigious list included some of the most impressive scientific studies of the period. Beginning with *The Evolution of Sex* (1889) by Patrick Geddes and J. Arthur Thomson, the series rapidly embraced translations of Lombroso's enquiries into the genius and the criminal, as well as analyses of such topics as sleep, manual education and hypnotism. Believing that his two *Problem* essays 'could very well be fused', he told Symons the time was ripe to show why 'the historical study of Greece' was 'absolutely essential to the psychological treatment of the subject now', because the subject was 'fearfully mishandled by pathologists and psychiatrical professors, who know nothing whatsoever about its real nature'.[56] A week later, he eagerly wrote to Ellis himself repeating the same points but this time suggesting the possibility of collaborating 'in the production of an impartial and really scientific survey of the matter'.[57] Symonds proposed he would take responsibility for the 'historical side of the analysis', while Ellis could 'criticize the crudest medical and forensico-medical theories'. There was, however, one issue on which both had to agree: 'the *legal* aspects of the subject'. The collaborative project would thus aim at reforming the law. Yet soon Ellis and Symonds were led into some tortuous negotiations on how to meet this objective.

Symonds's letter suggests that he did not entirely appreciate Ellis's own investment in the very 'psychiatrical' theories held by those pathologists and forensic anthropologists Symonds took to task. But if Symonds misjudged Ellis's position, then it is worth asking why Ellis himself responded positively to this proposal. The answer, I think, lies in the way Ellis had already begun to make his mark not just as a scientific researcher but also as a man of letters – as the largely literary essays collected in the volume titled *The New Spirit* attest. It is in this study that we find some clues to Ellis's readiness to become involved in subject matter that he admits had little previous interest for him. There Ellis reprinted 'The Present Position of English Criticism', an essay that first appeared in *Time* in 1885. Echoing Matthew Arnold's highly regarded 'The Function of Criticism at the Present Time' (1864), Ellis begins by attacking Arnold as a moralist; he then notes Pater's 'narrow range'; and by way of contrast he applauds the superiority of Symonds, who in his view 'represents to-day whatever is best in English criticism'.[58] In particular, Ellis accentuates Symonds's belief that Whitman was 'more truly Greek than any other man of modern times' – an opinion that, he rather affectedly observes, displays the '*cáractères essentiels*' of the American poet.[59] This essay, as one might expect, elicited a warm response from Symonds.

Later, when Ellis published his paper on Whitman, Symonds thought he saw his own opinions once again repeated in Ellis's prose: 'from the days when the Greek spirit found its last embodiment in the brief songs, keen or sweet, of the [Greek] "Anthology", the attitude which Whitman represents in "Song of Myself" has never lacked representatives'; yet as this statement makes clear, the Greek element in Whitman is, for Ellis, part of a revolutionary tradition that includes the 'profane and gay paganism' of Latin student-songs and the 'certain insane energy' of William Blake.[60] His main focus, then, was not on the homoerotic inflections of 'Calamus', although he remained unembarrassed by this sexual aspect to Whitman's celebration of comradeship, observing in a footnote that 'Whitman is hardy enough to assert' that 'manly love [. . .] will to a large extent take the place

of love between the sexes'.[61] This marginal comment, however, was suffi-
cient provocation for Symonds to write at once asking if Ellis thought
'modern society could elevate manly love into a new chivalry'.[62] Could
such desire be part of a 'new spiritual energy'? Was Whitman 'willing to
accept, condone or ignore the physical aspects of the passions'? Perhaps
not far from Symonds's mind was the prospect that Ellis too shared in
these thoughts as the result of experiencing the same desires.

But as Ellis's essay reveals, he applauded Whitman's 'vigorous masculine love'[63] because it enshrined the spirit of political rebelliousness that
inspired the generation of progressive thinkers to which Ellis belonged. In
the early 1880s, Ellis became involved in the Fellowship of the New Life,
a freethinking group established on somewhat mystical lines by Thomas
Davidson, from which the socialist Fabian Society would develop. The
fellowship brought Ellis into contact with Carpenter, whose long vision-
ary poem *Towards Democracy* (1884) emulated Whitman's *Leaves of
Grass*. Carpenter's poetry was part of a large corpus of pathbreaking nineteenth-century works that Ellis keenly absorbed to imagine a better social
order. In one of his first letters to the novelist and social theorist Olive
Schreiner – who would soon count among Ellis's closest friends – he sum-
marizes some of the writings that influenced his thought. He mentions,
for example, the Higher Criticism of David Friedrich Strauss, which viewed
the Bible as narrative not historical fact, and he adds that Herbert Spencer's *First Principles* (1862) – a work of social Darwinism that impressed
Schreiner deeply – did him 'much good'.[64] But the writer who interested
him more than any other was James Hinton, a contentious proponent of
free love (and even polygamy), whose posthumous *Life and Letters* (1878)
motivated Ellis to meet Hinton's followers, one of whom – Caroline
Haddon – provided funds for Ellis's medical education at St Thomas's
Hospital in London. Hinton, Ellis declares, was 'very good' for his 'soul –
as G[eorge]. Eliott [*sic*] said of Whitman (And so is Whitman, indeed).'[65]

Elsewhere in his correspondence with Schreiner, Ellis reveals that his
interest in Carpenter's and Whitman's respective works hardly rests on
the question of homosexuality. In September 1885, Ellis remarked: 'I have
never felt such a longing for anyone's friendship as for Carpenter's. I feel
so near to him. He could never say anything which wouldn't be mine too';
yet he added, perhaps with some caution: 'Only I have an idea that he
consciously imitates Whitman in all sorts of things.'[66] Such imitation, of
course, obliquely refers to the doctrine of 'manly love' that drew Carpenter and Symonds to Whitman's poetry. Here Ellis is not necessarily showing any fear of same-sex desire; indeed, he seems barely able to detect it.
The point is that *Leaves of Grass* provided an exhilarating literary medium in which both homosexual and heterosexual men could realize their
own different desires for sexual and social transformation. And in the

process, as we have seen in Ellis's essay on Whitman and in Symonds's letter of response, these divergent enthusiasms could lead to mutual misunderstandings. Such evidence goes some way towards elucidating why Ellis and Symonds's collaboration on *Sexual Inversion* was based on some confusion from the start.

As their plans took shape in 1892, their intellectual differences became apparent, though both made compromises. Symonds tried to persuade Ellis that although their 'object' was 'primarily a study of psychological anomaly', it was not possible to agree upon 'the part played in the phenomenon by morbidity'. 'I should', adds Symonds, 'be inclined to abolish the neuropathical hypothesis' because he regards 'neurosis in a Sexual Pervert as a *concomitant* not as a *cause*'.[67] As Symonds informed Carpenter, Ellis was 'too much inclined to stick to the neuropathical theory of explanation'.[68] Ellis, of course, made concessions on this point, since the most progressive aspect of *Sexual Inversion* lay in rejecting the neuropathic basis of homosexuality. He observes instead that same-sex desire is a 'biological variation', like colour-blindness – an analogy he attributes to Symonds.[69] Yet that does not stop Ellis from remarking that the 'sexual invert may thus be compared to the congenital idiot, to the instinctive criminal, to the man of genius'[70] – an assertion that firmly puts his analysis in close proximity to Lombroso's thinking, which Symonds disliked. Ellis's resistance to Symonds's historical approach is also based, if with far less clarity, on similar concepts. He rebuts the view that classical scholarship throws light on how homosexuality emerges in a modern English culture expressly opposed to such desires. 'It requires', he remarks, 'a very strong impetus to go against this compact social force which on every side constrains the individual into the paths of heterosexual love.'[71] But having made this thoughtful objection, he disappointingly concludes that it remains hard to know whether ancient Greek homosexuality could be referred either to 'an organic or racial disposition' or a 'state of social feeling'.[72] Puzzled by the nature or nurture of *paiderastia*, all Ellis can do is flatly refuse Symonds's tenet that ancient Greek customs could in any way account for homosexuality in 'a northern country like England'.[73]

No matter how much Symonds was troubled by Ellis's prevailing tendency to discard history and uphold heredity, he was not averse to conforming with one of the main structuring features of sexological writing. He willingly provided *Sexual Inversion* with data in the form of case histories that he may have felt would enhance the scientific authority of their joint study. Symonds, however, wished to distance these documents from the type commonly used by sexologists. 'You will', Symonds informed Ellis, 'observe my method in eliciting these confessions. I framed a set of questions upon the points which seemed to me of most importance after a study of Ulrichs and Krafft-Ebing.' Even though he certainly recognized that there was a bias towards a '"fixed style" in these confessions', he stressed that his were 'quite different from those collected by physicians'.[74] Doubtless he believed that his particular sympathies for homosexuality produced franker and thus more reliable insights into the phenomenon. But the format in which these cases appeared did not make them look different from those in the 'fixed style' garnered by doctors. Although Ellis notes that these histories were not collected by physicians, he declares that he presented them as a psychologist to show 'that in many cases we may fairly call acquired there is a congenital element, and that in many cases we may fairly call congenital some accident of environment had had an influence in developing latent tendency'.[75] Ellis says this is most plain to see in the one he characterizes as 'a very radical case of sexual inversion'[76] – namely, Case XVIII, featuring the anonymous Symonds. And it is only here that the frustrated voice of Symonds can at least be heard, though not exactly on his own terms.

For in furnishing his own case history Symonds speaks, as it were, in silence. The very nature of this document turns Symonds into anonymous material for not just Ellis's ruthless editing, but also the libel case against Bedborough. Here Symonds provides an autobiographical account of his childhood longings for sexual contact with other men, his perennial bouts of illness, the emotional hardship he suffered, his brilliance as a scholar, his homosexual practices, and his belief that has committed 'no wrong in his actions'.[77] His regret is that 'the perpetual conflict with' his 'inborn nature' led to masturbatory 'indulgence', thus ruining his 'moral repose'.[78] Even though Symonds implies that a paiderastic ethic would have saved his health, this account of his degeneration in many respects follows the path traced by Krafft-Ebing from onanism to neuropathic illness – for that, at least, is the kind of reading prompted by the conventions of the case history. It is a great irony that Symonds felt he needed to produce evidence of this kind to articulate the long-suppressed sufferings of the homosexual man. Yet as he said to Carpenter, he required the legitimacy of scientists like Ellis, otherwise he would merely have 'the effect of an eccentric'.[79] Appealing to a scientific figure such as Ellis to speak for him, however, had results that Symonds could not foresee, including the obliteration of his far-reaching critiques of sexology and the eventual charge of obscenity. In the process of elevating heredity at the expense of Symonds's history, Ellis did not anticipate that the state would also treat him as – if you will – an 'eccentric', if not perverted, man. Regardless of the claims Ellis made to scientific authority, in the late 1890s sexology held almost as precarious a position as homosexuality before the law. And that, I would claim, is perhaps the most significant aspect of *Sexual Inversion* that neither Symonds nor Ellis – given the marked differences between them – ever expected to share.

Notes

Research for this paper has been assisted immeasurably by generous advice given by the staffs of the University Research Library and the Biomedical Library at UCLA. My thanks to Lucy Bland and Laura Doan for their editorial guidance, and to Sandra F. Siegel for her generous responses.

1 Havelock Ellis, *My Life: Autobiography of Havelock Ellis* (Boston: Houghton Mifflin, 1939), p. 347. I have based my account of the Bedborough trial on two studies besides Ellis's autobiography: Phyllis Grosskurth, *Havelock Ellis: A Biography* (New York: Alfred A. Knopf, 1980), pp.191–204; and Arthur Calder-Marshall, *Lewd, Blasphemous and Obscene: Being the Trials and Tribulations of Sundry Founding Fathers of Today's Alternative Societies* (London: Hutchinson, 1972), pp.193–229.

2 Ellis, *My Life*, p. 371.

3 Burrill Friedman, 'The Contributions of Havelock Ellis to Sexology', *Psychoanalytic Quarterly*, 11 (1942), p. 378.

4 Havelock Ellis and John Addington Symonds, *Sexual Inversion* (London: Wilson and Macmillan, 1897; reprinted New York: Arno Press, 1975), p.137. As my discussion should make clear, although this first English edition bears the names of both Ellis and Symonds on the title page, it was left to Ellis to piece the manuscript together, and it is his authorship that is at stake when we analyse the main text of *Sexual Inversion*.

5 Jeffrey Weeks, 'Havelock Ellis and the Politics of Sex Reform', in Sheila Rowbotham and Jeffrey Weeks, *Socialism and the New Life: The Personal and Sexual Politics of Edward Carpenter and Havelock Ellis* (London: Pluto Press, 1977), p.155.

6 Ellis, *My Life*, p. 373.

7 Ellis, *My Life*, p. 368.

8 Ellis, 'To Edward Carpenter', 24 April 1896, quoted in Grosskurth, *Havelock Ellis* p.179.

9 I have been able to trace some of the papers on sexual inversion Ellis published in medical periodicals: 'The Study of Sexual Inversion', *Medico-Legal Journal*, 12 (1894), pp. 148–57; 'Sexual Inversion in Women', *Alienist and Neurologist*,16 (1895), pp. 141–58; 'Sexual Inversion: With an Analysis of Thirty-Three New Cases', *Medico-Legal Journal*, 13 (1895), pp. 255–67; and 'Sexual Inversion in Men', *Alienist and Neurologist*, 17 (1896), pp. 115–50.

10 Grosskurth, *Havelock Ellis*, p. 180.

11 Anonymous, Review of *Das Konträre Gesclechtsgefühl* (Leipzig: Wigand, 1896), *Journal of Mental Science*, 43 (1897), pp. 565–6. The British medical press was not altogether supportive of the first English edition, even though it expressed some anxiety about the legal ban on *Sexual Inversion*. The *British Medical Journal* – if recognizing the subject matter as 'extremely disagreeable' – none the less felt that there was 'certainly nothing about the book itself [. . .] to pander to the prurient mind': *British Medical Journal*, Volume 2 for 1898, p. 1466. The *Lancet* also carried an article, 'The Question of Indecent Literature', about the banning of *Sexual Inversion*, which stressed that it had not reviewed the English

edition because 'it was not published through a house able to take proper measures for introducing it to a scientific audience'. The writer was concerned that
'the book would fall into the hands of readers totally unable to benefit from it as
a work of science and very ready to draw evil lessons from its necessarily disgusting passages': *Lancet*, 19 November 1898, p. 1344.

12 Ellis, 'To Arthur Symons', 1 July 1892, quoted in Grosskurth, *Havelock Ellis*,
    p. 175.
13 Ellis, *My Life*, p. 373.
14 Ellis, *My Life*, p. 373.
15 Ellis, *My Life*, p. 373.
16 Ellis, *My Life*, p. 349.
17 Ellis, *My Life*, p. 349–50.
18 Ellis, *My Life*, p. 350.
19 On Ellis's depiction of lesbians, see Lucy Bland, *Banishing the Beast: English
    Feminism and Sexual Morality, 1885–1914* (Harmondsworth: Penguin, 1995),
    p. 263. Carroll Smith-Rosenberg observes that 'Ellis, while politically liberal
    and psychologically sensitive', nevertheless produced an analysis of female
    inversion that was limited by his inability to 'conceptualize sex except as part
    of a biological model': *Disorderly Conduct: Visions of Gender in Victorian
    America* (New York: Alfred A. Knopf, 1985), p. 277.
20 [Symonds,] *A Problem in Greek Ethics* (n.d. [1883]), number five in an edition
    of ten, Department of Special Collections of the University Research Library,
    UCLA. On the inside cover, Symonds has inscribed : 'This essay was written at
    Clifton Hill House about 1874, printed by Ballantyne and Hanson [maybe
    Harron] in 1883.' Symonds deleted the final six paragraphs from this essay, and
    it is this revised version that Ellis reprinted in the main text of the first German
    edition and appendix A of the first English edition; the concluding sentences of
    the 1883 text contain speculations that 'it is rational to predict that what may
    remain of an instinctive tendency toward paiderastia . . . will continue to be
    treated much in the same manner as we treat the inconvenient survival of the
    superfluous member in the corporeal organism' (p. 97). But as his later essay *A
    Problem in Modern Ethics* shows, Symonds was keen to distance himself from
    hereditarian arguments. By the second English edition, Ellis disposed of Symonds's
    essay in its entirety. On Ellis's gradual excision of some of Symonds's writings
    from the appendices to *Sexual Inversion*, see Percy L. Babington, *Bibliography
    of the Writings of John Addington Symonds* (London: John Castle, 1925), p.
    126.
21 Ellis and Symonds, *Sexual Inversion*, p. xii.
22 Ellis, 'Preface to *Sexual Inversion*', p. xii.
23 Symonds, 'To Havelock Ellis', 1 December 1892, in *The Letters of John
    Addington Symonds*, eds Herbert M. Schueller and Robert L. Peters, 3 vols
    (Detroit, MI: Wayne State University Press, 1969), III, p. 789.
24 Wayne Koestenbaum, *Double Talk: The Erotics of Male Literary Collabora-
    tion* (New York: Routledge, 1989), p. 51.
25 Ellis, *My Life*, p. 350.
26 Linda Dowling, *Hellenism and Homosexuality in Victorian Oxford* (Ithaca,
    NY: Cornell University Press, 1994), p. 64. Dowling's study builds on the

innovative research of Richard Dellamora, notably his chapter titled '"The New Chivalry" and Oxford Politics', in his *Masculine Desire: The Sexual Politics of Victorian Aestheticism* (Chapel Hill, NC: University of North Carolina Press, 1990), pp. 147–66.

27   Symonds, 'To Benjamin Jowett', 1 February 1889, in *The Letters of John Addington Symonds*, III, pp. 345–6.

28   R. St John Tyrwhitt, 'The Greek Spirit in Modern Literature', *Contemporary Review*, 29 (1877), pp. 556–7.

29   The first edition of Whitman's *Leaves of Grass* appeared in 1855, and the volume was revised and augmented in five further editions until 1881–82. The 'Calamus' poems appeared under that heading in the third edition of 1860; for detailed textual commentary on these works, see Whitman, *Leaves of Grass; A Textual Variorum of the Printed Poems*, 3 vols (New York: New York University Press, 1980), II, pp. 364–408.

30   Whitman, 'For You O Democracy', in *Leaves of Grass: A Textual Variorum of the Printed Poems*, II, p. 375.

31   Symonds, *Walt Whitman: A Study* (London: George Routledge, 1893), p. 89.

32   [Symonds], *A Problem in Modern Ethics. Being an Inquiry into the Phenomenon of Sexual Inversion. Addressed Especially to Medical Psychologists and Jurists*, n.d. [1891], p. 91.

33   Symonds, 'To Walt Whitman', 3 August 1890, in *The Letters of John Addington Symonds*, III, pp. 483, 482.

34   Walt Whitman, 'To John Addington Symonds', in Whitman, *Correspondence: 1890–92*, ed. Edward Haviland Miller (New York: New York University Press, 1969), p. 73.

35   [Symonds], *A Problem in Modern Ethics*, p. 91.

36   Edward Gibbon, *The History of the Decline and Fall of the Roman Empire*, ed. J. B. Bury, 3 vols (1776; New York: Heritage Press, 1946), II, p. 1475.

37   [Symonds], *A Problem in Modern Ethics*, p. 21.

38   [Symonds], *A Problem in Modern Ethics*, p. 27

39   Roy Porter and Lesley Hall, *The Facts of Life: The Creation of Sexual Knowledge in Britain, 1659–1950* (London: Yale University Press, 1995), pp. 162–3.

40   [Symonds], *A Problem in Modern Ethics*, p. 35.

41   [Symonds], *A Problem in Modern Ethics*, p. 37.

42   [Symonds], *A Problem in Modern Ethics*, pp. 37–8.

43   [Symonds], *A Problem in Modern Ethics*, p. 38.

44   Ellis, *The Criminal* (New York: Scribner's, 1890), pp. 39, 83.

45   [Symonds], *A Problem in Modern Ethics*, p. 52.

46   [Symonds], *A Problem in Modern Ethics*, p. 52.

47   [Symonds], *A Problem in Modern Ethics*, p. 66.

48   James D. Steakley, *The Homosexual Emancipation Movement in Germany* (New York: Arno Press, 1975), p. 5.

49   Hubert Kennedy, 'Karl Heinrich Ulrichs: First Theorist of Homosexuality', in Vernon A. Rosario, ed., *Science and Homosexualities* (New York: Routledge, 1997), p. 29.

50   Ellis and Symonds, *Sexual Inversion*, p. 27.

51   [Symonds], *A Problem in Modern Ethics*, p. 75.

52 There are many correspondences between Symonds's *A Problem in Modern Ethics* and the memoir he began in the late 1880s and worked on until the end of his life. A substantial proportion of this memoir – which Symonds's executors banned from publication for fifty years after it passed into the hands of the London Library in 1926 – has appeared as *The Memoirs of John Addington Symonds*, ed. Phyllis Grosskurth (London: Hutchinson, 1984).

53 Symonds, 'To Havelock Ellis', July 1891, in *The Letters of John Addington Symonds*, III, p. 587.

54 [Symonds], *A Problem in Modern Ethics*, pp. 103–4.

55 [Symonds], *A Problem in Modern Ethics*, p. 103.

56 Symonds, 'To Arthur Symons', 13 June 1892, in *The Letters of John Addington Symonds*, III, p. 691.

57 Symonds, 'To Havelock Ellis', 20 June 1892, in *The Letters of John Addington Symonds*, III, p. 694. The following two quotations appear on this page.

58 Ellis, 'The Present Position of English Criticism', *Time*, n.s. 12 (1885), pp. 671, 674, 677.

59 Ellis, 'The Present Position of English Criticism', p. 670.

60 Ellis, *The New Spirit* (1890; New York: Kraus Reprint Co., 1969), p. 107. It is worth noting that Symonds introduced and translated *Wine, Women, and Song: Mediaeval Latin Student's Songs* (London: Chatto and Windus, 1884).

61 Ellis, *The New Spirit*, p. 104.

62 Symonds, 'To Havelock Ellis', 6 May 1890, in *The Letters of John Addington Symonds*, III, p. 459.

63 Ellis, *The New Spirit*, p. 127.

64 Ellis, 'To Olive Schreiner', 3 April 1884, in *'My Other Self': The Letters of Olive Schreiner and Havelock Ellis, 1884-1920*, ed. Yaffa Claire Draznin (New York: Peter Lang, 1992), p. 40.

65 Ellis, 'To Olive Schreiner', 3 April 1884, in *'My Other Self'*, p. 40.

66 Ellis, 'To Olive Schreiner', 3 September 1885, in *'My Other Self'*, p. 378. (I have removed Draznin's non-traditional editorial sigla from this quotation.)

67 Symonds, 'To Havelock Ellis', 1 December 1892, in *The Letters of John Addington Symonds*, III, pp. 787–8.

68 Symonds, 'To Edward Carpenter', 29 December 1892, in *The Letters of John Addington Symonds*, III, pp. 797–8.

69 Ellis and Symonds, *Sexual Inversion*, p. 134.

70 Ellis and Symonds, *Sexual Inversion*, p. 134.

71 Ellis and Symonds, *Sexual Inversion*, p. 23.

72 Ellis and Symonds, *Sexual Inversion*, p. 24.

73 Ellis and Symonds, *Sexual Inversion*, p. 23.

74 Symonds, 'To Havelock Ellis', 12 February 1893, in *The Letters of John Addington Symonds*, III, p. 817.

75 Ellis and Symonds, *Sexual Inversion*, p. 42.

76 Ellis and Symonds, *Sexual Inversion*, p. 58.

77 Ellis and Symonds, *Sexual Inversion*, p. 63.

78 Ellis and Symonds, *Sexual Inversion*, p. 63.

79 Symonds, 'To Edward Carpenter', 29 December 1892, in *The Letters of John Addington Symonds*, III, p. 797.

6 'Educating the Eye': The Tattooed Prostitute

Jane Caplan

In the obscure history of the European tattoo, no figure is more obscure than that of the tattooed woman. At the risk of isolating one aspect of this history, I propose here to reanimate this almost invisible female figure, to explain the tattooed woman's identification with female prostitution as an effect of contemporary encounters between the new human sciences of sexual regulation and criminology. In ways that I will explore further below, the European tattoo was commonly seen as an emblem of the deviant and the primitive by the end of the century; in fact, it was only this pathologization that secured its otherwise surprising visibility in the new sciences of the human body. This double movement was accomplished especially through the writings of the Italian criminologist Cesare Lombroso, whose theorization of the born criminal and prostitute as manifestations of evolutionary atavism set the agenda for European criminology in the last two decades of the century. It was in continental Europe – Italy, France, Germany – that the tattoo attracted the greatest academic attention; this was in sharp contrast with England, where tattooing was both more widespread and less noticed. To trace this inequality is to track a path through an irregular series of encounters and appropriations in the continental and English human sciences, which I will epitomize here through the relationship between Lombroso and Havelock Ellis. Lombroso seized on the slender evidence of the prostitute's tattoo as support for his theory of female criminality; Ellis, intrigued by criminology but sceptical of Lombroso's indiscriminate enthusiasm, offered English readers a brief glimpse of the tattoo in his 1890 book *The Criminal*, but never integrated it into his sexology. Despite Ellis's continuing interest in criminal anthropology, he developed a theory of female prostitution that was almost the exact reverse of Lombroso's, for it was based on the proposition that the prostitute represented not an atavism, but 'the attraction of civilization [. . .] the fascination for the city [. . .] the brilliant fever of civilization [that] pulses round them in the streets'.[1] The terms of this brief encounter between continental criminology and English sexology illuminate the overlaps and differences in European intellectual cultures, as well as evoking the context in which female tattoos were made conspicuous beyond the community of those who bore them.[2]

Through the nineteenth century, the prostitute[3] epitomized the overlap between the disciplines of sexual and criminal science, understood both as scientific disciplines and as means of social discipline. She was the object of repeated regimes of inspection and regulation in the successive idioms of nineteenth-century morality and science, but the quality and effects of her visibility varied according to the local inflections of these pursuits. In England, where prostitutes were only briefly and incompletely liable to official regulation and medical surveillance, prostitution was more likely to be approached as a moral and social than police or criminal issue.[4] In much of continental Europe, however, prostitutes were subject to highly interventionist systems of police and sanitary registration and inspection. A limited legality for their trade was bought at the price of official surveillance and segregation from the 'normal' woman and regime of sexuality. As both policing and public health were scientized in the course of the century, so this system of regulation also established prostitutes as a collective subject for systematic research, rendering them readily assimilable to contemporary continental paradigms of deviance and criminality. The European prostitute thus became highly visible to criminology, to the extent of being seen as the female analogue to the male criminal and attracting the same apparatus of physical and psychological investigation and measurement. It was within this criminological field of vision that the tattooed woman, like the tattooed man, came into view.

While it took a considerable effort of scientific commentary to reduce the male tattoo to an automatic stigma of criminality, the tattooed woman was always represented as a figure of deviance, and identified almost exclusively with the prostitute. As the German ethnographer Wilhelm Joest wrote in 1887, in an ethnographic text which otherwise aimed to normalize tattooing, 'simply the facts that among European *women* only prostitutes of the worst sort tattoo themselves, and that *only* Europeans or whites [. . .] allow their skins to be imprinted with obscenities [. . .] demonstrate how this originally pagan custom can, like an exotic plant, degenerate into a loathsome weed on our Christian-European soil'.[5] Joest's association of prostitution and obscenity with a shift from exoticism to degeneration condemned women most strongly, but it also picked up a pervasive note in contemporary accounts of men's tattoos. For most of the nine-teenth century tattooing hovered in dominant cultural discourse some-where between the exotic and the disreputable, backed by the view that irreversible body-marking was a custom of pre-literate, savage cultures which stood below Europe on the evolutionary scale of human civiliza-tion. As a form of voluntary body decoration, tattooing had not been widespread in Europe for perhaps a millennium before the eighteenth cen-tury (though its actual incidence and character in this long period are disputed and hard to reconstruct).[6] Whatever the scattered survivals and indigenous character of European tattooing, these were overwhelmed by the exotic quality attached to the practice when it emerged into more distinct view in the course of the eighteenth century. The tattoo was, it appears, reimported into Europe by seamen who encountered it in Pacific and East Asian cultures, and who in deciding to become tattooed 'did not act on impulses which could be accounted for in purely European terms', hence were automatically exoticized.[7] By a process which is unclear but must surely have involved some convergence of imported and indigenous practices, the habit quickly spread among sailors and soldiers, and thence more widely into working-class culture by the turn of the century. But it was not until the 1880s that this schema of social, cultural and evolution-ary hierarchy hardened, forcing the tattoo into interpretation as an intrin-sically savage practice of mutilation whose recurrence within 'civilization' was a mark not just of social and cultural inferiority, but of atavism, de-generation and criminality.

The tattoo's (re)domestication into European popular culture in the course of imperial expansion was thus resisted by dominant interpreta-tions that repositioned it from an exotic exteriority to a pathological interiority (a traverse which also carries some of the anatomical ambigu-ity of the tattoo itself as both a surface script and an insertion).[8] Its history of discursive marginalization and devaluation is also the history of its migration from one intellectual discipline or practice to another, and of the reconstitutions and recombinations of those practices: in Foucaultian terms, the emergence of different configurations of power/knowledge. This was a journey that took the tattoo from the literatures of exploration and ethnography through forensic medicine and pathology to the emerging disciplines of criminology and sexual science. This trajectory also over-lapped with the shifts in the broader discursive status of the human body: essentially, a process of medicalization which made it available for new therapeutic interventions, in the name of both individual and social health. As this process made the body more transparent to scientific interpreta-tion and manipulation, so the tattoo became one of the abnormal physi-cal features that were coerced into legibility as signs of states and identities that were also themselves deemed pathological. It was in this context that the European tattoo was impelled, by an effort of medico-legal research, into its durable association with criminal and outcast status, as simultaneously a manifestation and a declaration of the bearer's exclusion from the norms of law-bound culture.

This pathologization of the tattoo was, however, almost entirely a project of continental European medico-legal and criminal science. There is no comparable English record, though not because tattooing was unknown in England: on the contrary, it was probably even more widespread and familiar than on the continent. But while contintental criminology devoted great efforts to 'reading' the tattoo, its greater dispersion and visibility in England, together with differences between continental and European medico-legal culture which will be discussed below, seem to have produced the opposite effect: the custom was apparently more normalized in its own time, but its residues were buried that much deeper in the historical archive.[9] The nineteenth-century tattoo makes one of its few appearances in English academic writing in Havelock Ellis's least characteristic work, his 1890 book The Criminal. This was one of a pair of publications with which Ellis first made his name in London's literary and scientific world, though it was a book by which he set no great store and for which he made no claims of originality.[10] In fact he described it as a task which he 'would willingly have given [. . .] to abler hands', and which he took upon himself only because of the English neglect of its subject, the new science of criminal anthropology and the work of Lombroso in particular.[11] Ellis's book was successful enough to merit four editions between 1890 and 1910, but it was not authoritative and is generally regarded as an oddity in the history of criminal science in England. It was a text that stood outside the dominant conventions of the field, and that was to some extent superseded by the translation a few years later of some of Lombroso's own work on female criminality.[12]

It was not accidental that Ellis titled his study of European criminology The Criminal: a deliberate echo of Lombroso's L'uomo delinquente (1876) that signalled his own objectives and perspective. But Ellis was not an unapologetic apostle of criminal anthropology. Although he struggled to give it a balanced account, his own attitudes towards it were distinctly ambivalent and incomplete: in fact, his text recapitulated the ambivalences of English criminal science in both embracing and hesitating before the physical indications of criminality. While he apparently concurred with the criminal anthropologists in accepting that the criminal was 'a natural phenomenon, the resultant of manifold natural causes', at the same time his study is marked by a persistent unease at its most extreme conclusions, and by repeated references to his own belief in the overriding significance of 'the social factor' in crime. Although he embraced the 'psychiatrization of crime' and was prepared to admit that 'every truly criminal act proceeds from a person who is, temporarily or permanently, in a more or less abnormal condition',[13] he remained sceptical that this abnormality could be read from the physical evidence of the criminal body, let alone that the criminal was a member of a distinctive human species or an atavistic throwback to a primitive or savage state of humanity. Yet he also reproduced in his text a series of line drawings of thirty-six misshapen and repulsive criminal physiognomies from British prisons, which were later unmasked as profoundly distorted caricatures of the very ordinary-looking photographic portraits from which they had been taken.[14]

Although Ellis's foray into criminology was derivative and tangential by comparison with his lifelong investment in sexual science, the two fields themselves are far from being unrelated. Both emerged in the same intellectual field of force in nineteenth-century Europe – the discourse of the body and its pathologies; both exhibited 'the great classificatory zeal'[15] that characterized the nineteenth-century biological sciences, isolating morphologies and types, demarcating and naturalizing the boundaries of abnormality; and both were more characteristic of continental European than of English intellectual enterprise. In England, Ellis acted as the transitional figure between the two fields of knowledge. When he returned to the continental literature in his account of the 'biological factor' in prostitution in the final volume of his *Studies in the Psychology of Sex*, he judged the anthropometrical evidence as incomplete, and ventured only the cautious conclusion that 'prostitutes are not quite normal representatives of the ranks into which they were born'.[16] But whereas he helped to domesticate sexology in England, it is usually accepted that he was unable to make much of a dent in English scepticism about late nineteenth-century developments in continental criminology. Despite his own efforts to foster contacts with the continental exponents of this emerging science, English academics and administrators, somewhat to Ellis's embarassment, seemed to show little enthusiasm for the positivist criminologies of the Italian, French and German scholars whose work he hoped to introduce them to.[17] English debates about criminality between the 1880s and 1914 owed little to continental positivist criminology, partly because English anxieties about criminality had arisen somewhat earlier and generated indigenous debates and responses.[18] Nevertheless, it was the new criminology that set the terms of European debate in this period: indeed the very concept of 'criminology' was a new one, and an exotic import as far as English usage was concerned.[19]

It is usually hard to resist placing Lombroso at the heart of this project, though in truth his basic arguments drew heavily on familiar and already contested claims about the physiological calculus of criminal identity. In developing his theory that the 'born criminal' could be classified through certain physical and psychical features 'as an anomaly, partly pathologi-

cal and partly atavistic, a revival of the primitive savage', he was subject-
ing to scientific discipline an older tradition of reading identity directly off
the surface of the body. It is therefore hardly surprising that Lombroso
grasped the tattoo, a form of writing directly onto the body, as central to
this project. Although eventually the tattoo was to become submerged in
an extensive and elaborate repertoire of anatomical and behavioural signs
of criminality, it was Lombroso's sight in 1864 of 'vicious' soldiers covered with numerous and indecent tattoos that first brought him to the
brink of his life's project.[20] However, the dissemination and elaboration
of Lombroso's theories in the 1880s and 1890s served largely to disclose
their inherent contradictions and weaknesses, and to reinstate less radically positivist though no less biologized images of the habitual or professional criminal.[21] In that sense, the culmination of criminal anthropology
was also the crisis of its own dissolution; and Ellis's introduction of
Lombroso into England occurred just as the critique of his work was gath-
ering force. However, if the Lombrosian project was in some respects an
elaborate detour in the history of criminology, it was a highly symptomatic one, and it undoubtedly organized the continental European debate
about the causes of criminality in the last two decades of the century. The
figure of Lombroso will therefore suffuse my discussion here, but always
understood in the compromising company of certain reservations and
caveats: for in depriving him of his originality and mastery, we also undermine his positioning as the paragon of positivist criminology, as the gran-
diose and dogmatic European other to an allegedly more restrained English
pragmatism. Against this background, English scepticism of Lombroso
emerges as the effect less of his repudiation than of his redundancy – in
the sense that the means of criminological debate were already adequately
supplied in England from indigenous sources, and did not need to engage
in the troublesome task of translation from another idiom.

The emergence of criminology in Europe was part of a broader movement in late nineteenth-century official interventions in the field of crime
and social disorder. From the mid-nineteenth century, 'deviance' underwent both a sociologization and a medicalization: a double translation
which substituted a language of social pathology for that of classical moral
individualism. Anxieties about social demoralization and disintegration
were not of course new in themselves in this period, but the pathologization
of social disorder was. The new discourses of 'social hygiene' represented
the attempt to find means of management appropriate to dangers that
were now grasped in terms of morbidity rather than morality; they subsumed a range of strategies to protect and cleanse society from the abnormal, the deviant, the unfit. By the 1880s, the danger was increasingly
conceptualized in the concept of 'degeneration' – a protean term whose
authority was secured as its specificity was disseminated across a great

range of cultural and scientific discourses, from fiction to social science to medicine and psychiatry.[22] It turned essentially on a linkage of hereditarian concepts from the biological and the social sciences to present an alarming scenario of potentially fatal national and racial decline that unfolded in the very process of individual and social reproduction: degeneration was, in a sense, decadence understood as pathological and hereditary. As Darwin wrote in his *Descent of Man* (1871), unless society found means to 'prevent the reckless, the vicious and otherwise inferior members of society from increasing at a quicker rate than the better class of men, the national will retrograde'.[23]

While 'degeneration' was a European-wide cultural discourse in the later nineteenth century, its precise sources, character and applications differed significantly from country to country. In terms of its application to the practical protection of the social order by means of medical, psychiatric and penal interventions, its authority was strongest in continental Europe, where the traditions of the disciplinary state and positivist social science provided a defensive environment that was much stronger than in England, with its heritage of liberal anti-statism, its more cautious negotiation of the boundaries between law and medicine, its practical rather than disciplinary approach to penal policy.[24] Continental Europe nurtured a culture of disciplinary practices and human sciences that, by the second half of the nineteenth century, had placed the degenerated physical body at the heart of its model of organic social health and disease. In England, by contrast, 'the shared emphasis was on degeneration more than the degenerate', on the process rather than the person.[25] Although this by no means precluded biologized and hereditarian concepts of criminality, it did not lead to the obsessively focused fixation on the body of the criminal apparent in continental criminology.

This divergence should not be be exaggerated, especially in relation to women, whose physicality was often thought to suffuse their identity more completely than in the case of men. In practice English debates on crime and criminality between the 1860s and World War I generated their own biologized concepts of the 'habitual criminal' and the 'moral imbecile', which paralleled and even preceded the shift of discursive focus in continental thought from the crime to the criminal and from the individual offender to the criminal type. The general proposition that deviant or criminal identity could be read from physical characteristics was a commonplace of nineteenth-century European social thought, both in England and on the continent. So too was the rarefaction of this idea into the later nineteenth-century postulates of a hereditarian pathology of deviance and crime, and of the incurable character of that residuum of offenders labelled as 'born' or 'habitual' or as the 'criminal class'; and so too the postulate of a resemblance between the habitual criminal and the prostitute. In England, they appeared equally impervious to social intervention, equally '"outcast from decent society", with scant hope of rehabilitation'.[26] To a Russian researcher in the 1880s, prostitutes differed from women thieves in the fact that they committed the same act repeatedly, thus in a sense embodying the very concept of recidivism.[27] In Italy at the same time, the female prostitute was seen as the counterpart to the thief, and as no less of a social threat.[28]

As in the discourse of male criminality, the push to explain at least a proportion of prostitution as the result of innate disposition was irresistible: some women were 'born' prostitutes just as some men were 'born' criminals. In Victorian England, 'women of the underworld were found especially repulsive and beyond all hope of redemption for, unlike men, they were said to have neither the physical strength nor the mental agility to reverse the tremendous pull of degeneracy'.[29] To Lombroso, the vice of prostitution proved a virtue for his research, for he was able to seize upon the statistics of prostitution to resolve the apparent anomaly that women criminals were not only vanishingly few in number but also failed to display the expected accumulation of anatomical and behavioural anomalies, including tattoos, that his theory of criminal atavism would have predicted.[30] This problem was resolved by asserting the equivalence of prostitution to male habitual criminality; the addition of prostitutes to the category of female deviants not only bumped up the numbers, but more importantly enhanced the evidence of atavistic anomalies in this enlarged group.

It was thus virtually inevitable that, just as the male tattoo was at its most visible on the criminal, so also it was the body of the prostitute that yielded a record of the female tattoo. This was partly a matter of opportunity. Criminals were exposed to scientific investigation in prisons and penitentiaries, along with similarly confined male communities in barracks, hospitals, asylums and clinics. Comparable access to female prostitutes was guaranteed in continental Europe by their compulsory inscription on official registers and their partial segregation in officially licensed brothels (the *maisons tolérées* and the *postriboli tollerati* of France and Italy). Even though many women evaded inscription, the existence of the system further institutionalized their moral status as a group outside society. And the registration of female prostitutes was a measure of medical as well as social hygiene, and included the compulsory medical inspection of registered women for evidence of venereal disease.[31] The signs of venereal infection were read from symptoms on the skin: dermatology and syphilology were linked as a single medical specialism in the nineteenth century (the Italian medical term for which was *dermosifilopatia*). This linkage exposed the skin of prostitutes to intense and regular scrutiny which must have rendered their tattoos particularly conspicuous: as an Italian specialist wrote in 1884, 'if medical lessons should be practical and empirical, this necessity is especially obvious in the case of skin and venereal diseases, for which it is first necessary to educate the eye'.[32] It may also have helped to underwrite the sense that tattoos were surface eruptions that indicated organic conditions; even, given contemporary medical confusion about the congenital character of syphilis, that tattoos were symptoms of hereditary disturbances.[33] The skin figured, moreover, in the repertoire of sexual differentiation as the site of experiments to test comparative sensitivity: thus Lombroso claimed that prostitutes were more insensible to pain than normal or criminal women, and in general exhibited a greater 'dulness of sense'.[34]

It is instructive that the first and most celebrated account of tattooing among prostitutes – in A.-J.-B. Parent-Duchatelet's pioneering study of Parisian prostitutes in 1836 – was not only one of the earliest studies of any tattooed community in Europe, but was also intended to highlight the dangers of syphilis and recommended minute physical examination of women's bodies.[35] Although the custom of tattooing among soldiers and sailors had already been noticed in France,[36] the deviance of the female tattoo thus appears to have preceded and underwritten the later pathologization of men's tattoos. Parent claimed that only prostitutes 'of the lowest class' were in the habit of getting tattoos, and that they picked up the taste 'for these more or less bizarre images' from the type of men with whom they associated or to whom they wished to make themselves attractive – soldiers and men of the same social class. Prostitutes' tattoos differed from men's, however, in being smaller, less figurative and less conspicuous. They were to be found on parts of the body that were not 'normally' uncovered, as Parent put it – on the upper arm, the back of the shoulder, the region below the breast – and were usually inscriptions of proper names, sometimes set between flowers or entwined hearts, or accompanied by the words 'pour la vie' or just 'PLV'. On younger women, the names and initials referred to their male lovers; but older women inscribed the names of their female lovers, and in a location in which men's names were never found, between the navel and pubis.[37] Apparently to his surprise, Parent found virtually no images 'offensive to honesty and decency'. The worst that could be said of them was that they were acquired as the consequence of imitation and idleness – concomitants of life inside a closed community that also figured prominently in later accounts of men's motivations.

Fragmentary and impressionistic, these observations made the tattooed prostitute visible for the first time, establishing her as a fit subject for repeated examination. The longest series of studies was made in Italy, where Parent's research was integrated into the systematic investigation of tattoos launched by Lombroso in the 1870s.[38] These studies produced vastly inconsistent findings on the incidence of tattooing among prostitutes, including percentages that were either very close or very different in each case, or that ranged from the vanishingly small to the measurable but modest. Most research disclosed only a handful of tattooed women, unless the fashion for tattooed facial beauty spots was included, in which case the proportions rose somewhat, but rarely above 1 per cent. Only in a few studies were somewhat larger proportions found – from 5 to 18 per cent – and many of these were also beauty spots rather than names or figures.[39] One of the most extensive analyses, a 1905 study of 720 Italian prostitutes, 121 of whom were tattooed, included research data indicating that the tattooed prostitutes exhibited significantly more cranial and other anatomical anomalies than those without tattoos, thus supporting the inference that the tattooed prostitute was at the extreme of the degenerative scale.[40] The imagery (which was more rarely illustrated than in the case of men)[41] remained strikingly similar to that reported earlier in the century by Parent: lovers' initials or names predominated, occasionally in association with other sentimental figures or inscriptions. There were few or no obscene images, and most tattoos were on parts of the body that were normally covered rather than exposed (a description that left unsaid the circumstances of 'normal' clothing among prostitutes).[42]

The inconclusive and often anecdotal character of the evidence did not deter Lombroso and his collaborator Guglielmo Ferrero from asserting that 'we have here [. . .] yet a further proof that phenomena of atavism are more frequent among prostitutes than among ordinary female criminals'.[43] Nor were they disconcerted by the fact that women's tattoos were less diverse and impassioned than those of male criminals: this could be explained by reference to the claim that in primitive cultures it was men who were elaborately tattooed, while women, according to Lombroso, remained content with simpler or just painted designs and cosmetics. The paucity and simplicity of tattoos borne by modern European prostitutes, compared with male criminals, were thus repetitions of this primitive divergence between men and women.

> [The] absence of epigrams, obscene signs, and cries of vengeance, and the presence of ordinary symbols and initials only [are] another effect of of the smaller ability and fancy, the lower degree of differentiation in the female intellect; for even the female criminal is monotonous and uniform compared with her male companion, just as woman is in general inferior to man. Once again, then, we must seek an explanation of the type in atavism.

Thus 'even simplicity of tattooing is a sign of atavism in the criminal prostitute', confirming that among women it was the prostitute rather than the criminal who was the embodiment of degeneracy.[44]

If these conclusions were no more than consistent with the fundamental Lombrosian position, they also carried an echo of the almost universal inference, from Parent onwards, that women were not even fully responsible for their own tattoos, but owed them to some involuntary or external impulse. These ranged from references to the 'instinct for imitation and the frivolity of these women' by the Danish physician R. Bergh in 1891,[45] to the shocking case of Sidonie N. in 1894, allegedly forcibly tattooed by a spurned and vengeful lover with the demeaning inscription 'J'aime Louis T. . .pour la vie, celui qui m'aura après n'aura qu'un c. . .'.[46] Among the 80 tattooed Copenhagen prostitutes out of a total of 800 examined by Bergh, more than half had been tattooed by a young ex-sailor who had set up shop there in the 1880s; he had revived a fashion that had otherwise allegedly been declining among prostitutes.[47] The women's suggestibility was underlined by the typical maritime motifs described on them, including a ship in full sail, anchors, and 'a patriotic flag decoration with cannon'. The case of Sidonie N. represented an extreme inscription of male ownership, which was repeated in less sadistic forms in the names and initials that were almost always assumed to have been imposed on women by their male lovers and pimps.[48] A much-cited French study admitted only two ways in which the prostitute acquired her tattoo, both representing 'the moral ruin of this victim of mutilation': either she was tattooed under the influence of a male lover (often himself tattooed), or 'by enticement' in a *café de nuit* where the professional tattooist plied his trade.[49]

These nineteenth-century accounts of prostitutes' tattoos thus exhibit a certain ambivalence about their origin and status. They are understood both as the expression, on the surface of the skin, of something innate to the prostitute herself, in this akin not only to the symptoms of the venereal infections to which her occupation exposed her, but also to the blush of the normal woman or the spontaneous stigmata of the hysteric.[50] At the same time, they are ascribed to the influence of a male milieu, operating either through an impulse to imitation or through a more baleful coercive power. The French historian Alain Corbin barely emancipates the prostitute from these same ascriptions of male power and desire when he suggests that her tattoos are:

> the most moving documents available [. . .] indisputable evidence of the depth of feeling and love that the women felt for their *souteneurs* or for their *amants de coeur* [. . .] The simplicity and intensity of the love felt by these women bound to the men on whom they depended was expressed in a naive and childish but indelible symbolism [. . .] taking the form of a concern to redeem the sold body.[51]

But whether the 'sold body' was redeemed (let alone for whom) or was, rather, certified and abjected by its surface marks is debatable, for the meaning of the tattoo was expropriated in advance of any decision to acquire one. The tattooed woman thus shared the fate of the tattooed man in becoming the emblem of her deviance, but doubly so: it was a mark of her subjection both to men, and to her own inferior will.

Notes

I am grateful to the Rockefeller Foundation's Bellagio Study and Conference Center and to the John Simon Guggenheim Foundation for their support of the research on which this essay is based.

1 Havelock Ellis, *Studies in the Psychology of Sex*, vol. 6: *Sex in Relation to Society* (F. A. Davis, Philadelphia, 1910), pp. 295, 298.

2 Tattooed women do not figure in the handful of attempts to interpret European tattooing directly in terms of sexual science: '"Erotische Tätowierungen."' Eine Umfrage von Krauss', *Anthropophyteia*, 1 (1904), pp. 507–13; Hugo Ernest Luedecke, 'Erotische Tätowierungen', ibid., 4 (1907), pp. 75–83.

3 For the sake of simplicity, I will use this word without further qualification to refer to female prostitutes.

4 For the history of regulation and abolition in England, see Judith R. Walkowitz, *Prostitution and Victorian Society* (Cambridge University Press, Cambridge, 1980).

5 Wilhelm Joest, *Tätowiren, Narbenzeichen und Körperbemalen* (A. Asher, Berlin, 1887), p. 105.

6 The literature on the subject is large and uneven. In default of a comprehensive bibliography here, see for England before the eighteenth century Juliet Fleming, 'The Renaissance Tattoo', *RES: Anthropology and Aesthetics*, 31, Spring 1997, pp. 34–52; and for nineteenth-century Europe Jane Caplan, '"Speaking Scars": The Tattoo in Popular Practice and Medico-Legal Debate in Nineteenth-Century Europe', *History Workshop Journal*, 44 (Autumn 1997), pp. 107–42. The best general history is Stefan Oettermann, *Zeichen auf der Haut. Die Geschichte der Tätowierung in Europa*, 2nd edn (Europäische Verlagsanstalt, Hamburg, 1994); and see Ronald Scutt and Christopher Gotch, *Art, Sex and Symbol. The Mystery of Tattooing*, 2nd edn (Cornwallis, New York/London, 1986).

7 Alfred Gell, *Wrapping in Images. Tattooing in Polynesia* (Clarendon Press, Oxford, 1993), p. 10.

8 These qualities of the tattoo are explored in ibid., ch. 1. See also Terence S. Turner, 'The Social Skin', in *Reading the Social Body*, eds K. Burroughs and J. Ehrenreich (University of Iowa Press, Iowa City, 1993), pp. 38–9; Didier Anzieu, *The Skin-Ego. A Psychoanalytic Approach to the Self* (Karnac, London, 1989); Elizabeth Grosz, *Volatile Bodies. Towards a Corporeal Feminism* (Allen & Unwin, London, 1994), chs 5 and 6.

9 Generally, one must construct the evidence, for both men and women convicts, from 'raw' sources such as the Habitual Criminals Registers issued by the Metropolitan Police after 1869, which include descriptions of tattoos

under the column 'Distinctive marks and peculiarities' (Public Record Office, MEPO 6). The only systematic account I have discovered for this period is Mary Gordon, *Penal Discipline* (George Routledge & Sons, London, 1922), ch. 9, a report on women prisoners' tattoos which takes a generally benign attitude. The author describes the finest tattoo work as 'having a beauty of its own [. . .] on the perfect background furnished by the human skin [. . .] [rivalling] the work on old china in its delicate drawing, and depth and transparency of colour [. . .] It seems to me to be in harmony with nature's scheme' (pp. 131–2).

10 See Phyllis Grosskurth, *Havelock Ellis. A Biography* (Allen Lane, London, 1980), pp. 114–16, 131; the other book was *The New Spirit*.

11 Havelock Ellis, *The Criminal*, p. vii.

12 Leon Radzinowicz and Roger Hood, *A History of English Criminal Law*, vol. 5: *The Emergence of Penal Policy* (Stevens & Sons, London, 1986), describe the book as 'a slight publication, with no originality and little critical acumen' (p. 12); a heavily abbreviated version of Cesare Lombroso and Guglielmo Ferrero, *La donna delinquente, la prostituta e la donna normale* (Turin, 1893) was translated as *The Female Offender* (T. Fisher Unwin, London, 1895).

13 Ellis, *The Criminal*, p. 233.

14 Charles Goring, *The English Convict. A Statistical Study* [1913] (Patterson Smith, Montclair, NJ, 1972), frontispiece illustrations. For further discussion, see Mary Cowling, *The Artist as Anthropologist. The Representation of Type and Character in Victorian Art* (Cambridge University Press, Cambridge, 1989), pp. 312–16.

15 The phrase is Jeffrey Weeks's in *Sex, Politics and Society. The Regulation of Sexuality since 1800* (Longman, London, 1981), p. 144.

16 Havelock Ellis, *Sex in Relation to Society*, pp. 266–80.

17 Ellis attended the 1894 International Congress of Criminology, but the sole official English delegate was Arthur Griffiths, inspector of prisons, in 1896; see Radzinowicz and Hood, *The Emergence of Penal Policy*, pp. 12–13.

18 See ibid.; V. A. C. Gatrell, 'Crime, Authority and the Policeman-State', in *The Cambridge Social History of Britain 1750–1950*, ed. F. M. L. Thompson (Cambridge University Press, Cambridge, 1990), vol. 3, pp. 243–310; David Garland, 'British Criminology before 1935', *British Journal of Criminology*, 28, 2 (1988), pp. 1–17; Clive Emsley, *Crime and Society in England 1750–1900* (Longman, London, 1987).

19 The terms 'criminal anthropology' and 'criminology' (*antropologia criminale* and *criminologia*) were put into circulation in Italy in the 1880s, and were adopted into other European languages around 1890.

20 Cesare Lombroso, 'Introduction', in Gina Lombroso Ferrero, *Criminal Man, According to the Classification of Cesare Lombroso* (G.P. Putnam's Sons, London, 1911), pp. xii, xiv f. As Lombroso put it, he was first 'struck by a characteristic that distinguished the honest soldier from his vicious comrade: the extent to which the latter was tattooed and the indecency of the designs that covered his body', but could make nothing of this observation; it was the animal-like cranial anomalies he subsequently identified in a post-mortem on the brigand Villela that persuaded him that the criminal was 'an atavistic be-

ing who reproduces in his person the ferocious instincts of primitive humanity and the inferior animals'. His research on tattooed soldiers was first published in the *Giornale de medicina militare* in 1864; and see his 'Sul tatuaggio in Italia, in ispecie fra i delinquenti', *Archivio per l'antropologia e la etnologia*, 4 (1874), pp. 389–402.

21 For these points, see Marie-Christine Leps, *Apprehending the Criminal. The Production of Deviance in Nineteenth-Century Discourse* (Duke University Press, Durham, NC, 1992) and David G. Horn, 'This Norm Which is Not One: Reading the Female Body in Lombroso's Anthropology', in *Deviant Bodies. Critical Perspectives on Difference in Science*, eds Jennifer Terry and Jacqueline Urla (Indiana University Press, Bloomington, IN, 1996), pp. 109–28.

22 The most comprehensive and perceptive study is Daniel Pick, *Faces of Degeneration. A European Disorder, c. 1848–c. 1918* (Cambridge University Press, Cambridge, 1989); see also Sander Gilman and J.E. Chamberlin, eds, *Degeneration. The Dark Side of Progress* (Columbia University Press, New York, 1985), and Greta Jones, *Social Darwinism and English Thought* (Harvester Press, Brighton, 1980). For the links to sexual science, see Weeks, *Sex, Politics and Society*, chs 7 and 8; Lucy Bland, *Banishing the Beast. English Feminism and Sexual Morality 1885–1914* (Penguin, Harmondsworth, 1995), ch. 6.

23 Quoted in Radzinowicz and Hood, *The Emergence of Penal Policy*, p. 28.

24 For these differences, see Gatrell, 'Crime, Authority and the Policeman-State', and Garland, 'British Criminology before 1935'. For an alternative interpretation, see Leps, *Apprehending the Criminal*.

25 Pick, *Faces of Degeneration*, p. 9.

26 Stefan Petrow, *Policing Morals. The Metropolitan Police and the Home Office 1870–1914* (Clarendon Press, Oxford, 1994), p. 119.

27 Pauline Tarnowsky, *Étude anthropologique sur les prostituées et voleuses* (Lecrosnier et Babé, Paris, 1889), p. 202.

28 Mary Gibson, *Prostitution and the State in Italy, 1860–1915* (Rutgers University Press, New Brunswick, NJ, 1986), p. 3.

29 Lucia Zedner, *Women, Crime and Custody in Victorian England* (Clarendon Press, Oxford, 1991), p. 79.

30 For a perceptive reading of Lombroso's strategy, see Horn, 'This Norm Which is Not One'; and Mary Gibson, 'The "Female Offender" and the Italian School of Criminology', *Journal of European Studies*, 12 (1982), pp. 155–65.

31 For the regulation and medical inspection of prostitution in France, see Jill Harsin, *Policing Prostitution in Nineteenth-Century Paris* (Princeton University Press, Princeton, NJ, 1985), and Alain Corbin, *Women for Hire. Prostitution and Sexuality in France after 1850* (Harvard University Press, Cambridge, MA, 1990); for Italy, Gibson, *Prostitution and the State in Italy*; for Russia, Laurie Bernstein, *Sonia's Daughters. Prostitutes and their Regulation in Imperial Russia* (University of California Press, Berkeley, Los Angeles and London, 1995).

32 Professor Pellizzari, quoted in Gibson, *Prostitution and the State in Italy*, p. 172; Gibson also points out the importance of the supply of diseased prostitutes to Italian medical schools for teaching purposes.

33 See Claude Quétel, *History of Syphilis* (Polity Press, Cambridge, 1990), pp. 136–7; John T. Crissey and Lawrence C. Parrish, *The Dermatology and Syphilis of the Nineteenth Century* (Praeger, New York, 1981). Jean-Thierry Maertens describes the symptoms of syphilis as a 'tegumentary counter-inscription', in *Le dessin sur la peau* (Aubier, Paris, 1978), p. 115.

34 Lombroso and Ferrero, *The Female Offender*, pp. 139, 146; cf. Havelock Ellis, *Man and Woman* (Walter Scott, London, 1894), ch. 6, and Havelock Ellis, *Studies in the Psychology of Sex*, vol. 4: *Sexual Selection in Man* (F. A. Davis, Philadelphia, 1906), ch. 1.

35 A.-J.-B. Parent-Duchatelet, *De la prostitution dans la ville de Paris, considérée sous le rapport de l'hygiène publique, de la morale, et de l'administration*, 2 vols (J.B. Baillière, Paris, 1836), ch. 2, p. 5: 'De l'habitude qu'ont certaines prostituées de s'imprimer sur le corps des figures et des inscriptions'. Quotations below are from this chapter, pp. 119–22; and see Harsin, *Policing Prostitution*, ch. 3.

36 See the account by the naval physician R.P. Lesson, 'Du tatouage chez les différens peuples de la terre', *Annales maritimes et coloniales*, 1820, part II, pp. 280–92; Pierre Rayer, *Traité theorique et pratique des maladies de la peau*, 2nd edn (J. B. Baillière, Paris, 1835), vol. 3, pp. 602–12.

37 Parent-Duchatelet's hypothesis was that most women remained prostitutes for only a few years, leaving a much smaller contingent of lifetime prostitutes who were almost always tribades (lesbians); see *De la prostitution*, pp. 161–72.

38 See the summaries tabulated in Lombroso, 'Sul tatuaggio in Italia' (1874), p. 389, in the first edition of his *L'uomo delinquente* (Ulrico Hoepli, Milan, 1876), pp. 43–4, and in the fourth edition (Bocca, Turin, 1889), p. 289, where proportions range from nil to 'a handful [*qualcuna*]' – against figures among various male criminal groups ranging as high as 40 per cent. Of 1,007 Turin prostitutes studied by G. Salsotto in 1887, for example, only four were tattooed with initials or names, eighteen more with beauty spots: 'Il tatuaggio nella donna criminale e nella prostitute', *Archivio di psichiatria, scienze penali ed antropologia criminale* (hereafter cited as *Archivio di psichiatria*), 8 (1887), pp. 102–3. French research in the same period often referred to the practice among female prostitutes, but rarely presented detailed findings; an exception is Albert Le Blond and Arthur Lucas, *Du tatouage chez les prostituées* (Société d'éditions scientifiques, Paris, 1899); on the more frequently studied North African prostitutes see, e.g., Dr Bazin, 'Étude sur le tatouage dans le régence de Tunis', *L'Anthropologie*, 1 (1890), pp. 566–79.

39 Orazio de Albertis, 'Il tatuaggio in 300 prostitute liguri', *Archivio di psichiatria*, 9 (1888), pp. 569–72; I. Callari, 'Prostituzione e prostituta in Sicilia', *Archivio di psichiatria*, 24 (1903), pp. 347ff. See also summaries in Lombroso and Ferrero, *The Female Offender*, pp. 115–21, and Lombroso and Ferrero, *La donna delinquente*, 3rd edn (Biblioteca antropologico-giuridico, Milan, 1915), pp. 220–1.

40 Abele de Blasio, *Il tatuaggio* (Gennaro M. Priore, Naples, 1905), pp. 229–40.

41 For some examples, see R. Bergh, 'Über Tätowierungen der Prostituierten', *Monatshefte für praktische Dermatologie*, 12 (March 1891), pp. 205–17; de

Blasio, *Il tatuaggio*, p. 237; Le Blond and Lucas, *Du tatouage chez les prostituées*.

42 Cf. Gordon, *Penal Discipline*, p. 130: 'The women, at any rate, are seldom to be seen doing honourable work with uncovered arms.'

43 This and the following quotations are from Lombroso and Ferrero, *The Female Offender*, pp. 122–4. For a similarly unconstrained argument, from a single case, see the report 'Cas de tatouage chez une femme, observé et illustré par M. le Dr. De Albertis', *Actes du premier Congrès International d'Anthropologie Criminelle, Biologie et Sociologie, Rome 1885* (Turin, 1886–7), pp. 456–8; also de Albertis, 'Il tatuaggio', p. 572.

44 See Horn, 'This Norm Which is not One', pp. 117–18.

45 Bergh, 'Über Tätowirungen der Prostituierten', p. 211.

46 Marcel Baillot, *Du détatouage. Différents procédés de destruction des tatouages* (G. Steinheil, Paris, 1894), p. 33. This was one of five case studies of de-tattooing described by Baillot, all of them women who wanted to remove the names of presumably abandoned lovers.

47 The fashion survived his death a few years later, when two other tattooists took up the Copenhagen trade; in a second article, 'Über Tätowierungen bei Frauenzimmern der öffentlichen und geheimen Prostituierten', *Monatshefte für praktische Dermatologie*, 35 (1902), pp. 370–7, Bergh noted that no fewer than 37 per cent of the 397 registered prostitutes he had examined in 1901 bore tattoos. It is a testament to the brevity of the Lombrosian moment that in this second article Bergh made no reference to the degenerationist interpretation he had derived from Lombroso and Tarnowsky in his earlier account.

48 See, e.g., Abele de Blasio, 'Il tatuaggio dei camorristi e delle prostitute di Napoli', *Archivio di psichiatria*, 15 (1894), pp. 199–204, and 'Sul tatuaggio di prostitute e pederasti', *Archivio di psichiatria*, 27 (1906), pp. 42–5; 'Cas de tatouage', p. 457; Le Blond and Lucas, *Du tatouage*, pp. 19–20.

49 Ibid., pp. 19–20.

50 See Vieda Skultans, 'Bodily Madness and the Spread of the Blush', in *The Anthropology of the Body* (Academic Press, London, 1977), ed. John Blacking, pp. 145–60; Dr Mesnet, 'Autographisme et Stigmates', *Revue de l'hypnotisme et de la psychologie physiologique*, 4 (1890), pp. 321–35; and Régine Plas, 'Tatouages et criminalité (1880–1914)', in Laurent Mucchielli, ed., *Histoire de la criminalité française*, L'Harmattan, Paris, 1994, pp. 164–6.

51 Corbin, *Women for Hire*, pp. 157–8.

7 Transsexuals and the Transsexologists: Inversion and the Emergence of Transsexual Subjectivity

Jay Prosser

'About this time I read a book where a girl was represented as saying she had a 'boy's soul in a girl's body.' The applicability of this to myself struck me at once, and I read the sentence to my mother who disgusted me by appearing shocked.

Havelock Ellis, *Sexual Inversion*

[U]nfortunately, we are often falsely considered to be homosexuals.

Magnus Hirschfeld, *Transvestites:
The Erotic Drive to Cross Dress*

If sexual inversion is key to late nineteenth- and early twentieth-century sexology, the dominant and most enduring category of this extensive field, then the dynamic of transgender, of gender identifications that cross ('trans') at angles to bodily sex, is arguably sexology's main subject. The overwhelming tendency among critics and historians of sexology has been to read the sexual invert as homosexual. Even though it is acknowledged that the sexual invert is *not* equivalent to the homosexual, even sometimes that inversion is a definitively cross-gendered category (as George Chauncey states, 'Sexual inversion [. . .] did not denote the same conceptual phenomenon of homosexuality. "Sexual inversion" referred to a broad range of deviant gender behavior, of which homosexual desire was only a logical but indistinct aspect'[1]), homosexual desire has continued to dominate work uncovering the invert – including Chauncey's own. Concomitantly inversion's cross-gendered paradigms have been considered the 'discursive frame' for homosexuality, transgender demoted to a conceit for thinking homosexual desire at a conceptual moment before Freud's theory of the drive had separated sexual object choice from sexual aim, and at a cultural moment when the rigidity of gender roles necessitated that a woman who desired women be represented as really a man, and a man who desired men as really a woman.[2] Transgender has thus been configured – with the emphasis on figure – as homosexuality's fictional construct: not referential of actual transgendered subjects but metaphoric of homosexuals falsely transgendered. Foucault's famous assertion that inversion represents the homosexual's origins as a 'species' sets the tone for this relegation of transgender to indexical sign for (absolute construction of) homosexuality.[3] Even a recent essay by Gert Hekma, which promises in its title to read gender inversion back into sexual inversion, describes gender inversion as the sexologists' conjured restraint on *homosexual* identities.[4] True testimony to the thoroughness of this critical imposition of homosexuality onto inversion, Hekma manages to write an entire essay on sexual inversion as gender inversion without once mentioning transgender, without upsetting in the slightest the equation of invert with homosexual.

Yet as Hekma intuits and Chauncey notes, what sexologists sought to describe through sexual inversion was not homosexuality but differing degrees of *gender* inversion. My contention is that sexual inversion *was* transgender, and while homosexuals certainly number among inverts, the category described a much larger gender-inverted condition of which homosexuality was only one aspect. In fact (a fact crucial to our understanding of inverted identity) on occasions, homosexuality was not indicated in inverts' desire at all. Even when ostensibly directed towards the 'same' sex, given the profound degree of identification with the '*other*' sex embraced and lived by many inverts, it is questionable to what extent we may accurately classify this desire as '*same*-sex'. Such subjects need to be mapped along the axis of gender, and as it re-emerges as an identity category in our own *fin de siècle* in a striking echo of sexual inversion in the last, specifically along the axis of transgender. Their identifications recorded in the autobiographies and biographies of sexology's case histories, sections of sexology which have been underread in comparison with the sexologists' theoretical passages – this is, I think, the pivotal reason for the belief that cross-gender in inversion represents nothing more than the sexologists' 'construction' of homosexuality – these inverted subjects need to be re-read in the light of our own current shifts in sexual and gender labels, the elucidation of transgender as a category irreducible to homosexuality. Understood as gender inverted, the invert is not *de*historicized but *re*historicized; for in sexual inversion, gender inversion is not an appurtenance to homosexuality but rather vice versa.

The reading of sexual inversion as about homosexuality is profoundly ironic. As lesbian and gay commentary itself often evidences, the 'heterosexist' paradigms of sexual inversion, and above all sexology's medicalization of transgender in the body of the invert, have not fitted easily with the homosexual subject. In lesbian and gay history, medicalization is the ideological bogey, and in its pathologizing fixation on transgender, sexual inversion is often cast as the most well-known if not the worst offender.[5] In transgendered history on the contrary, sexology's pathologizing fixation on transgender not only makes historical sense, it was productive, absolutely necessary for one key transgendered subject to emerge. The category of sexual inversion allowed the transsexual to emerge as a sex-changeable subject. The first full sex transition (hormonal and surgical combined) took place in the early 1940s, critically and subtly underwritten by sexual inversion. The label 'transsexual' appeared at the end of the 1940s, and would be carefully refined in the following two decades; but as this later sexological work evidences, the labelling of transsexual bodies and desires would not have been possible without the isolation and medicalization of transgender undertaken in the earlier sexological work on sexual inversion. What is thoroughly 'cultural' about sexology in the case of the transsexual's emergence is, first, its continuity: the material ways in which the second-wave sexologists recycled and recited their precursors' texts in their quest for a term for the subject who felt compelled to change sex. Reading the literature on sexual inversion with the later work on transsexuality, we get a sense of the shared focus on transgender, the importance of the transmission of theories from one sexologist to the next in the attempt to label the transsexual subject. And second, what is cultural about the sexological material pertinent to transsexuality is the way in which it recorded in the form of case histories, and prompted in its being taken up and read in turn by transgendered subjects, the unique narrative shape of transsexual lives: the overwhelming desire to be, the feeling of already being, and/or the attempt to transition and become the 'other' sex; the crossing of sex for the sake of self-identity. These case histories (medicine intersecting with real lives) proved crucial to the labelling of transsexual desire. The value of sexology for transsexuals lies precisely in the implications of these two cultural aspects. Together they challenge not only the belief that transgender in sexual inversion was a misrecognition of homosexuality, but the assumptions of construction upon which transsexuality's popular and critical derogation even today turns.

The term 'transsexual' appeared for the first time in an American popular sexology magazine in 1949.[6] In the next decade, it was taken up and depathologized by Harry Benjamin, often dubbed the 'father of transsexualism', to establish what remains one of the major strands of sexological work: research into transsexuality.[7] Yet the category was not conjured out of nowhere, but shaped by a century of prior sexological work on cross-gender identity. Indeed transgender is central to sexology's origins.

Writing in Germany in the 1860s, Karl Heinrich Ulrichs has been credited with initiating the thinking of same-sex desire through cross-gender identification and, in his correspondence with contemporary sexologists, inadvertently enabling the medicalization of homosexuality.[8] Yet although derived from the Platonic 'urning', Ulrichs's typology of inverted identities represents an elaborate schematization of cross-gender identification. The 'weibling urning' (the womanly male invert) and the 'mannlinge urningin' (manly female invert)[9] represent the most extreme cases not of homosexuality but of transgenderism. Ulrichs was measuring not same-sex desire as his commentators contend (an invariable among all urnings) but transgender identification; and his description of his own inverted identity as 'anima muliebris virile corpore inclusa' ('a feminine soul confined by a masculine body')[10] opens up the conflict between sex and gender by using the identical trope that would come to define transsexuality: the woman/man trapped in the wrong sexed body. Similarly Carl Westphal's description of 'die konträre sexualempfindung' (contrary sexual feelings), his 1870 article which Foucault selects to stand for the 'date of birth' of homosexuality, described not same-sex desire but radical gender inversion.[11] In Westphal's earlier 1869 essay, 'die konträre sexualempfindung' were represented by two profoundly cross-gendered subjects: in Vern L. Bullough and Bonnie Bullough's description, 'a young woman who from her earliest years enjoyed dressing like a boy and engaging in boy's games. She was sexually attracted only to women. [. . .] [And] a man who wanted to wear women's clothing and live as a woman all the time. *His sexual orientation is not clear.*'[12] The female subject of this case had written to Westphal expressly articulating her wish to become a man: 'Ich [. . .] möchte gern ein Mann sein' ('I would like to be a man').[13] Had she realized h/er *transsexual* desire to become the other sex, even *h/er sexual* desire for women would of course have been not 'homo' but 'hetero'.

Richard von Krafft-Ebing's 1886 *Psychopathia Sexualis* developed these early formulations of sexual inversion into the 'antipathic sexual instinct'.[14] Even though this label would appear to describe the trajectory of sexual desire, in Krafft-Ebing's nosology same-sex desire remains subordinate to cross-gender and now also cross-sex features:

In so-called antipathic sexual instinct there are degrees of the phenomenon which quite correspond with the degrees of predisposition of the individuals. Thus, in the milder cases, there is simple hermaphroditism; in more pronounced cases, only homosexual feeling and instinct, but limited to the sexual life; in still more complete cases, the whole psychical personality, and even the bodily sensations, are transformed so as to correspond with the sexual inversion; and in complete cases, the physical form is correspondingly altered.[15]

Current terminology would differentiate Krafft-Ebing's four 'degrees' of inversion as respectively, bisexuality, homosexuality, transgender/transsexuality and intersexuality; but, as in Ulrichs and Westphal, what Krafft-Ebing is seeking to map – what the 'degree' represents – is the presence of transgender. Same-sex desire (and given the transgendered character of the overall paradigm, the term again appears a misnomer) constitutes only one of four (and the second least extreme) symptoms of inversion. Krafft-Ebing's most influential successor, Havelock Ellis, in his 1897 *Sexual Inversion* crucially names both sexual inversion *and* homosexuality, suggesting strongly that they were *not* coextensive.[16] And indeed, though *Sexual Inversion* generally conflates them, the work opens with their differentiation: 'Sexual inversion, as here understood, means sexual instinct turned by inborn constitutional abnormality toward persons of the same sex. It is thus a narrower term than homosexuality.'[17] The statement importantly sustains in sexual inversion sexology's somatization of transgender, even as, in configuring inversion as 'a narrower term than homosexuality', it simultaneously paves the way for Freud's subsuming of homosexuality into inversion and *his* repudiation of sexual inversion as myth, the clearest statement of which is surely this: 'The mystery of homosexuality is therefore by no means so simple as it is commonly depicted in popular expositions, e.g., a feminine personality which therefore has to love a man, is unhappily attached to a male body; or a masculine personality, irresistibly attracted by women, is unfortunately cemented to a female body.'[18] If, Freud goes on, we break apart sexual inversion into three axes: 'Physical sexual characteristics (physical hermaphroditism) – Mental sexual characteristics (masculine, or feminine, attitude) – Kind of object choice' – roughly, we might say, sex, gender and sexuality – 'then, to be sure, the supposition that nature in a freakish mood created a "third sex" falls to the ground'.[19] It is no coincidence that Ellis was writing contemporaneously with Freud. Explicitly critical of psychoanalysis, *Sexual Inversion* was none the less implicitly caught up in psychopathology's shift of attention from inversion to homosexuality, and interconnectedly, from gender to sexuality.

Yet while psychoanalysis made its subject sexuality (its role in founding the unconscious), sexology, perhaps enabled by this emergence of sexuality as a discrete object of study, began to produce labels that more successfully isolated transgender desire. In his 1910 *Transvestites*, Magnus Hirschfeld provided a comprehensive description of cross-dressing.[20] His case histories and analyses make eminently clear that his subject is not homosexuality; most of his subjects were not homosexual but heterosexual. In a pre-emptive critique of the notion of fetishism as a defence against homosexuality which Freud was to propound, Hirschfeld writes that in transvestism,

> we at first were inclined to assume that we again had homosexuality before us, perhaps unconscious. However, more accurate testing revealed that this was not the case, because the main marker of homosexuality, as its root word – *homos,* or 'same' – indicates, is the direction of the sex drive toward persons of the same sex. We saw in most of our cases that there was not a trace of it.[21]

Hirschfeld's coinage 'transvestite' instead refers to an exclusively *cross-gendered* subject: 'taken from the Latin "trans" = across and "vestitus" = dressed, used also by the Roman classical writers as "transvestite"'.[22] Yet Hirschfeld is clearly not happy with this term, and this is because of its connoted externalization of transgender, its emphasis on clothes: 'One disadvantage of the term is that it describes only the external side, while the internal is limitless.'[23] And thus at the end of 'The Theory of Intermediaries' chapter, we find Hirschfeld running through a number of labels, ultimately finding none that is 'universally satisfactory' for the phenomenon he seeks to describe: and this is because his category of transvestite *includes* the transsexual. Identifying transsexuality, he writes that for 'the condition that [. . .] is not simply a matter of cross-dressing, but rather more of a sexual drive to change', 'sexual metamorphism' would be a better, though again (because ungainly and already connected by Krafft-Ebing in one case study to paranoia) not ideal, term.[24]

Hirschfeld's 'transvestite' was pivotal to the discursive emergence of the transsexual. The first subject to change sex and earn the diagnosis of transsexual, the subject who introduced transsexuality into the popular and medical lexicon, Christine Jorgensen, changed sex in 1952 under the diagnosis of 'genuine transvestite'; her case was described by her doctors in an article on 'transvestism' in May 1953.[25] In August 1953, also in response to Jorgensen's 'conversion operation', Benjamin distinguished between transvestism and transsexuality by portraying transsexuality as a severe form of transvestism.[26] Reading back genealogically to earlier sexology from these two articles marking the origins of transsexual sexology as a named field, we discover that such 'conversion operations' had already been attempted by subjects under Hirschfeld's label 'transvestite' – and this not only before the medical diagnosis of transsexuality but before the development of plastic surgery and endocrinology as medical technologies.[27] In 1922, Hirschfeld himself had described a female who had managed to obtain a bilateral mastectomy; and in 1928–9, *Zeitschrift für Sexual Wissenschaft* published under the rubric of transvestism the case of a natal female, Herman Karl (born Sophia Hedwig), whose genitals had been surgically reconfigured as early as 1882.[28] In so far as their subjects use medicine to bring soma into line with transgendered identification, here to masculinize their female bodies, both cases illustrate that sexology recorded the presence of transsexual desire before the label 'transsexual' appeared in the late 1940s. (Vern Bullough has even credited Hirschfeld with coining the term 'transsexual' in 1923, though it would seem the label was not deployed in English until D. O. Cauldwell in 1949.)[29] We thus need to reread Hirschfeld's *Transvestites*, like other putatively pre-transsexual work on sexual inversion, according to this recursive model of history, keeping in mind that Hirschfeld's transvestites are not identical to our own post-transsexual transvestite. Exemplifying such a method of rereading, Bullough and Bullough reproduce in a useful table Hirschfeld's seventeen transvestite cases, suggesting that because of their evident commitment to a full-time opposite sex role, 'four [of Hirschfeld's transvestites] might have become transsexuals had they lived at a later time'.[30]

I would emphasize the significance of Hirschfeld's entire theory of intermediaries for recognizing the central place of transgender in sexology. As with earlier theorists of inversion, Hirschfeld in effect maps degrees of transgender, the crossing of sex (Hirschfeld's groups 1 and 2: '1. the sexual organs, 2. the other physical characteristics') with gender ('3. the sex drive, 4. the other emotional characteristics').[31] Sexual orientation or object choice is implied in group 3. However, the fact that group 4, 'the other emotional characteristics', surely what we now understand as gender identity (transcribed as 'D' in the tables), is the dominant variable in the tables – it is the one characteristic that remains consistent within each table and varies only across the three tables (in the first, 'm', in the second, 'w', and in the third 'm + w', determining therefore the 'absolute' ideals within each table; respectively, man, woman and hermaphrodite) – illustrates with a truly mathematic precision the dominance of gender identity over sexuality. And as the transgendered subject (transvestite and 'sexual metamorphotic') is represented by D/group 4, and the homosexual thrown together with the bisexual into the demoted B/group 2, the tables also evidence the prioritization in this sex/gender system of transgender over homosexuality. What is remarkable about the theory of intermediaries is Hirschfeld's multiplication of categories to the effect that *all* subjects are revealed in some sense as transgendered: there is no absolute man or woman but only degrees of sex and gender crossing – a vision binding transgender to sexology's premise of an essential bisexuality.

When the transsexual was named, transsexual sexologists traced the history of their subject by returning to their precursors' work on sexual inversion. Cauldwell's 'Psychopathia Transexualis' ends its description of a female subject who lived as a man and desperately sought hormonal and surgical treatment by citing Hirschfeld's case from his *Sexual History of the World War* of a woman who enlisted as a male solider.[32] (Cauldwell's title, of course, is an overt re-citation of Krafft-Ebing's *Psychopathia Sexualis*.) Benjamin's 1953 essay and his even more seminal 1966 *The Transsexual Phenomenon* begin by mobilizing for transsexuality Ellis's term for cross-dressing, 'eonism'.[33] Similarly, later sexologists Ira Pauly, Richard Green and Leslie Lothstein all return to late nineteenth- and early twentieth-century work on sexual inversion to document the first medical records of transsexuality: Pauly and Lothstein first to Westphal's 1869 case, while for Green, a case in Krafft-Ebing is key.[34] This later work on transsexuality *is* sexology of course: a fact that, in the privileging of homosexuality in sexual inversion, we tend to overlook. For transsexuality, sexology – and sexual inversion – are far from being a defunct discourse.

Material connections between earlier and later sexologists also facilitated the transsexual's emergence. Benjamin's first transgendered patient, whom he began treating in the 1920s, was Otto Spengler; and Spengler, so Hirschfeld had told him, was the inspiration for *Transvestites*.[35] (Another filigree to this sexological tapestry is that Benjamin's first 'true transsexual' was referred in 1948 by Alfred Kinsey.)[36] But what most holds together the argument for the presence of transsexual subjects among sexology's categories of sexual inversion before the late 1940s' naming of the transsexual, what forms the warp and the woof to this tapestry of transsexual history in sexology, is the case histories of sexual inversion: the narratives of inverts' lives and identification preserved in their autobiographical recounting or translated into biography by the sexologist. In either format, given transsexuality's continued definitive narrative shape – the fact that transsexuals must tell a transsexual autobiography to present-day psychiatrists and psychologists in order to become transsexual, the fact that transsexuality *is* a narrative – these individual cases are precious and indispensable as transsexual texts.[37] As Bullough argues in a crucial note on a nineteenth-century transsexual (diagnosed at the time as homosexual), 'Publicizing such cases and bringing them to the attention of others in the sex field is important because it serves to confirm that transsexualism existed before it was an accepted diagnosis. It also serves to emphasize that individuals of the past often expressed themselves in ways similar to today's preoperative transsexuals.'[38]

Reading sexual inversion for transsexual subjects is a diagnostic exercise: like contemporary psychiatrists and psychologists who must decide whether a presenting subject is transsexual on the basis of his or her autobiography alone, we are faced with the problem of how to 'tell' (read and convey) who is transsexual through narrative. In an earlier essay, Bullough argues that '[f]or historical purposes, the best way to distinguish transvestism from transsexualism [and implicitly homosexuality] is to adopt the definition of Benjamin, who [. . .] labeled transsexualism as the most severe manifestation' ('of sex and gender disturbance').[39] Within this project of reading for 'severity', beyond those early subjects who actually reconfigured their sex surgically, the surest way to *read* the transsexual in inversion is to trust his or her narrative. Those subjects who expressly wished to change sex (Westphal's 'I-want-to-be-a-man' female is our first instance), identified profoundly with the 'other' sex, and struggled against the odds without medical aid to live their lives in their gender identity opposed to their sex are the best place to begin this work of documenting transsexual lives in history.

In Krafft-Ebing's *Psychopathia Sexualis*, the most likely male-to-female is the Hungarian doctor who feels h/imself to have actually undergone sex change. H/e experiences h/is body as a woman's ('I feel like a woman in a man's form. [. . .] I feel the penis as clitoris; the urethra and vaginal orifice [. . .] the scrotum as *labia majora*; in short, I always feel the vulva').[40] H/is desire to realize this sensory transformation even prefigures the transsexual's: 'I am sure that I should not have shrunk from the castration knife, could I thus have attained my desire.'[41] Pointedly, Krafft-Ebing labels the case 'transmutio sexus', a change of sex.[42] However, as this case is tangled with paranoia, it has caused some confusion in later classification. While Green selects it to stand for Krafft-Ebing's transsexual and Bullough suggests that Krafft-Ebing's '"metamorphosis sexualis paranoica" [. . .] today would be described as transsexualism', remember that Hirschfeld much earlier had troubled over the label 'sexual metamorphosis' precisely because of its prior impacting by Krafft-Ebing with paranoia.[43] More transparently transsexual in *Psychopathia Sexualis* is the case of Count Sandor/ Sarolta, the aristocratic female who lived his life as a man (hence I refer to him as such) – and, marrying twice and seducing women on the side, evidently with great panache. Yet that Sandor was cross-living not simply for the purpose of sexuality – side-stepping the taboo on homosexuality as the lesbian and gay reading of gender inversion as a heterosexist construct would have it – is evidenced by his blatant dysphoria over his own female sex. 'Love led me to take the step I took', Sandor waxes lyrical; but though 'love' – and the need to keep this tabooed sexual desire a secret – might be argued to motivate his refusal to let the other touch his body (Krafft-Ebing's theory), Sandor's disgust at touching himself ('Such a thing seemed very disgusting to her, and not conducive to manliness') and his 'horror' at even *speaking* of his own menstruation ('it was a thing repugnant to her masculine consciousness and feeling') makes clear that a much more fundamental rejection of bodily sex is at work than can be explained through (homo)sexuality.[44] In the first formulation of female-to-male transsexuality as such, Pauly will specify such a refusal of sex via sexuality as a key point on which the transsexual diverges from the lesbian: the transsexual avoids stimulation 'because it confronts her with her own female anatomy', the female anatomy that, as a transsexual man, s/he is *not*.[45] Sandor's case reads like a late nineteenth-century sexological Brandon Teena's: the female subject so desperate to change sex, yet without access to the medical technology, that he lived his life as a man anyway, binding and packing this body into the desired male surround, even in the face of dangerous and, in the case of Teena in 1993 Nebraska, fatal discovery.[46]

In Ellis's *Sexual Inversion*, the most unambiguous transsexual cases are similarly female to male, cases 38 and 39, the transsexual desire again symptomized in the inverts' narratives here maintained in their autobiographical form. The feelings of a profound gendered difference from other children, particularly around other girls; the disabling shame over one's own female body, its form and its functions; the sense of this female body 'as a mysterious accident';[47] the fantasies about reconforming this body to the imaginary male morphology (case 38's attempts to urinate through a tube); the unshakable experience of womanhood as a role and the wrong one; the unambivalent masculine identification and behaviour; the expressed regret at not being a man, in excess of social gender roles and linked to a profound sense of somatic lack: the features that make these life-stories read as classical transsexual plots make up a long, almost formulaic list. What is remarkable is the incredible stability of these narrative features, the consistence with which they reappear in contemporary transsexual autobiographies. The sole difference is that today transsexuals can resolve that 'hiatus [. . .] between [. . .] bodily structure and feelings' which case 39 identifies as the root of h/er suffering.[48] But the fact that inverts did not really have the technology to change sex does not bar them from the label 'transsexual'. Because even today, the diagnosis of transsexuality is required before correctly supervised medical sex transition, the transsexual is necessarily transsexual *before* changing sex. To refuse the invert a transsexual label is not simply to stick (in a way that refuses the very operation of history) over historical labels, it is to mistake the effect of transsexuality (sex change) for its cause: a profound sex dysphoria and a proportionate, compelling transgendered identification.[49]

Hence the reason why the case of the first fully transitioned (hormones and surgery) transsexual is so significant. Michael Dillon, born Laura in England in 1915, started testosterone therapy in 1939, underwent a double mastectomy in 1942, and began in 1945 a series of operations to construct a penis.[50] Notably, he did all this – achieved the first transsexual transition proper – without the label 'transsexual', years *before* this category had come into circulation. Author and doctor himself, Dillon published among his books one key to revealing how he undertook his transition, how he understood his identity, before the label 'transsexual'.

Self: A Study in Ethics and Endocrinology (1946) stands at a crossroads in the history of transsexual and homosexual subjects.[51] Because, as has often been noted, homosexuality began to replace inversion in the medical literature from around the 1910s and concomitantly psychoanalysis and psychology appeared as the more up-to-date discourse for analysing psychopathologies, Dillon is required to articulate transsexuality under the rubric of homosexuality. Yet his complex mapping of degrees of *gender* inversion *within* this rubric is definitively informed by sexology's taxonomies of sexual inversion as gender inversion. In the finest and most important point of distinction in Dillon's system, the 'feminine male homosexual' and 'masculine female homosexual' are differentiated from the 'effeminate male homosexual' and the 'mannish female homosexual':

> Now, most psychologists draw no distinction. [. . .] Yet there is a clear distinction. Where the one imitates and acquires, the other seems to develop naturally along the lines of the other sex [. . .] Invariably the cry is 'I have always felt as if I were a girl'; or alternatively from the girl comes the cry: 'I always felt as if I were a man.' In these instances the body may approximate in essentials to one sex, male or female, but the personality is wholly peculiar to the opposite one.[52]

The psychologist's strategy is to align mind with body; Dillon argues that in the case of the masculine/feminine homosexual, if we take our lead from Dillon's own labels, what we might term the ontologically as opposed to the performatively transgendered subject, the patient's answer is simpler. With a logic that prefigures Benjamin's and indeed the whole of the late twentieth-century approach to treating transsexuality, Dillon writes: 'Surely where the mind cannot be made to fit the body, the body should be made to fit, approximately at any rate, the mind.'[53] And as if to recognize the provisionality, the inappropriateness of the label, Dillon has by the end of this chapter for these now undeniable transsexual subjects inserted '"homosexuals"' in inverted commas.[54]

In addition, in discarding psychology for the condition he seeks to describe, Dillon turns for explanations – and solutions, as he did in his own life – to the then emergent field of endocrinology. This turn, with his classification of this form of 'homosexuality' as a glandular abnormality, is identical to that which Benjamin will make in his 1953 essay. Indeed both Dillon and Benjamin refer to the same study performed by a key figure in developing endocrinology, the Viennese anatomist/gynaecologist Eugen Steinach, in which laboratory animals of one sex were castrated and treated with the gonadal tissue of the other – in other words, transsexed – with the effect that (in the example cited by both Dillon and Benjamin) male rats suckled their young.[55] Steinach's *Sex and Life* was published in 1940: at the beginning of the decade then, with endocrinology having isolated and now able to redistribute sex hormones, ushering in a medical technology that would bring with it new possibilities for transsexuals, as anticipated by Dillon; and a revitalized role for sexology.[56]

Yet the focus on hormones and the glands was not so radically new. As noted by Bernice L. Hausman, Ellis and Hirschfeld both argued that sexual inversion was caught up with 'internal secretion', (indeed, Hausman states that it was Hirschfeld who suggested to his friend Steinach that he experiment with animal gonads).[57] Early sexology's hunches about the correlation between 'inversion' and 'the glands' are even now being followed through in studies of transsexual aetiology on the interaction between transsexual brains and sex hormones.[58] Dillon's life and work as a transsexual sit on the cusp of this earlier sexological work on sexual inversion and later sexological work on transsexuality, articulating succinctly and satisfyingly their join.

In an interview, Gayle Rubin conveys her enthusiasm for the 'amazing voices' in turn-of-the-(last)-century sexology and suggests that Freud has 'overshadowed' the sexological context in which he was writing.[59] That overshadowing of sexology by psychoanalysis in feminist and queer studies has amounted to an overshadowing of the transgendered subject by the homosexual; and even when sexology has been read, it is Freud's reading of sexual inversion (as a myth about homosexuality) that has been overwhelmingly, uncritically embraced. Yet although Freud positioned his theory of homosexuality explicitly against sexological paradigms of sexual inversion, as Rubin's comments suggest, his assumptions about sexuality remain at points profoundly invested in sexology, even sometimes a *continuation* of his predecessors' sexological work, so that Freud may himself be seen as a sexologist. In spite of that much-acclaimed separation of object choice and sexual aim, certain of Freud's 'homosexual' subjects are thoroughly transgendered (return, for instance, to 'Psychogenesis of a Case of Homosexuality in a Woman' where female homosexuality is predicated on a transgendered identification with the father). And Freud's very base for thinking sexuality in the first place was surely provided by sexology, a telling marker of the extent of this enablement being the first footnote to Freud's *Three Essays on the Theory of Sexuality*, where Freud states his debt to, among other sexologists, Krafft-Ebing, Havelock Ellis and Hirschfeld.[60] As Henri F. Ellenberger has remarked in his history of psychiatry, which makes clear Freud's place as a medic of sexual psychopathologies, 'the origin of psychoanalysis cannot be understood without taking into account several scientific trends of the last decades of the nineteenth-century', among them, 'the new science of sexual pathology that was given its decisive impetus by Krafft-Ebing'.[61]

In *The Transsexual Phenomenon*, Benjamin provides us with this less familiar, more sexological Freud. In 1930, Benjamin called on Freud in

Berggasse 19 in Vienna. The meeting was arranged by a mutual friend – one Dr Eugen Steinach – who had recently discovered the 'puberty gland', 'the hormone-producing part of the testicle'.[62] Of the unforgettable hour he spent with Freud, Benjamin writes: 'Among other topics, we discussed the body–mind relationship (suggested by Steinach's researches) and when the pun came to my mind that the "disharmony of the emotions may well be due to a disharmony of our endocrine glands," Freud laughed and fully agreed.'[63] It is a startling and again, immensely satisfying picture: an encounter over puns and the body between two men who had so much in common, European Jews soon to be forced to emigrate by Nazism to continue their study of sex, Freud of course to England, Benjamin to the USA; the one the founder of psychoanalysis, the other a key player in transsexual sexology, whose name even today denotes the most professional body in this field (the International Harry Benjamin Gender Dysphoria Association). Perhaps opening up sexology to more various subjects, re-reading the works to see how labels in addition to that of homosexual emerge, opens the way for similar re-readings of psychoanalysis. Perhaps it may be found that psychoanalysis is less to blame for the disappearance of the transgendered subject than it has itself been subject to similarly sublimating readings on this subject.

In the case of sexology, reading transgender back radically challenges what I call the 'market theory' of transsexuality: the critical commonplace that the term 'transsexual' and the availability of the medical technologies of plastic surgery and endocrinology conjoined to create transsexuality, that the transsexual did not exist until s/he was named.[64] Such absolutist constructionism in malignant form underlies the popular derogation of transsexuals as literally constructed: that is, not real men and women but ersatz, fake, made up – with no 'real' gendered history. Sexology's value as a cultural discourse lies in intervening in such a representation. In its rich and dense history, it demonstrates that though labels change, our desires (and desires for re-embodiment) as transsexual subjects remain astoundingly consistent.

Notes

1 George Chauncey, 'From Sexual Inversion to Homosexuality: Medicine and the Changing Conceptualization of Female Deviancy', *Salmagundi*, 58/59 (1982–3), p. 116.

2 For critical embraces of Freud against sexology, see Chauncey, 'From Sexual Inversion to Homosexuality', p. 137, Teresa de Lauretis, *The Practice of Love: Lesbian Sexuality and Perverse Desire* (Indiana University Press, Bloomington, IN, 1994), pp. 15–18, and Esther Newton, 'The Mythic Mannish Lesbian: Radclyffe Hall and the New Woman', *The Lesbian Issue: Essays from* Signs,

(eds) Estelle B. Freedman, Barbara C. Celpi, Susan L. Johnson, Kathleen M. Weston (Chicago University Press, Chicago, 1985), p. 18, n. 30.

3 Michel Foucault, *The History of Sexuality,* vol. 1: *An Introduction,* tr. Robert Hurley (Vintage, New York, 1990), p. 43.

4 Gert Hekma, '"A Female Soul in a Male Body": Sexual Inversion as Gender Inversion in Nineteenth-Century Sexology', *Third Sex, Third Gender: Beyond Sexual Dimorphism in Culture and History,* ed. Gilbert Herdt (Zone Books, New York, 1994), pp. 213–40.

5 See Jennifer Terry's work on the medicalization of homosexuality, especially, 'Anxious Slippages Between "Us" and "Them": A Brief History of the Scientific Search for Homosexual Bodies', in *Deviant Bodies: Critical Perspectives on Difference in Science and Popular Culture,* eds Terry and Jacqueline Urla (Indiana University Press, Bloomington, IN, 1995), pp. 129–69.

6 D. O. Cauldwell, 'Psychopathia Transexualis', *Sexology* (Dec. 1949), pp. 274–80.

7 Harry Benjamin, 'Transvestism and Transsexualism', *International Journal of Sexology,* 7.1 (1953); Benjamin, *The Transsexual Phenomenon* (Julian Press, New York, 1966).

8 Hubert Kennedy, *Ulrichs: The Life and Works of Karl Heinrich Ulrichs, Pioneer of the Modern Gay Movement* (Alyson, Boston, 1988); David F. Greenberg, *The Construction of Homosexuality* (Chicago University Press, Chicago, 1988), pp. 408–9.

9 Cited in Kennedy, *Ulrichs,* p. 73

10 Cited in Hugh C. Kennedy, 'The "Third Sex" Theory of Karl Heinrich Ulrichs', in *Historical Perspectives on Homosexuality,* eds Salvatore J. Licata and Robert P. Petersen (Haworth, New York, 1981), p. 106.

11 Foucault, *The History of Sexuality,* p. 43.

12 Vern L. Bullough and Bonnie Bullough, *Cross-Dressing, Sex, and Gender* (University Press of Pennsylvania, Philadelphia, 1993), p. 204; my emphasis.

13 Cited in Leslie Lothstein, *Female-to-Male Transsexualism: Historical, Clinical and Theoretical Issues* (Routledge, Boston, 1983), pp. 21–2.

14 Richard von Krafft-Ebing, *Psychopathia Sexualis, with Especial Reference to the Antipathic Sexual Instinct: A Medico-Forensic Study,* 10th German edn, tr. F. J. Rebman (Rebman, London, 1901).

15 Ibid., p. 188.

16 Havelock Ellis, *Studies in the Psychology of Sex,* vol. 2: *Sexual Inversion* (Random, New York, 1936).

17 Ibid., p. 1.

18 Sigmund Freud, 'Psychogenesis of a Case of Homosexuality in a Woman' (1920), in *Sexuality and the Psychology of Love,* ed. Philip Rieff (Macmillan, New York, 1963), p. 157.

19 Ibid., pp. 157–8

20 Magnus Hirschfeld, *Transvestites: The Erotic Drive to Cross Dress,* tr. Michael A. Lombardi-Nash (Prometheus, Buffalo, 1991).

21 Ibid., p. 147; Freud, 'Fetishism' (1927), in *Sexuality and the Psychology of Love,* pp. 214–19.

22 Hirschfeld, *Transvestites,* p. 233

23 Ibid., p. 233.

24 Ibid., pp. 233, 234.

25 Christian Hamburger, Georg K. Stürup and E. Dahl-Iversen, 'Transvestism: Hormonal, Psychiatric, and Surgical Treatment', *Journal of the American Medical Association*, 152 (1953), pp. 391–6.

26 Benjamin, 'Transvestism and Transsexualism', p. 12.

27 For a history of these fields but *not* in relation to transsexuality, see, respectively, Kathy Davis, *Reshaping the Female Body: The Dilemma of Cosmetic Surgery* (Routledge, New York, 1995), and Nelly Oudshoorn, *Beyond the Natural Body: An Archaeology of Sex Hormones* (Routledge, London, 1994).

28 Hirschfeld's case is cited in Lothstein, *Female-to-Male Transsexualism*, p. 22, and Ira Pauly, 'Adult Manifestations of Female Transsexualism', in *Transsexualism and Sex Reassignment*, eds Richard Green and John Money (Johns Hopkins University Press, Baltimore, 1969) p. 59; Herman Karl in Bullough and Bullough, *Cross-Dressing, Sex, and Gender*, p. 255.

29 Vern L. Bullough, 'A Nineteenth-Century Transsexual', *Archives of Sexual Behavior*, 16.1 (1987), p. 84.

30 Bullough and Bullough, *Cross-Dressing, Sex, and Gender*, p. 211(for table, see p. 210).

31 Hirschfeld, *Transvestites*, p. 219.

32 Cauldwell, 'Psychopathia Transexualis', p. 280.

33 Benjamin, 'Transvestism and Transsexualism', p. 12; Benjamin, *The Transsexual Phenomenon*, p. 16.

34 Lothstein, *Female-to-Male Transsexualism*, pp. 21–2; Pauly, 'Adult Manifestations of Female Transsexualism,' p. 59; Richard Green, 'Transsexualism: Mythological, Historical, and Cross-Cultural Aspects', in *The Transsexual Phenomenon*, Benjamin, p. 178.

35 Leah Cahan Schaefer and Connie Christine Wheeler, 'Harry Benjamin's First Ten Cases (1938-1953): A Clinical Historical Note', *Archives of Sexual Behavior*, 24.1 (1995), p. 77.

36 Ibid., p. 78.

37 For a discussion of transsexual narratives, see my *Second Skins: The Body Narratives of Transsexuality* (Columbia University Press, 1998). Chapter 4 discusses many of the sexological texts cited here but focuses on the narrative significance of sexual inversion for transsexuality, reading Radclyffe Hall's 1928 invert novel, *The Well of Loneliness*, as a transsexual novel from this premise.

38 Bullough, 'A Nineteenth-Century Transsexual', p. 81.

39 Vern L. Bullough, 'Transsexualism in History', *Archives of Sexual Behavior*, 4.15 (1975), p. 562.

40 Krafft-Ebing, *Psychopathia Sexualis*, pp. 301–2

41 Ibid., p. 294.

42 Ibid., p. 311.

43 Green, 'Transsexualism', p. 178; Bullough, 'A Nineteenth-Century Transsexual', p. 81; Hirschfeld, *Transvestites,* p. 234.

44 Krafft-Ebing, *Psychopathia Sexualis*, pp. 422, 424

45 Pauly, 'Adult Manifestations of Female Transsexualism', p. 83.

46 The case of the previously unknown Brandon Teena – of Teena's narrative of passing without hormones or surgery; above all of Teena's murder – is now legendary in the contemporary transgender movement (indeed, one of the mythic origins of the movement), and reference can be found to it throughout current transgender literature. For the fullest account of Teena's story, see Aphrodite Jones, *All She Wanted* (Simon & Schuster, New York, 1996).

47 Ellis, *Sexual Inversion*, p. 235

48 Ibid., p. 240

49 One of the problems with Bernice L. Hausman's *Changing Sex: Transsexualism, Technology, and the Idea of Gender* (Duke University Press, Durham, NC, 1995).

50 For Dillon's biography, see Liz Hodgkinson, *Michael née Laura* (Columbus, London, 1989).

51 Michael Dillon, *Self: A Study in Ethics and Endocrinology* (Heinemann Medical Books, London, 1946).

52 Ibid., pp. 50–1

53 Ibid., p. 53.

54 Ibid., p. 54.

55 Dillon, *Self*, p. 35, Benjamin, 'Transvestism and Transsexualism', p. 13. Oudshoorn, *Beyond the Natural Body*, discusses these experiments.

56 Eugen Steinach, *Sex and Life* (Faber and Faber, London, 1940).

57 Hausman, *Changing Sex*, pp. 30, 223 n. 9.

58 Jiang-Ning Zhou, Michael A. Hofman, Louis J.G. Gooren and Dick Swaab, 'A Sex Difference in the Human Brain and its Relation to Transsexuality', *Nature*, 378 (1995), pp. 68–70.

59 Gayle Rubin with Judith Butler (Interview), 'Sexual Traffic,' *differences*, 6.2–3 (1994), pp. 80, 81.

60 Sigmund Freud, *Three Essays on the Theory of Sexuality*, tr. and ed. James Strachey (Basic Books, New York, 1975) p. 1 n. 1.

61 Henri F. Ellenberger, *The Discovery of the Unconscious: The History and Evolution of Dynamic Psychiatry* (Basic Books, New York, 1970), p. 537.

62 Benjamin, *The Transsexual Phenomenon*, p. 41.

63 Ibid., p. 41.

64 See Janice M. Irvine, *Disorders of Desire: Sex and Gender in Modern American Sexology* (Temple University Press, Philadelphia 1990); and after her, Hausman, *Changing Sex*.

Part III

Constructing Desires

8 Feminist Reconfigurations of Heterosexuality in the 1920s

Lesley A. Hall

In making a case for the influence of sexology on culture, arguments have been advanced, particularly by Sheila Jeffreys's *The Spinster and her Enemies* and Margaret Jackson's *The Real Facts of Life*,[1] that a radical feminist discourse critiquing heterosexuality, which had burgeoned in the earlier years of the century, was overturned during the 1920s. They attribute this to the agency of women who, though allegedly feminists, were the passive dupes of male sexologists. These men, the writers claim, had a definite if concealed misogynist agenda to impose a retrogressive (and male-defined) model of compulsory heterosexuality under the pretence of affirming female sexual desire. Following the grant of the limited suffrage in 1918 and the upheavals of World War I, a 'New Feminism' is alleged to have arisen, laying an emphasis on the requirements of female difference, rather than promoting female claims to equality. This has been claimed as asserting women's sexual rights at the expense of wider political and social interests.

Feminist debates on sexuality prior to the post-war legislation which granted the (still restricted) right to the vote and removed various other sexual disqualifications on women were not quite as clear-cut as this formulation suggests, as Lucy Bland has pointed out in her recent book *Banishing the Beast*.[2] Some figures who have been (somewhat anachronistically) identified as exemplars of a radical new feminist discourse on sexuality had rather politically dubious views on eugenics and racial purity, whereas others were active campaigners for birth control. Sexology and feminism both emerged from a questioning of conventional mores which arose during the later nineteenth century, resulting from the campaign against the

Contagious Diseases Acts and changes in the social roles of the sexes. Sexologists might sometimes base their arguments on unexamined assumptions about 'natural' gender characteristics, but involvement with the social purity movement was not necessarily the only choice any self-respecting late nineteenth-century feminist might make. Although voices within the movement radically critiqued contemporary sexual mores, this was not necessarily characteristic of social purity as a whole. Many of its activities were less about making the streets safer for women than about men, and indeed, middle-class women, policing women who did not conform to the requirements of middle-class respectability, censoring literature, etc.

Furthermore, few British sexologists were unthinking adherents, let alone uncomplicated champions, of conventional assumptions about sexual difference and hierarchy. They were on the margins of medical and scientific orthodoxy, something which is not always recognized. They were committed to promoting social change, and in favour of improving the position of women in society.[3] The degree to which women were themselves involved in the critical exploration of sexual questions should not be underestimated. As well as debates in the columns of journals such as *Shafts*, *The Adult* and *the Freewoman*, there were active discussion groups in which women participated. Leading British sexologists such as Havelock Ellis and Edward Carpenter drew on experiences volunteered by women friends, and did not invent misogyny (which had been almost universally prevalent for many centuries), but were in fact doing their best to fight it, even if their weapons may not now seem always appropriate or correctly aimed.

It is an immense condescension by present-day feminists to assume that those of the past were blank wax imprinted with the ideas of male sexologists, rather than independent women who felt that sexology might have tools to offer to women struggling with patriarchal attitudes. Feminists were themselves participating in sexological debates and endeavouring to give voice to women's own experiences, and were less suggestible than Jeffreys's model implies. Interesting questions about how exactly individuals engage with and use new forms of knowledge, and for what purposes, have not been addressed. It is also far from obvious that the distinction made between feminism and sexology would have been apparent to protagonists of debates on these subjects during the early twentieth century: they were frequently perceived as facets of the same struggle.[4]

This discussion of attempts in the 1920s to theorize (and put into practice) a form of heterosexuality acceptable to feminists focuses on two women, Marie Stopes and Stella Browne, who were particularly articulate on sexual questions and have been named as particularly guilty of getting feminists off the barricades and onto their backs. Both were far from being 'Bright Young Things' or jazz babies, being in their forties by the 1920s and having served their time in the suffrage movement. Some attention will also be given to writings by Dora Russell and Naomi Mitchison, feminists of a slightly younger generation who contributed to the same debates.

Marie Stopes is well known to many as a pioneer of birth control and sex advice. A distinguished scientist in the field of botany, she turned to sex as a result of the debacle of her first marriage to a fellow-botanist who had, she convinced the court which granted her an annulment, failed to consummate their union. She had built up her case by a course of research in the books on sex kept locked up in the section still known as 'Cupboard' in the British Museum. 'Knowledge gained at such a cost' ought, she believed, to be made available for the public benefit, and she published *Married Love: A New Contribution to the Solution of Sex Difficulties* early in 1918; it became a runaway best-seller and was followed by works on *Wise Parenthood* (1918), *Radiant Motherhood* (1921) and *Enduring Passion* (1928) as well as other books, plays and journalism. Her writings, and her much-publicized presence as a public personality, encouraged thousands to write to her for advice and counsel.

Stella Browne, her almost exact contemporary, is a rather less well-known figure, primarily remembered as a founder of the Abortion Law Reform Association (1935), a cause which she had been publicly advocating for two decades during which even birth control had come only grudgingly to be accepted. She was born in Halifax, Nova Scotia, educated in Germany, at the pioneering girls' school St Felix Southwold, and at Somerville College, Oxford. An early career in teaching led to health breakdown, but in 1907 she became librarian at Morley College, the adult education institute in South London. She was a member of the militant suffragettes, the Women's Social and Political Union (Stopes was in the Women's Freedom League), but regarded the political struggle for the vote as only one aspect of feminism and was also active in movements for the reform of divorce law, birth control, legitimacy laws, and a wide-ranging agenda of other sexual matters, as well as humanitarianism, socialism and pacifism. Living in Chelsea with her mother and sister, after leaving her post at Morley College she eked out a meagre living in translating, reviewing and journalism, supplemented by occasional clerical and editorial jobs. Throughout the 1920s she led a busy life of writing and lecturing on a range of topics, predominantly to do with the struggle for birth control. An early member of the British Communist Party, she resigned in 1923 because of its lack of interest in birth control. In both principle and practice she believed passionately in free love and women's bodily and sexual autonomy.

That determinedly independent women such as Stopes and Browne were, as Jeffreys alleges, brainwashed by 'male sexologists such as Ellis' and therefore 'forced to redefine [. . .] and repudiate' their own experiences seems highly improbable.[5] Browne was widely read in sexological literature, including French and German texts, but her own conclusions were, she stated, 'based on life, not on books', drawn from her 'own experience, or the observation and testimony of people I know well'.[6] The same applied to Stopes, who could cite in witness the vast quantities of correspondence she received in response to her writings and on which she drew in modifying or expanding her own ideas. Both believed in particular that there were important aspects of female experience which had been overlooked, which they felt it their duty to voice.

Sexology, it is claimed, was a male knowledge construct which could only co-opt and distort what women were saying. However, any set of discourses available to women in the early twentieth century carried some patriarchal baggage: women were often aware of this and endeavoured to manipulate it for their own ends. The misogynistic bias of medicine and science in the later nineteenth and early twentieth centuries was hardly unique to those fields, being perhaps even more deeply inscribed in the legal system and forming a significant if often barely conscious element in popular thought.

Early twentieth-century feminists were not blind to the sexist elements within knowledge creation. Browne was alert to the potentially masculine bias of, for example, psychoanalysis, in 1925 praising the 'admirably close and detailed criticism of Freud's androcentric view of sex and mis-interpretation of the sexual impulse in women' of Paul Bousfield's Sex Civilisation.[7] She did not fail to critique androcentric tendencies and the temptation to be doctrinaire when she found them among sexologists. She gently suggested that eminent sexologist Havelock Ellis had failed to realize the 'moral value of [the] active and articulate revolt against tradition as well as present conditions' embodied in the militant suffrage movement.[8] She was less gentle to Walter Heape's Sex Antagonism: 'neither exhaustive nor unbiased [. . .] unqualified assumption[s] [. . .] discounts all the activities of women, except motherhood [. . .] dogmatising on women's nature.[9] Jeffreys's depiction of Browne as 'suffer[ing] from constraint and the need for men's approval when writing about sex'[10] would astonish anyone who reads her reviews of works by male writers, or her trenchant article 'Women and the Race' responding to an anti-feminist article by male socialist S.H. Halford.[11]

Browne was sensitive to women's lack of appropriate sexual vocabulary, and indeed of a suitable language generally for the discussion of sexual topics. Men had at least acquired 'all the slang of the streets' but well-brought-up girls completely lacked 'terms to define many of [their] sensations and experiences'.[12] She herself was struggling to find an appropriate form of expression, and drew largely on contemporary discourses of sexology and psychology, sometimes employing terminology which has now acquired connotations very far from her intentions. It was not necessarily naive of women to appeal to the authority of science. In its ideals, if not its practice, science seemed to hold the potential for a free and frank consideration of new ideas, as opposed to the reiteration of religious or political dogma to silence debate.

Stopes and Browne represented two rather different possibilities within feminism, their significant differences having been occluded by the tendency to lump them together. Stopes was a best-selling author with a (second) husband and child who placed great importance on her right to be presented at court as a married woman, even though her first marriage had been dissolved, but, she emphasized, by annulment rather than divorce. Browne was a far more marginal figure, poor, unmarried, politically radical, whose views were disseminated through often obscure publications and through personal contacts, lectures to a range of organizations, and private correspondence and conversation.

Stopes believed that if people followed her 'New Gospel' of good conjugal sex with effective birth control, society would be transformed and there would be no need for political revolution. Browne, however, believed that women's lot would never be significantly improved under the existing unjust social and economic system, even though she worked fervently for its amelioration through campaigns such as those for greater access to safe birth control and abortion: thus her ideas derived at least as much from socialism as sexology. Both women, as well as having been active in the suffrage movement, continued to voice strongly feminist views on a range of issues. In Stopes's case, apart from her birth-control crusade these involved concerns largely of the middle-class professional woman (e.g., separate taxation, protests against marriage bars to employment), while Browne's reflected her more radical position.

Margaret Jackson has conceded Stopes's feminism, devoting an entire chapter in *The Real Facts of Life* to 'The Unhappy Marriage of Feminism and Sexology: Marie Stopes and the "Laws of Love"'. Given the high degree of formal and informal censorship of the works of Ellis and others, she makes the justifiable claim that most individuals' access to the current ideas of sexology would have been via marriage manuals such as those of Stopes, but fails to differentiate between scholarly works on the subject and the more populist genre in which Stopes was working, that of the advice manual. This was a genre with its own distinctive imperatives: rather than aiming to make people think, it was intended to make people act. Jackson attacks what she perceives as the 'deeply contradictory nature of [Stopes's] model of sexuality, which was, from a feminist perspective, both radical and reactionary', presented in an 'idiosyncratic blend of science, religion, mysticism, romanticism and feminism'.[13] She claims that this attempt to '"marry" sexology and feminism' was a failure, any feminist potential being undercut by the 'phallocentric model of sexology'[14] (though whether a text which became an international best-seller can be regarded as a failure is rather moot). Stopes's visions may not stand up to rigorous intellectual analysis, but the question is whether this is an appropriate demand to make of the kind of text *Married Love* is.

Stopes herself was (like everyone) a creature of contradictions, and this was one of the sources of her strength and success as a writer of sex advice. Indeed, it is far from obvious that the contradictions of *Married Love* can be attributed to any deliberately perverse attempt to yoke feminism with contemporary sexology. Stopes's combination of the assertion of women's rights to careers and intellectual life as well as sexual pleasure, with a romantic vision of women as mysterious coy nymphs always and alluringly escaping, was undoubtedly very attractive to both men and women, and owed far more to Stopes's self-perceptions than to any insights she might have gained from sexology. She provided a programme for change within the context of post-Great War society which did not threaten too much upheaval or subversion of societal norms of marriage. To combine in this way both 'radical and reactionary' elements within the message being put across was a recipe for success in this particular genre.

Stopes's ideology of marriage was much more seductive to a much wider audience than Browne's far more searching analysis of the economic, social and political system which continued to deny women their equal rights and persisted in oppressing them. Browne saw her own position as representing 'a very small minority' arguing for 'social and sexual freedom for women' on combined feminist and socialist grounds.[15] Her sense of fighting firmly entrenched powers of conventional attitudes accounts for what can seem exaggerated attacks on individuals, groups and ideas. Her opinions, far from slavish adherence to some modish set of approved ideas, appeared to her profoundly and dangerously oppositional. As late as 1951 she wrote to Janet Chance, her colleague in the Abortion Law Reform Association, that: 'It is not ALRA's business – in my humble view – to raise objections and suggest limitations to the right of maternal choice. Other persons and organizations will do that soon enough.'[16] She was not advancing her ideas into a vacuum but into a space she perceived as already occupied by hostile forces.

Unlike Stopes, who believed that marriage, and ultimately society, could be transformed by the application of her prescriptions, Browne persistently repudiated marriage as it existed in contemporary society, suggesting that:

In love as in religion, we have no infallible prescription. [. . .] We are working out standards and codes with pain and stress, with mistakes, no doubt, but with an unalterable 'No' to the lies and fears of the former dispensation.[17]

It should be noted that she saw this working out of a new dispensation as an ongoing process, rather than something which had already been laid down as a revealed truth in the writings of sexologists only needing to be put into practice. Her views, like Stopes's claim that 'only by loosening the bonds can one bind two hearts indissolubly',[18] belong to a long-standing feminist tradition critiquing marriage and were not modish assent to fashionable theories of 'free love'. The younger feminist Dora Russell similarly defined marriage as, too often, 'degraded and humiliating slavery' and saw feminism as engendering women 'armed and unsubdued to make marriage tolerable'.[19]

In her own time, Browne found that 'women of independent minds and ardent natures can find no publicly recognised and honoured form of sex union which meets both their needs'.[20] She herself never married, and may be contrasted with contemporaries such as Dora Russell, Vera Brittain, Naomi Mitchison, Janet Chance, and even Marie Stopes herself, who were trying to create new models of relationship, but within the relative security of marriage (not always trustworthy, as Russell discovered).

Browne claimed that 'an ardent temperament does not necessarily imply indulgence in indiscriminate promiscuity. The passionate woman may be, and often is, as fastidious in her choice of a lover as her placid sister.'[21] She herself had a number of lovers: in 1907 she became involved with a man whom she described as being a 'demi-semi-lover' until 1910, and after that her 'technically complete, though very intermittent and occasional lover' for at least a further dozen years. However, she also had two other serious liaisons between 1915 and 1922, as well as 'three very slight occasional and mainly physical episodes'. She consistently put a case for women's right to experimentation and variety in her relationships. In describing these experiences in a letter to Havelock Ellis, she was referring specifically to male lovers, in the context of thoughts about the sexual requirements of 'nervous sensitive mentally active working women of "modern" and mentally evolved types' generated by Margaret Sanger's recent marriage to Noah Slee.[22]

While Stopes and Browne believed that there was great positive potential in heterosexual relations, they were both, contrary to Jeffreys's and Jackson's inferences, extremely critical of the male-dominated way these were normally defined, suggesting that this was equally damaging to the male, though less obviously so than to the female. As Stopes put it, the 'abysmal and universal [. . .] mists and shadowy darkness' of sexual ignorance were rife,[23] so that 'physical passion, so swiftly stimulated in man, tends to over-ride all else, and the untutored man seeks but one thing – the accomplishment of desire', leading to 'scorn and loathing for the act which should have been a perpetually recurring enchantment' in the woman.[24]

Stopes saw the central problem as neglect of the woman's side of the question. Woman's nature, Stopes argued, was 'set to rhythms over which man has no more control than he has over the tides of the sea',[25] which had been occluded by 'the tradition of [. . .] [woman's] flower-like innocence'.[26] While Stopes was transparently deploying pervasive notions of women as closer to nature, she identified them with powerful and sweeping tides, not small and fading flowers. Husbands' routine habits of intercourse, negligent of their wives' desire or indifference, Stopes claimed, 'tended to flatten out the billowing curves of the line of her natural desire',[27] and they thus lost 'realms of ever-expanding joy and tenderness'.[28] '[T]he essentials', which Stopes made known in 'simple, direct, and scientific language', were that 'stiffening and erection of the penis did not *necessarily* call for relief in the ejaculation of sperm',[29] and that unless women were physically aroused before sexual union took place, the man was likely to cause 'actual pain, apart from the mental revolt and loathing'.[30]

In *Married Love* Stopes assumed the problem to be one of ignorance, and that providing clear information about sexual functioning, in a way which innumerable readers of *Married Love* praised as 'clean', would solve the majority of problems. Those whose problems were amenable to reading Stopes's works and their implicit giving of permission needed no more: those whose problems were more intransigent took them to Stopes herself. This created difficulties. By the time of *Enduring Passion*, 1928, Stopes was increasingly relying upon the discoveries about the sex hormones for her explanatory models, rooting her thoughts about sexuality in physiology rather than social forces or individual psychology – she was implacably hostile to psychoanalysis. In her resort to the latest glandular theories, one discerns a desire for certainty, a strong resistance to ambiguity, a wish to be an authority with definite answers, all antipathetic to more sensitive exploration of the complex issues around sexuality. This owed little, however, to sexology: it had much more to do with Stopes's own ideas and personality and the position she had attained (and enjoyed) as an expert authority.

Browne, however, retained a more open mind. Perhaps the essential difference between the two is encapsulated in the opposition between Stopes's overriding emphasis on the normal and the natural and Brownes's statement that 'I have never met the normal woman. I have seen a lot about her in print [. . .] but I have never met her.'[31] Browne's surviving writings deal less with specific details of intimate sexual praxis, and rather more with wider factors militating against women enjoying emotionally fruitful sexual experiences. She was explicitly committed to a wide-ranging agenda of reform of what she described as:

A political system which denies women alike equality of opportunity and adequate special protection; an economic system which is iniquity and waste incarnate; and sexual institutions founded on the needs and preferences of a primitive type of man.[32]

True reformation of sexual morals and attitudes demanded 'redistribution of wealth and the reconstruction of our institutions'.[33]

There is little justification for the claims made by Jeffreys and Jackson that Browne uncritically advocated sexual indulgence and 'did not seek to transform men or agitate about the sexual abuse of women and girls'.[34] She was quite adamant about the need for a radical transformation of an oppressive patriarchal society and was active in inciting protests against legislation such as Regulation 40D under the Defence of the Realm Act in 1918, widely regarded as reinstituting the Contagious Diseases Acts under the guise of wartime necessity, since it penalized women for the transmission (or alleged transmission) of venereal disease to members of the armed forces. She abhorred prostitution and continually condemned the conventional division of women into 'two arbitrary classes [. . .] the prospective or actual private sex property of one man' or 'the public sex property of all and sundry'.[35]

The promiscuity which flourished during World War I was far from the ideals she advocated. Browne wrote to Bertrand Russell in 1917:

a great deal of the newer manifestations of sexual liberty are very far from encouraging or attractive, but [. . .] [o]ne cannot expect people to develop *real* responsibility, or refinement and discrimination of feeling, in one generation, especially with prostitution so firmly rooted in our social order.[36]

Women's needs, according to Browne, had never been expressed either by '[p]rostitution and promiscuity' or by 'enforced celibacy and cast iron monogamy'. The very 'variety and variability of the sexual impulse' in women militated against promiscuity, since 'the most passionate women have sexual repulsions and aversions as strong as their preferences'.[37] If few women were absolutely monandrous, fewer still were promiscuous. (Even male promiscuity, Browne suggested, was less an innate instinct than a reaction to social conditions or the result of commercialized exploitation.) She added the proviso that all women should enjoy access to contraception, 'a most important part of women's real emancipation', and economic security.[38] Similar views were expressed by Dora Russell: 'that thirty shillings a week, which stands between her and the abyss of primeval submission', enabled a woman to take a lover who would not 'tyrannize'.[39]

In 1927 Browne suggested that men of 'creative vigour and intelligence [. . .] sympathy and imagination' who did not feel any necessity to 'fetter and further handicap women' but were able to 'attract and satisfy women as mates, without [. . .] bribery or bullying' were an 'interesting and delightful minority'.[40] What a woman required in a man, she believed, was 'splendid physical vitality and virility [. . .] *just as necessary in a sex partner* as ideal and intellectual sympathy [. . .] warm lifequickening ardour and dash and aggressiveness that are so intoxicating in a lover'.[41] That was the ideal. Browne had plenty of criticisms to make of contemporary heterosexual relations as they were widely practised. The law's outrageous concept of 'conjugal rights' flagrantly failed to prevent 'exploitation or violation' within marriage.[42] A vast amount of sexual anaesthesia among married women was caused by 'lack of skill, control and sympathy on the husband's part',[43] and many underwent the 'ordeal of parturition' having enjoyed 'very little definite pleasure in the act of intercourse'.[44] The 'large percentage of sterility in women [. . .] due to venereal infection by their husbands [. . .] [was] a tremendous indictment of men's government of society'.[45]

Browne's condemnation of the 'cold woman', which has been the subject of much criticism, should be understood within her perception that women had internalized the standards of a patriarchal social system which valued and rewarded chastity and indeed sexual apathy in women, judging themselves and other women on the basis of 'ascetic superstitions' with deep misogynistic roots. Her respect for diversity led her to recognize 'natural nuns' for whom celibacy was appropriate, and also to assert the rights of the 'inverted' (i.e., homosexual) to the enjoyment of their passions.

The paper 'Studies in Sexual Inversion', published in 1923 but first given as a lecture in 1917, tends to be cited as if it represented Browne's final views on lesbianism, engraved in stone, but it was quite explicitly advanced as a preliminary study to stimulate discussion and investigation, and occupied a transitional place in her own thinking. Over the following decade and a half she gave an increasing amount of respect to the choice of a woman partner, and even in this early paper placed 'inverted' passions on a level with the heterosexual.[46]

In no way can Browne be said to have repudiated passionate feelings for women and to have denigrated lesbians. She publicly and privately expressed the warmest appreciation for women friends and acquaintances, and certainly did not, as Jeffreys has alleged, 'twist [herself] into knots by rejecting [her] own experience of loving women'.[47] A strong case can be made that her personal commitment to variety and experimentation included sexual relationships with women, and that by the late 1920s she was increasingly identifying as bisexual rather than as indulging in 'that episodical homosexuality on the part of women who are normally much more attracted to men'.[48] Reviewing Katharine Bement Davies's *Factors in the Sex Life of Twenty-Two Hundred Women* in 1930 Browne hypothesized 'a type of articulate, vigorous and adventurous woman who is inherently bisexual. She is active and positive, yet a sexual epicure as well.'[49] In 1935 Browne placed love for a woman alongside love for a man or commitment to a career as something many women might understandably find more compelling than maternity.[50] For her, the genuine choice of a female partner (as opposed to a *faut-de-mieux* solution imposed by women's lack of sexual opportunities) was certainly one option, and within her formulation of the diversity of desire, being a minority rendered no choice any the less acceptable. She did not regard even the still widely stigmatized practice of masturbation as necessarily deleterious or pathological, claiming in 1917 that 'A certain amount of self-excitement, and solitary enjoyment, seems inevitable in any strongly developed sexual life',[51] and arguing in 1930 that it was 'very moot' to suppose it necessarily less 'beneficial and preferable' than heterosexual relations.[52]

Her take on lesbianism differed quite distinctively from that of Stopes, very much a 'man's woman' seeking out male admiration, although there are hints of warm female friendships prior to her marriage. In *Enduring Passion*, Stopes claimed that women deprived of satisfying sexual union by their husband's ineptitude or impotence were in danger of succumbing to 'homosexual vice'. This tended to 'unfit women for real union. [. . .] This corruption spreads.' Stopes was firmly convinced that the soothing of 'surface nervous excitement' by lesbian caresses could not compete with the exchange of bodily secretions in heterosexual intercourse.[53] She doubtless found anathema Naomi Mitchison's contention that there are 'many kinds of mutual caresses and pleasures' available to the (heterosexual) couple besides full intercourse, and would have been even more appalled by Mitchison's recommendation of 'romantic affections for persons of their own sex up to the end of adolescence' as a desirable alternative to early heterosexual affairs.[54]

There were many reasons why a new, radical and feminist vision of the possibilities of sexuality failed to be realized in the post-suffrage era. On a practical level, contraception remained hard to obtain and unreliable, while abortion was still criminalized and potentially lethal. There was little support for the single mother, and divorced women were widely shunned. Formal and informal marriage bars on female employment are relatively well known, but a woman known to be openly living with a man would also have found her livelihood in danger. Dora Russell commented on the 'fear of starvation' which compelled 'outward acceptance of old codes and conventions'. She suggested that 'a good deal of freedom in action' had been matched with 'less boldness in speech, because of the heavy penalties involved', and 'dread of the scandal that will end the work Aspasia loves'.[55] Françoise Lafitte was a specific instance: separated, the mother of two children, employed by the London School Board, she had to resort to elaborate expedients to ensure that no gossip ever arose concerning her liaison with Havelock Ellis: 'I, a teacher, must not be thought "immoral". My children's bread depended on my behaviour, and also my own independence.'[56] Even without what Jeffreys and Jackson perceive as the malign influence of sexology, the likelihood that the grant of the limited suffrage in 1918, or even of the 'flapper vote' ten years later, would usher in a feminist millennium was vanishingly small. There was still an enormous deadweight of institutional oppression and inertia, and social custom, to contend with.

Marie Stopes was indubitably the most influential female voice in sexual matters during the 1920s. Her ability to market herself and her ideas, and to express these in writing accessible to a range of different audiences, was phenomenal. Unlike Browne, she did not challenge often scarcely conscious assumptions about marriage, but reinforced the idea that heterosexual marriage, along middle-class lines, was and ought to be a central institution of society, even while promoting its sweeping reform in a more woman-friendly direction. Stopes knew exactly the limit to which she could go, and usually went right up to it, but not beyond, almost mediumistically attuned to the requirements and taboos of her audience. Her vision of change was a matter of interior decor and furnishing rather than architecture and town planning, of private rather than public spaces, of bedrooms rather than barricades. Within that area, and within her limitations, she was a great success. Unquantifiable numbers of readers owed her enormous gratitude for the relief of marital difficulties and a greater measure of conjugal happiness.

Browne, however, clearly felt that such limits were part of the oppressive structures of the patriarchal capitalist society she wanted to overthrow. In a largely favourable review of Married Love, she pointed out that the book was 'based on observation of, and addressed to, the educated, prosperous, and privileged classes' and ignored the 'immense industrial, social and legislative changes [. . .] necessary, before the majority of her fellow-citizens are able even approximately to [. . .] follow her suggestions'. Furthermore, Stopes overlooked the connection between women's economic dependence and their sexual ignorance.[57]

Browne's rather more complex vision of the roots of sexual oppression and the diversity of changes necessary to bring about liberation was presumably one reason why her work was so marginalized, although her commitment to activism, and quite probably a reluctance to market herself as Stopes did, are further possible explanations why someone conceded by several authorities to be a good writer never published a book. Her body of work consists of numerous but scattered articles and letters in a range of often obscure periodicals. Also, her programme was almost certainly far too challenging for the majority – much happier with the circumscribed degree of change advocated by Stopes. Within society as it existed, as Browne herself was aware, living out her agenda involved considerable risk; she commented in 1929 that 'the woman of the transition so often wants to have it both ways – to enjoy the privileges of subjection and the rights of freedom!'[58]

While Marie Stopes's message resembled refurnishing an existing Victorian house in modern 1920s' style, even this apparently minor degree of change had major implications for the increased happiness of many women, and her work relieved much appalling suffering, just as apparently minor domestic alterations made home life more pleasant. Stella Browne advanced a much more structurally radical agenda, decoupling sex from marriage and maternity, and placing sex with men as one option (rather than an obligation) among a range of possibilities, including freely chosen celibacy, lesbian relationships, masturbation and single (including lesbian) motherhood. It is less easy to assess the influence of her work than Stopes's, but quite apart from her writings she is reported as a distinctive and memorable lecturer and addressed many groups. What invisible seeds might she have sown?

Credit should be given to women who, during the interwar years, struggled with varying degrees of success to voice the needs and pleasures of women and sought ways in which these could be fulfilled, against what was less a backlash than the deadweight of enduring, massive structures of a still profoundly patriarchal and deeply sex-negative culture. They were part of the attempt, characteristic of both feminism and sexology, to think consciously and critically about matters which were too often taken as given and assumed to be the 'natural' way things were.

Notes

1 Sheila Jeffreys, *The Spinster and her Enemies: Feminism and Sexuality 1880–1930* (Pandora Press, London, 1985); Margaret Jackson, *The Real Facts of Life: Feminism and the Politics of Sexuality c1850-1940* (Taylor and Francis, London, 1994).

2 Lucy Bland, *Banishing the Beast: English Feminism and Sexual Morality, 1885–1914* (Penguin, London, 1995).

3 Lesley Hall, 'Heroes or Villains? Reconsidering British *fin de siècle* Sexology and its Impact', in *New Sexual Agendas*, ed. Lynne Segal (Macmillan, London, 1997), pp. 3–16.

4 Lesley Hall, 'Suffrage, Sex and Sciences', in *The Women's Suffrage Movement,*

New Feminist Perspectives, eds Maroula Joannou and June Purvis (Manchester University Press, 1998).

5 Jeffreys, *The Spinster and her Enemies*, p. 115.

6 F.W. Stella Browne, *The Sexual Variety and Variability Among Women, and their Bearing upon Social Reconstruction* (British Society for the Study of Sex Psychology, London, 1917), p. 13.

7 F.W. Stella Browne, 'Reviews: Concerning Women and Children', *New Generation*, 4 (1925), p.33.

8 *English Review*, 13 (1912), p. 157.

9 *English Review*, 14 (1913), p. 665.

10 Jeffreys, *The Spinster and her Enemies*, p. 159.

11 F.W. Stella Browne, 'Woman and the Race', *Socialist Review: A Quarterly Review of Modern Thought*, 14 (1917), pp. 151–7.

12 Browne, *Sexual Variety and Variability*, p. 13.

13 Jackson, *The Real Facts*, p. 132.

14 Ibid., p. 155.

15 F.W. Stella Browne, 'The Feminine Aspect of Birth Control', in *Report of the Fifth International Neo-Malthusian and Birth Control Conference [. . .] London [. . .]1922*, ed. R. Pierpoint (William Heinemann (Medical Books) Ltd, London, 1922), pp. 40–3.

16 Stella Browne to Janet Chance, 12 December 1951, Abortion Law Reform Association archives in the Contemporary Medical Archives Centre, Wellcome Institute for the History of Medicine, CMAC: SA/ALR/B.5.

17 F.W. Stella Browne, 'A Modern Programme', *New Generation*, 8 (1929), p. 41.

18 Marie Stopes, *Married Love: A New Contribution to the Solution of Sex Difficulties* (A. C. Fifield, London, 1918), p. 124.

19 Dora Russell, *Hypatia, or Woman and Knowledge*, first published 1925, in *The Dora Russell Reader*, ed. Dale Spender (Pandora, London, 1983), pp. 17, 21.

20 F.W. Stella Browne, Review of *The Sexual Crisis: A Critique of our Sex Life*. By Grete Meisel-Hess, *Malthusian*, 1917, p. 39.

21 'A New Subscriber' (F.W. Stella Browne), 'Who are the "Normal"?', *Freewoman*, 7 March 1912, pp. 312–13.

22 Stella Browne to Havelock Ellis, 25 December 1922, Ellis papers in the British Library Department of Manuscripts, Additional Manuscripts 70539.

23 Stopes, *Married Love*, p. 8.

24 Ibid., p. 13.

25 Ibid., p. 19.

26 Ibid., p. 22.

27 Ibid., p. 28.

28 Ibid., p. 39.

29 Ibid., pp. 40–2.

30 Ibid., p. 47.

31 Minutes of Evidence at Eighth Meeting of the Interdepartmental Committee on Abortion, Ministry of Health, 17 November 1937: Evidence of Miss F.W. Stella Browne. Ministry of Health records at the Public Record Office: PRO: MH71/23.

32 F.W. Stella Browne 'Women and Birth Control', in *Population and Birth-Control: A Symposium*, eds Eden and Cedar Paul (Critic and Guide Company, New York, 1917), pp. 247–57.

33 F.W. Stella Browne, 'Letter to the Editor, with a copy of a letter (unpublished) to *The New Statesman*', *Malthusian*, 1915, p. 92.

34 Jeffreys, *The Spinster and her Enemies*, p. 5.

35 Browne, *Sexual Variety and Variability*, p.4.

36 Stella Browne to Bertrand Russell, 12 September 1917: Russell papers in the William Ready Division of Archives and Research Collections, Mills Memorial Library, McMaster University, Hamilton, Ontario.

37 F.W. Stella Browne, 'Some Problems of Sex', *International Journal of Ethics*, 27 (1916/17), pp. 464–71.

38 Browne, *Sexual Variety and Variability*, p. 6.

39 Dora Russell, *Hypatia*, pp. 17–18.

40 'F.W.S.B.', 'Reviews: A Brilliant Boomerang', *New Generation*, 6 (1927), p. 34.

41 Stella Browne to Havelock Ellis, 25 December 1922, BL Add Mss 70539.

42 Browne, 'Some Problems of Sex'.

43 Browne, 'Women and the Race'.

44 Browne, 'Women and Birth Control'.

45 Browne, 'Women and the Race'.

46 Browne, 'Studies in Feminine Inversion', *Journal of Sexology and Psychoanalysis*, 1 (1923), pp. 51–8.

47 Jeffreys, *The Spinster and her Enemies*, p. 121.

48 F.W. Stella Browne, 'Studies in Feminine Inversion'.

49 F.W. Stella Browne 'Women Bear Witness', *New Generation*, 9 (1930), pp. 127–8.

50 F.W. Stella Browne, 'The Right to Abortion', in *Abortion (3 essays)*, F.W. Stella Browne, A. M. Ludovici and Harry Roberts (G. Allen and Unwin, London, 1935), pp. 13–46.

51 Browne, *Sexual Variety and Variability*, p. 10.

52 F.W. Stella Browne, 'Some Books that Help', *New Generation*, 11 (1932), p. 66.

53 Marie Stopes, *Enduring Passion: Further New Contributions to the Solution of Sex Difficulties, Being the Continuation of Married Love* (Putnam, London, 1928), pp. 41–2

54 Naomi Mitchison, *Comments on Birth Control* (Faber and Faber, London, 1930).

55 Russell, *Hypatia*, 'Aspasia', pp. 16–22.

56 F. Delisle (Françoise Lafitte-Cyon), *Friendship's Odyssey* (Delisle, London, 1964), pp. 116–17.

57 F.W. Stella Browne, Review of *Married Love*, *International Journal of Ethics*, 29 (1918/19), pp. 112–13.

58 F.W. Stella Browne, 'A Year of Indiscretion', *New Generation*, 8 (1929), p. 7.

9 Sex, Love and the Homosexual Body in Early Sexology

Suzanne Raitt

She said she could not conceive of any other way of being in love, but she added that for her parents' sake she would honestly help in the therapeutic attempt, for it pained her very much to be the cause of so much grief to them.[1]

I separate my loves into two halves: Harold, who is unalterable, perennial, and *best*; there has never been anything but absolute purity in my love for Harold, just as there has never been anything but absolute bright purity in his nature. And on the other hand stands my perverted nature, which loved and tyrannised over Rosamund and ended by deserting her without one heart-pang, and which now is linked irredemiably with Violet.[2]

In 1920, in different countries, and in very different domestic settings, the two young women whose voices we hear in the extracts found themselves struggling with the consequences of their desire for other women. The protagonist of my first quotation is the 'beautiful and clever girl of eighteen' who, at her parents' instigation, was treated briefly by Freud after an unsuccessful suicide attempt. Resonating through Freud's puzzled words we hear the echo of the girl's sad but sceptical common sense, of her 'cool reserve', as Freud calls it (p. 391). Despairing of ever getting through to her, he eventually broke off the treatment and recommended that she see a woman analyst. In response the girl performed her own act of renunciation: she promised her father that she would stop seeing the woman with whom she was obsessed. Freud records in the case history that he does not know whether she did in fact give up her lover, or, indeed, whether she ever saw another analyst. The case history is thus an account not of the 'successful' treatment, but of the aetiology, and partial analysis, of a case of 'congenital homosexuality' (p. 398). My interest in this chapter is in what Freud's account has to say about love. As we shall see, discourses that deal with homosexuality – books by sexologists, psychoanalytic case histories, and autobiographical accounts like Vita Sackville-West's, the source of my second extract – invariably also develop, either explicitly or implicitly, their own systems of sexual morality. I shall be asking what role love plays in these systems. How do early twentieth-century analyses of homosexual feeling represent the relationship between sex, the emotions and ethics?

In the summer of the year in which Freud published his lesbian case history, another lesbian, this time a young Englishwoman, Vita Sackville-West, lay down in a field in Sussex and began to write her autobiography. She was 28 years old, a published poet and novelist, wife of diplomat Harold Nicolson, mother of two small boys, and – in her most recent incarnation – lover and travelling companion of Violet Trefusis. As readers of *Portrait of a Marriage*, and viewers of the BBC and PBS, will know, her various identities were in radical conflict with one another. As she took up her pen, her marriage was shaky, her sons scarcely knew who she was, and her future with Trefusis was in doubt. The writing of her memoirs was a kind of rescue operation, an attempt to draw a functional narrative of identity out of the chaos of her emotional history. Like Freud's analysis of her Viennese counterpart, Sackville-West's autobiography is a project of reparation. In it she anatomizes her own guilt and insistently exonerates her husband of any blame. It is as if she is trying to make amends – to take responsibility for all the hurt she has caused him. Freud and his patient begin her analysis at the instigation of the girl's father, who wants them to 'cure' her homosexuality, and to make up for all the humiliation and pain his daughter has caused him. But from the beginning Freud holds out little hope. The truth is, he says, that the girl feels morally perfectly justified. In spite of the co-operative tone of the remarks I quoted in the extract, Freud notes that she has no real feeling of guilt, no anxiety on which together they might build a transference. Where Vita Sackville-West describes herself as sadistic and perverse, Freud's patient enters analysis without any sense of past wrongdoing. Indeed, Freud discovers that, if anything, it gives her pleasure to cause her parents pain. He is sceptical about the outcome of the analysis: 'in general, to undertake to convert a fully developed homosexual into a heterosexual does not offer much more prospect of success than the reverse, except that for good practical reasons the latter is never attempted' (p. 376). Both he and the patient start the analysis already half convinced that it will not give the father what he wants. There are complicated and intractable reasons for the patient's sexual make-up, and her investments in them are too intense either for her to want to change, or for Freud to believe that she can.

Although Freud refers in the case history to 'a fully developed homosexual' (p. 376), he also acknowledges that the patient's attachment has its origins in a bisexual disposition:

> Her lady's slender figure, severe beauty, and downright manner reminded her of the brother who was a little older than herself. Her latest choice corresponded, therefore, not only to her feminine but also to her masculine ideal; it combined satisfaction of the homosexual tendency with that of the heterosexual one. (p. 382)

Sackville-West too, as we saw in the extract, conceived of herself in terms of a fundamental dualism, but in her hands the concept has a number of ramifications. 'I see now that my whole curse has been a duality with which I was too weak and too self-indulgent to struggle' (p. 38). Much later in the manuscript (p. 108) Sackville-West will gloss 'duality' as an alternation between masculinity and femininity. Here, however, it seems to refer both to her desire for women (against which, it is implied, she should have struggled), and to a moral schizophrenia in which her 'pure' side is associated with Harold and heterosexual marriage, and her 'perverted nature' with her relations with women. In 'loving' Rosamund she also tyrannized over her, and in leaving her she failed to feel any remorse or sympathy. The 'perversion' she describes is a moral, emotional and sexual dereliction.

Vita Sackville-West went to books for an explanation of her puzzling sexual identity. Victoria Glendinning, in her biography of Sackville-West, comments that on her bookshelves at the time of her death in 1962 were Havelock Ellis's *Sexual Inversion* (1897), inscribed by Harold Nicolson, a copy of Edward Carpenter's *The Intermediate Sex* (1908), and a heavily annotated copy of Otto Weininger's *Sex and Character* (1903). Sackville-West apparently read Weininger during the very early days of her affair with Trefusis.[3] Ellis and Weininger are also cited in Freud's earliest systematic account of human sexuality, the *Three Essays on the Theory of Sexuality* (1905). Even though names such as these are absent from the much later 'Case of Homosexuality in a Woman', it is clear that throughout his career Freud's elaboration of concepts such as the sexual object and the sexual aim owes much to earlier sexologists. Arnold I. Davidson has argued that in the *Three Essays* Freud paradoxically both shared the assumptions of earlier theorists of perversion such as Richard von Krafft-Ebing and Albert Moll, *and* overturned their conceptual underpinnings: 'by claiming, in effect, that there is no natural object of the sexual instinct, that the sexual object and sexual instinct are merely soldered together, Freud dealt a conceptually devastating blow to the entire structure of nineteenth-

century theories of sexual psychopathology'.[4] But, as Davidson points
out, Freud did of course also share 'conceptual space' with many of the
theories his work overturned.[5] One of those shared spaces was a vision of
the homosexual body as an emotional as well as a sexual entity. Even
though in the *Three Essays* homosexuality is classed as a *sexual* rather
than an emotional aberration, in the case history of a lesbian that followed fifteen years later, Freud is clear that his patient had no sexual
contact with the woman she pursued, or indeed with any other. But unlike
Ellis and Carpenter, Freud did not celebrate the ability to love. In 'A Case
of Homosexuality in a Woman' and elsewhere, he defines love itself as an
aberrational behaviour.

The manuscript that Sackville-West started writing on that July evening
in 1920 was finally finished about nine months later in March 1921. It is
structured as a journal in which, day by day, Sackville-West recalls and
records the events of the years leading up to its writing. Its formal features
are those of conventional autobiography: a first section describing Sackville-
West's family history, her childhood, her marriage, and the birth of her
children, and a second section, in which the sensational (and *sensational-
ized*) events for which the first section is a preparation unfold. In these
pages, she is seduced by Violet Trefusis, elopes with her to France, and
after three tortured years together, including repeated attempts to break
entirely with their husbands (who are meanwhile in hot pursuit of them),
the women return to their homes. At the end of the manuscript, Sackville-
West expresses her uncertainty about the future. In fact, she remained
married, and continued to sleep with women, for the rest of her life.

After she wrote the closing words, on 28 March 1921, Sackville-West
placed the notebook in a leather bag, locked the bag, and hid it in a corner
of the little book-lined turret-room which opens off her sitting-room at
Sissinghurst. No-one ever entered this room except Sackville-West. Even
when she was wanted on the telephone, or for meals, family members
would merely come to the foot of the turret staircase and call up to her.
The elaborate secretion of the manuscript, then, was a form of theatre, a
dramatization for herself of the story's status as a secret that must never
be told. It implied that the manuscript must be hidden both for her own
protection and for the protection of others whose names were concealed
in it (she used pseudonyms throughout). But in fact she and Trefusis had
been anything but discreet, and their story was already widely known and
gossiped about. Her disposition of the manuscript was as much a symptomatic performance of her own shame as a genuine effort at discretion.

That theatre of shame would continue to play itself out in the encounters that followed. The manuscript remained unread and presumably un-
touched by anyone but Sackville-West for the next forty years. Then, after

Sackville-West's death in 1962, her son Nigel, sorting out her belongings in the once-forbidden room, stumbled on the leather bag. 'The bag contained something – a tiara in its case, for all I knew. Having no key, I cut the leather from around its lock to open it' (PM, p. 1). The Oedipal, or even pre-Oedipal, reverberations of this scene – the son taking a knife to his mother's locked bag – are hardly deflected by Nicolson's defensive fantasy that the bag will contain only his mother's jewels.[6] Disingenuously, he seems to want his readers to know that his mother was an aristocrat who might carelessly leave her tiara lying around in an old bag. In a classically reparatory move, Nicolson attempts to give his mother back some of her authority (and to warn readers of his own superior class status) even as he prepares to expose her vulnerability and her shame.

Nicolson's shame, though, is as theatrical as his mother's. In saying this I do not mean to impugn the sincerity of either one of them. As Eve Kosofsky Sedgwick has shown us, shame is always a form of theatre, a kind of exhibitionism agonizingly turned in on itself:

> Shame effaces itself; shame points and projects; shame turns itself skin side outside; shame and pride, shame and dignity, shame and self-display, shame and exhibitionism are different interlinings of the same glove: shame, it might finally be said, transformational shame, is *performance*.[7]

The worst thing about being ashamed, as everyone knows, is that shame draws attention to itself: it is a kind of performance, like Sackville-West's elaborately unnecessary concealment of her manuscript. Nicolson's lengthy justification of his publication of his mother's manuscript is perhaps another case in point. 'Let not the reader condemn in ten minutes', he admonishes, 'a decision which I have pondered for ten years' (p. 2). Whose shame is he performing here, his mother's or his own? Each person who comes into contact with the manuscript is anxious to contain or to ward off its contagion. Nicolson remarks that although he had long known the story Sackville-West tells in the autobiography, he had not known it from her (p. 2), and suggests too that as she wrote, she increasingly told the story 'as if it were not her own experience that she was describing but another's' (p. 2). As Nicolson describes it, each transmission of the narrative is also a process of estrangement: his mother tells it as if it had happened to someone else, and he learns it in a way that only confirms his distance from her. Nowhere does he say that reading her intimate history first-hand made him feel closer to her or helped him to understand her better. This story of marital estrangement, then, has its own power to estrange. Its claim to truth ('I [write] urged', Sackville-West says, 'by a necessity of truth-telling, because there is no living soul who knows the complete truth' (p. 9)) is also a well-rehearsed gesture from the theatre of confession: a declaration of emotional authenticity rather than an invitation to intimacy.

Although the story is ritually disowned by both mother and son, Sackville-West also claims it as typical. It belongs to no one, perhaps, because it could belong to anyone. Sackville-West invokes this possibility when she says that she is not writing the manuscript 'for fun' (p. 107), but partly because she believes that as time goes on, 'the psychology of people like myself will be a matter of interest' (p. 107):

> I advance, therefore, the perfectly accepted theory that cases of dual personality do exist, in which the feminine and the masculine elements alternately preponderate. I advance this in an impersonal and scientific spirit, and claim that I am qualified to speak with the intimacy a professional scientist could acquire only after years of study and indirect information, because I have the object of study always to hand, in my own heart, and can gauge the exact truthfulness of what my own experience tells me. (p. 108)

Sackville-West claims a representative status for her sexual make-up: in an odd locution she argues that her story 'advances' – presumably, develops – a well-established theory of dual personality. She claims to examine herself as if she were a kind of scientific experiment, a newly evolving species, or 'sport', as Ellis would have it.[8] But Sackville-West argues that, unlike a professional scientist, she can enhance her 'case' with the spice of intimacy, a spice that paradoxically only intensifies her claim to scientific detachment.[9] The tone of her narration is thus a complex negotiation of the impersonal – she tells her own story as if it were someone else's – and of the chaotically personal. But in spite of her disclaimers the autobiography makes few attempts, other than that quoted above, to analyse lesbianism as a sexuality. Most of it is taken up with a kind of defiantly penitential self-justification: of her love-making with Trefisis during her honeymoon, she writes of the inexcusability of her behaviour and the depth of her suffering; of Nicolson's parents she comments: '[I] felt my alienation from them and my affinity with Violet so keenly that I only wanted to fly where I would not pollute their purity any longer' (p. 119). 'I am so frightened', she writes; and 'I say this with deep shame' (p. 39). It is tempting to argue that Sackville-West has fleshed out the skeletal stories of sexological science with the substance of her own shame. But to read things this way would be to miss the point of much contemporary sexology, and especially of that which Sackville-West was reading. For Carpenter, Ellis and Weininger rarely distinguish between sexual and emotional feelings. Personal narratives – accounts of intimate emotion – are the stuff of their scientific work. Ellis wrote to Carpenter in 1894, for example, that: 'I shall make my cases the kernel of my book, [. . .] and shall simply argue, so far as I argue, from the cases I present.'[10] Sackville-West's history of her body in *Portrait of a Marriage*, like many of Ellis's case histories, is also the story of her guilty soul and mind, the staging of a public confession.

The role of the emotions – guilt, fear, shame, love – in psychic life was increasingly a cause of controversy in psychiatric and sexological circles as Ellis laboured on *Sexual Inversion* and the succeeding volumes of his *Studies in the Psychology of Sex*. Attempts to define and locate the unconscious became entangled in endless debate about the nature of the instincts and their relation to the emotions. William McDougall, reader in mental philosophy at the University of Oxford, and founder member of the Medico-Psychological Clinic in London in 1913, maintained that instincts were essentially emotional phenomena:

> We may, then, define an instinct as an inherited or innate psycho-physical disposition which determines its possessor to perceive, and to pay attention to, objects of a certain class, to experience an emotional excitement of a particular quality upon perceiving such an object, and to act in regard to it in a particular manner, or, at least, to experience an impulse to such action.[11]

Instincts for McDougall always involve the emotions: they are part of the life of the feelings as much as of the life of the body. He commends psychoanalysis for the attention it pays to instincts and their vicissitudes, but also criticizes it for its emphasis on the primacy of the sexual instinct (for McDougall, it was fear, not sexual feeling, that was the most forceful and most complex emotion).[12] It is important to note, though, that in defining sexual feeling as an instinct, McDougall is implicitly stating its imbrication with emotional, as much as somatic, states. American psychiatrist Morton Prince developed McDougall's theories even further to argue not only that instinctual experiences were always emotional, but also that psychic energy was primarily emotional rather than libidinal.[13] Even as Freud intensified his stress on the libido as the motive force of psychic life, other eminent psychologists were elaborating a theory of the instincts that subordinated sexual feeling to the power of the emotions.

This philosophy seems partly to have shaped Ellis's work. Although his *Sexual Inversion* categorizes homosexuality (or 'inversion') as a form of sexual behaviour, his case histories (especially those of lesbians) tend to concentrate not on anatomy (although some of his patients did undergo internal examinations), but on stories of romantic attachment and acute emotional sensibility. Many of his studies are of subjects whose sexual histories did not include any sexual activity at all. Take Miss M., for example, who fell in love first with a teacher's face in a window, then with the sight of a visitor in the next-door garden, and finally with an invalid friend to whom she gave the most devoted care. 'Love is with me a reli-gion', she wrote.[14] Sexual feeling, for Miss M., was a way of approaching and intensifying the holiness of emotion. Ellis includes her in his chapter on sexual inversion in women without any sense of incongruence.

This was in itself a revisionary practice. Ellis's main contribution to homosexual rights has usually been taken to be his critical attitude to the work of such earlier sexologists as Krafft-Ebing, whose 1886 *Psychopathia Sexualis* had argued that homosexuality was a form of pathological degeneration.[15] Ellis argued that inversion was congeni-tal, but he diverged from Krafft-Ebing in his insistence on its non-degenerative nature. Inverts for Ellis (whose own wife Edith was a lesbian) were often characterized by their capacity for mental work, and their ability to form devoted and sustained attachments, like Miss M.'s. Freud wrote in 1914 that 'we must begin to love in order that we may not fall ill' (although elsewhere, as we shall see, he described love itself as a kind of illness); Ellis likewise assumed that if we loved wisely and well we were by definition in good psychic and moral health.[16] Part of his challenge to the degenerate theory lay in his emphasis on wom-en's love, rather than their desire, for one another. Ellis defended lesbi-anism as a moral behaviour even as he implicitly – and perhaps unwittingly – eclipsed its sexual possibilities. For women like Miss M., love *was* sex; or, as Freud said of his hysterics, 'the symptoms of the disease are nothing else than *the patient's sexual activity*'.[17] This mobil-ity of erotic feeling, its chameleon-like quality, became the cornerstone of Freud's thinking about sexuality, but it was already implicit in much of the work on which he built. Indeed the conflation of sex and emotion was one of early sexology's gifts to psychoanalysis, the formulation which made it possible for Freud to think of sexual desire as a labile and mutable appetite.[18]

It would be wrong, however, to assume that later sexologists were not themselves concerned about the role of the emotions in sexual life; indeed, some were specifically anxious to draw distinctions be-tween emotional and sexual feeling. Carpenter, the gay socialist and freethinker who wrote a number of books in defence of homosexu-ality, introduces one of his most significant publications with an an-nouncement of his intention to sort out the sexological confusion of love and sexual feeling. At the beginning of *The Intermediate Sex* (1908) he writes:

> The word Love is commonly used in so general and almost indis-criminate a fashion as to denote sometimes physical instincts and acts, and sometimes the most intimate and profound feelings; and in this way a good deal of misunderstanding is caused. In this

book [. . .] the word is used to denote the inner devotion of one person to another; and when anything else is meant – as, for instance, sexual relations and actions – this is clearly stated and expressed.[19]

The linguistic demarcation that Carpenter sets up between loving feelings and sexual acts is partly, of course, strategic rather than scientific. Carpenter is concerned to defend homosexual men. By stressing the significance of the emotional, rather than the physical, aspect of sexual relations, he can also argue, as Beverly Thiele comments, for 'the greater moral rectitude' of gay love, which was, in his experience, often unconsummated.[20] Eroticism between men, in his version of things, easily reaches a state of transcendence not because of its sexual possibilities, but because of its tendency 'to run along *emotional* channels'.[21] Most gay men, he says, have intensely emotional temperaments: 'extremely complex, tender, sensitive, pitiful and loving, "full of storm and stress, of ferment and fluctuation" of the heart; [. . .] intuition is always strong; [. . .] often a dreamer, of brooding, reserved habits'.[22] In spite then, of his avowed desire to differentiate between emotional states of being and sexual acts, Carpenter describes inversion as an emotional, rather than a sexual, morphology, and even if we allow for his investment in desexualizing gay relations as a kind of PR operation, the gay body in his texts is still primarily a phenomenon of the life of the feelings.

In valuing this sentimental body, Carpenter also values the cultural contribution of women. His vision of a 'third sex', which was taken over by Vita Sackville-West in her account of herself as both masculine and feminine, celebrates 'feminine' talents such as understanding, mediation and support: he urges that 'urnings' (as he terms homosexuals) have a specific part to play as reconcilers of the sexes to one another.[23] Ellis's refusal to condemn 'feminine' men or 'masculine' women shifts in Carpenter's work into a gay politics that partly depends on feminist assumptions. Carpenter welcomes, for example, the possibility of a political community organized around sexuality, and notes that already many lesbians have found a common interest in the suffrage movement.[24] This incipient consonance of gay and feminist interests in the discourse of sexology is in tension, however, with many of the assumptions of other contemporary sexual philosophers including – or perhaps especially – those of Weininger and, to a lesser extent, of the later Freud. While Freud, by 1920, still imagined the homosexual body primarily in emotional terms, he no longer saw those emotions as its saving grace. A politics that does not value love finds it hard to value women, so persistently associated with the capacity to love. Women may have paid the price for Freud's development of a model for a non-pathologized gay body, by his simultaneous investment in a language that pathologized both love and femininity itself.

Weininger's infamous *Sex and Character* was first published in 1903, two years before the first edition of Freud's ground-breaking *Three Essays*. Many critics have commented on the anticipation of Nazi ideologies in Weininger's radically anti-semitic comments; Freud himself, footnoting Weininger in a 1924 edition of the *Three Essays*, notes that *Sex and Character* is 'somewhat unbalanced', although he does credit Weininger with the popularization of the notion of a universal bisexuality.[25] The bisexual body is indeed about the only one that escapes excoriation in Weininger's philosophy. Jews and women, for example, are identified as sharing one 'non-moral', irreligious temperament: 'the homology of Jew and woman becomes closer the further examination goes. [. . .] Greatness is absent from the nature of the woman and the Jew, the greatness of morality, or the greatness of evil.'[26] This imbrication of misogyny with anti-semitism is linked to a bleakly nihilistic vision of a body which is incapable of bringing together sexual feeling and love:

> It is quite erroneous to say that sexuality and eroticism, sexual impulse and love, are fundamentally one and the same thing, the second an embellishing, refining, spiritualising sublimation of the first; although practically all medical men hold this view, and even such men as Kant and Schopenhauer thought so.[27]

Weininger's evidence for this is anecdotal: 'sexual attraction', he remarks, 'increases with physical proximity; love is strongest in the absence of the loved one'.[28] In fact, Weininger argues that it is impossible to love actual women; men who love women can do so only by projecting onto them their own narcissistic ideal. Women, conversely, who have 'no existence and no essence', cannot love. Their only function in the world is as the 'pairing agent': 'when man became sexual he formed woman. That woman is at all has happened simply because man has accepted his sexuality. Woman is merely the result of this affirmation; she is sexuality itself.'[29] Women, like Jews, are assigned bodies whose only valence is sexual. They have no moral or ethical agency; and they have no emotional reality of their own. In distinguishing between sex and love, Weininger places women squarely on the side of sex; and men, uncomfortably, on the side of the emotions, endlessly struggling and failing to reconcile their capacities to desire and to love.

Freud himself had remarkably little to say specifically about love. In the *Three Essays* he classes it among the sexual aberrations, defining it as a mode of 'overvaluation' of the love object.[30] Like Weininger, he implies that it is a pathology; and like Weininger, he emphasizes the narcissistic dimension of the experience of love. But Freud was far more circumspect than Weininger in his characterization of women's moral inadequacies. Famously, he remarked in the 1933 essay on femininity that women inevitably had less well-developed super-egos than men, and were therefore inferior moral beings.[31] The battle over Freud's usefulness for feminism has been fought long and hard, and I do not intend to rehearse it here.[32] My interest lies rather in Freud's extension of the concept of perversion to cover love itself, an extension which paradoxically allowed him to write relatively neutrally, at least by the 1920 case history, about homosexuality as a *sexual* identity. This neutrality derives, as I have suggested, both from Freud's scepticism about love as a redemptive capability and, in this particular case history, from the patient's own refusal to adopt a confessional mode. Sackville-West's framing of her own story as 'confession' (p. 9) means that even in *Portrait of a Marriage* lesbianism is inevitably read within an ethical framework.

Freud, like Havelock Ellis before him, notes that his patient has not had sexual relations with the woman she loves. Their relationship revolved around a romantic courtship in which the girl expressed her 'devoted admiration' for her beloved by 'waiting for her for hours outside her door or at a tram-halt, [by] sending her gifts of flowers, and so on' (CH, p. 372). It is not because the girl is capable of such an ardent attachment that he refuses to concur with the girl's father that she is either 'vicious', 'degenerate' or 'mentally afflicted' (p. 373). Rather, he argues that 'the girl was not in any way ill (she did not suffer from anything in herself, nor did she complain about her condition) [. . .] the girl had never been neurotic, and came to the analysis without even one hysterical symptom' (pp. 375, 381). As Mandy Merck points out, Freud's own terms (at least if we follow the taxonomies of the 1905 *Three Essays*) would classify the girl as perverse, rather than neurotic.[33] In some ways, of course, this formulation continues to frame homosexuality as a non-normative, aberrant sexuality, and it is significant that in fact, Freud, anxious here to defend homosexuality as a functional way of being, refrains from using the word 'perversion' in the case history itself (the nearest he gets is 'abnormality' (p. 380)). What interests me here, though, is Freud's characterization of the girl's emotional make-up. It becomes part of her 'abnormal' development that her attachment to the woman she loves is extravagantly sensitive and romantic:

> I mentioned the fact that in her behaviour to her adored lady the girl had adopted the characteristic masculine type of love. Her humility and her tender lack of pretensions, '*che poco spera e nulla chiede*', her bliss when she was allowed to accompany the lady a little way and to kiss her hand on parting, her joy when she heard her praised as beautiful [. . .], her pilgrimages to places once visited by the loved

one, the silence of all more sensual wishes – all these little traits in
her resembled the first passionate adoration of a youth for a celebrated actress whom he regards as far above him, to whom he
scarcely dares lift his bashful eyes. (p.387)[34]

In this image of a lesbian relationship the self-forgetful form of the girl's
love is part of its anomalous nature. Far from redeeming her as a noble
and loving presence, as it would have done for Carpenter or for Ellis, it
becomes symptomatic of the girl's maladjusted relationship to her own
gender. Her 'masculinity complex', with its attendant capacity for courtly
love, is responsible also for her feminist opinions, ascribed later in the
case history to her 'pronounced envy for the penis' (p.397). Freud manages to suggest, then, both that the girl's feminism is a perverse formation, and that her capacity for devotion, as much as her choice of a sexual
object, is what marks her out as abnormal. She loses both ways: if she
asserts herself in love she is a perverse feminist; if she effaces herself she is
behaving like a man. It is hard to imagine a version of femininity that does
not partake at least partly of one of these scenarios. As Jacqueline Rose
puts it in her discussion of this case, 'either the girl is neurotic (which she
clearly is not) or all women are neurotic (which indeed they might be)'.[35]
As in the work of Weininger, it is not lesbians but *women* who are
pathologized here. It seems as if both Weininger and Freud could develop
a gay politics (admittedly, of a very attenuated kind) only by virtue of
intensifying their tendencies to misogyny.

Freud's patient then, although not condemned for her sexuality, is not
redeemed by her capacity to love, either. We have been used to thinking of
late nineteenth- and early twentieth-century sexology as the discursive
moment in which a systematic science of sexuality – and particularly gay
sexuality – was born. But in fact, in these writings it is the definition of
love, as much as of sexuality, which is at issue. Ellis and Carpenter looked
to love to redeem the fallen nature of their homosexual patients and subjects; but for Freud, as for Weininger, love – and women – were part of the
problem. Nigel Nicolson defended Vita Sackville-West, who, he says,
'fought for the right to love' (PM, p. 173). But even if we believe this, by
the time she was fighting, 'love' was considered, in some quarters, no
longer to be worth fighting for.

Notes

1 Sigmund Freud, 'The Psychogenesis of a Case of Homosexuality in a Woman',
   in *Case Histories II*, ed. Angela Richards, Penguin Freud Library, vol. IX (Penguin, Harmondsworth, 1979), p.378. All subsequent references to this text
   (CH) will be to this edition.

2 Nigel Nicolson, *Portrait of a Marriage*, 1973 (repr. Futura, London, 1974), p. 38. All further references to *Portrait of a Marriage* (PM) will be to this edition.

3 See Victoria Glendinning, *Vita: A Biography of Vita Sackville-West* (Quill, New York, 1983), p. 405.

4 See Arnold I. Davidson, 'How to Do the History of Psychoanalysis: A Reading of Freud's *Three Essays on the Theory of Sexuality*', in *The Trial(s) of Psychoanalysis*, ed. Françoise Meltzer (University of Chicago Press, Chicago, 1988), pp. 39–64, 51–2. Richard von Krafft-Ebing was the author of *Psychopathia Sexualis, with Especial Reference to the Antipathic Sexual Instinct: A Medico-Forensic Study* (1886), and Albert Moll published *Perversions of the Sexual Instinct: A Study of Sexual Inversion* in 1891.

5 Davidson, 'How to Do the History of Psychoanalysis', p. 44.

6 See Freud, 'Fragment of an Analysis of a Case of Hysteria ("Dora")', 1905, in *Case Histories I*, tr. James Strachey, Penguin Freud Library, vol. VIII (Penguin, Harmondsworth, 1977), p.105. Freud tells Dora: 'perhaps you do not know that "jewel-case" (*"Schmuck-Kästchen"*) is a favourite expression for [. . .] the female genitals'.

7 Eve Kosofsky Sedgwick, 'Shame and Performativity: Henry James's New York Edition Prefaces', in *Henry James's New York Edition: The Construction of Authorship*, ed. David McWhirter (Stanford University Press, Stanford, 1995), pp. 206–39, 211.

8 See Havelock Ellis and John Addington Symonds, *Sexual Inversion*, 1897 (repr. Arno, New York, 1975), p. 133: 'thus in sexual inversion we have what may fairly be called a "sport" or variation, one of those organic variations which we see throughout living nature, in plants and in animals'.

9 Sackville-West's image of alternation, of a serially gendered personality, combines the beliefs of late nineteenth-century homosexual activists, such as Karl Heinrich Ulrichs, with the findings of contemporary psychiatric practice. Ulrichs argued in the 1860s that homosexuality was the result of the development of a masculine sexual drive in a feminine body (or *vice versa*); American psychiatrist Morton Prince wrote extensively about the case of Miss Beauchamp, whose three personalities sometimes communicated with each other by pinning notes to the mirror. See Morton Prince, *The Dissociation of a Personality: A Biographical Study in Abnormal Psychology*, 1905, 2nd edn (1908; repr. Longman, London, 1910). The detail about the notes comes from Miss Beauchamp's own autobiographical account, published under the acronym B.C.A. (Prince named her personalities A, B and C). See B.C.A., *My Life as a Dissociated Personality* (Richard C. Badger, Boston, 1909), p. 13. Sackville-West describes a personality in which feminine and masculine appear, not simultaneously, as in Ulrich's model, but in sequence, as in Prince's.

10 Havelock Ellis to Edward Carpenter, 22 January 1894, cited in Scott McCracken, 'Writing the Body: Edward Carpenter, George Gissing, and Late-Nineteenth-Century Radicalism', in *Edward Carpenter and Late Victorian Radicalism*, ed. Tony Brown (Frank Cass, London, 1990), pp. 178–200, 181.

11 William McDougall, *An Introduction to Social Psychology*, 1908, 15th edn. (Methuen, London, 1920), p. 29. The Medico-Psychological Clinic, founded

in 1913 by Jessie Murray and Julia Turner, was the first institution in Britain to offer psychoanalytic therapy and training. See Theophilus E. M. Boll, 'May Sinclair and the Medico-Psychological Clinic', *Proceedings of the American Philosophical Society*, 106 (1962), pp. 310–26.

12 McDougall, *An Introduction to Social Psychology*, pp. viii–ix, 55. During five years of military service during World War I, McDougall treated numerous soldiers who were suffering from various neurotic disorders, and post-war editions of *An Introduction to Social Psychology* stress the significance of fear for psychic development (see ibid., p. xvii).

13 See Morton Prince, *The Unconscious: The Fundamentals of Human Personality Normal and Abnormal* (Macmillan, New York, 1914), p. 447.

14 Ellis and Symonds, *Sexual Inversion*, p. 89.

15 See Jeffrey Weeks, *Coming Out: Homosexual Politics in Britain, from the Nineteenth Century to the Present*, 1977 (repr. Quartet, London, 1983), p. 26.

16 See Freud, 'On Narcissism: An Introduction', 1914, in *General Psychological Theory*, ed. Philip Rieff (Collier, New York, 1963), p. 66. The complex arbitration between diseased and healthy psyches is amply illustrated in the twists and turns of the Miss Beauchamp case. Morton Prince decides that the third personality to appear is 'the real Miss Beauchamp', because she is 'a natural person with whom one [can] talk frankly and freely without arousing angry opposition on the one hand, and without inducing depression on the other, who [is] ready to co-operate intelligently and efficiently for her own good' (Prince, *The Dissociation of a Personality*, p. 520). Here psychic health is equated with a compliant attitude to psychotherapy.

17 See Freud, 'Fragment of an Analysis of a Case of Hysteria', p. 156.

18 See, for example, Freud's distinction between hunger and the libido in this regard: 'a light is thrown on the nature of the sexual instinct by the fact that it permits of so much variation in its objects and such a cheapening of them – which hunger, with its far more energetic retention of its objects, would only permit in the most extreme instances' (Freud, *Three Essays on the Theory of Sexuality*, 1905, tr. James Strachey (Basic Books, New York, 1962), p. 14).

19 Edward Carpenter, *Selected Writings: Volume I: Sex*, ed. Noel Greig (Gay Men's Press, London, 1984), p. 188.

20 Beverly Thiele, 'Coming-of-Age: Edward Carpenter on Sex and Reproduction', in Brown, *Edward Carpenter and Late Victorian Radicalism*, pp. 100–25, 107.

21 Carpenter, *Selected Writings*, p. 214.

22 Ibid., p. 197.

23 Ibid., p. 240.

24 Ibid., p. 219.

25 Freud, *Three Essays on the Theory of Sexuality*, p.9. See the essays in *Jews and Gender: Responses to Otto Weininger*, ed. Nancy Harrowitz (Temple University Press, Philadelphia, 1995) for a full discussion of Weininger's views on Jews and Judaism. Weininger was himself both Jewish and a homosexual.

26 Otto Weininger, *Sex and Character*, 1903, 6th edn (Heinemann, London, 1972), p. 309.

27 Ibid., p. 237.

28 Ibid., p. 239.
29 Ibid., pp. 286, 298, 299.
30 Freud, *Three Essays on the Theory of Sexuality*, pp. 16–17.
31 See Freud, 'Femininity', 1933, in *New Introductory Lectures on Psychoanalysis*, tr. James Strachey, Penguin Freud Library, vol. II (Penguin, Harmondsworth, 1973), p. 163: 'In the absence of fear of castration the chief motive is lacking which leads boys to surmount the Oedipus complex. Girls remain in it for an indeterminate length of time; they demolish it late and, even so, incompletely. In these circumstances the formation of the super-ego must suffer; it cannot attain the strength and independence which give it its cultural significance.'
32 See, for example, Juliet Mitchell's defence of Freud in *Psychoanalysis and Feminism* (Penguin, Harmondsworth, 1974). Other relevant texts include Teresa Brennan, ed., *Between Feminism and Psychoanalysis* (Routledge, New York, 1989), and Rachel Bowlby, *Still Crazy After All These Years: Women, Writing and Psychoanalysis* (Routledge, New York, 1992).
33 Mandy Merck, 'The Train of Thought in Freud's "Case of Homosexuality in a Woman"', in *Perversions: Deviant Readings* (Virago, London, 1993), p. 15.
34 The quotation is from Tasso, *La Gerusalemme Liberata*, Canto II, Stanza 16, and is translated in the Penguin edition of Freud's 'The Psychogenesis of a Case of Homosexuality in a Woman' as 'hopes for little and asks for nothing'.
35 Jacqueline Rose, 'Dora: Fragment of an Analysis', in *In Dora's Case: Freud, Hysteria, Feminism*, eds Charles Bernheimer and Claire Kahane (Virago, London, 1985), pp. 128–48, 136.

10 Havelock Ellis, Sigmund Freud and the State: Discourses of Homosexual Identity in Interwar Britain

Chris Waters

In the English-speaking world, psychoanalytic accounts of the aetiology of homosexuality had, by the 1950s, come to dominate much 'official' thinking on the subject. Nowhere was this more the case than in the United States, where faith in modern science led not only to the valorization of psychoanalytic expertise, but to the marginalization of earlier sexological models of erotic desire that were based on premises quite distinct from those of Freud and his followers. In Britain, where doctors remained cautious about the 'cures' for homosexuality being advocated by American Freudians, discussion of the subject was, nevertheless, increasingly couched in Freudian terms. Gordon Westwood's *Society and the Homosexual*, along with D.J. West's *Homosexuality*, were both indebted to a model of psychosexual development that originated with Freud. West's study was prefaced by Dr Hermann Mannheim, a psychoanalytically oriented criminologist; Westwood's by Dr Edward Glover, who had established the Institute for the Scientific Treatment of Delinquency in 1932, a Freudian-inspired treatment centre through the doors of which passed a number of so-called 'homosexual offenders'. Moreover, in their calls for an end to criminal sanctions against most forms of homosexual activity, both West and Westwood borrowed the findings of Sir William Norwood East. Contributing to the debate around the work of the Wolfenden Committee, which urged the decriminalization of homosexuality in 1957, East offered his own study of the subject, an outgrowth of his 1930s, quasi-Freudian, investigation of the psychological treatment of crime.[1]

The psychoanalytic discourse of homosexuality not only came to provide many of the categories through which the topic was debated in the

1950s, but it also influenced the self-understanding of those gay men who 'came out' and took their case to the public. Notable in this respect was the journalist Peter Wildeblood, who was found guilty of homosexual offences and imprisoned in 1954. Upon his release, he published the story of his life, a life cast awkwardly in a language derived both from Freud and from the writings of Havelock Ellis. At times he spoke of an 'innate condition', of the 'congenital invert', of a 'tragic disability' for which there was no cure, casting himself in terms that were ascendant until the 1930s in Britain, terms consolidated by Ellis in his classic study, *Sexual Inversion*. But Wildeblood also spoke the language of Freud: he referred to friendships between boys which had 'an unconsciously homosexual basis'; he dissected individuals who went through a homosexual stage before making 'the natural transition into normality'; and he conceived of homosexuality in terms of 'arrested development'. In short, his life-story is an awkward story – a life defended by a psychiatrist in court, a story that moved uneasily back and forth between two, distinct understandings of homosexuality.[2]

It is this phenomenon – this homosexual self-fashioning born of both Freudian theory and a sexological discourse that was largely antithetical to the Freudian project – that is very much a post-war phenomenon in Britain. While the psychoanalytic language of homosexuality was certainly available between the wars, rarely did it inform those life-stories, or pleas for tolerance, written by gay men and lesbians during these years. Homosexual selfhood, as narrated by well-educated writers, was *not* cast in Freudian terms; rather, it depended on models of ancient Greek male friendship, reworked by Victorian Hellenists, or on ideas of a third sex – the homosexual as the embodiment of a male soul trapped in a female body, or vice versa – put forward by Karl Heinrich Ulrichs and Richard von Krafft-Ebing and circulated in Britain by Edward Carpenter. It was also indebted to the work of Havelock Ellis, who both documented homosexual experience and provided the terms through which that experience was often understood between the wars. It is well known, for example, that the novelist Radclyffe Hall ignored Freud and embraced the image of the mannish lesbian advanced by Ellis.[3] Equally important, though much less well known, is the case of 'anomaly', the pseudonymous author of the 1927 study, *The Invert and his Social Adjustment*, whose choice of a name – 'anomaly' – reflected Ellis's preferred term for homosexuality, a term that for him avoided any taint of pathology.[4]

Although writing at a time when Freudian ideas circulated widely in Britain, and when, as we shall see, criminologists were making use of Freud in their own attempts to classify and treat homosexuality as a form of pathological behaviour, 'anomaly' was very much a pre-Freudian subject. While he had encountered the Freudian view that adult homosexuality was an outcome of arrested psychosexual development, he insisted that such ideas were 'stretched beyond the bounds of probability'. Rejecting Freud, 'anomaly' remained sympathetic to Ellis, believing homosexuality to be an innate condition: inversion, he wrote, 'is one of those strange things which happened when God was not looking'.[5] If we turn to other gay men who came of age between the wars but who, unlike 'anomaly', did not document their lives in writing, we also discover Freud's name to be conspicuous by its absence in their subsequent recollections. In the 1970s, several gay men born between 1897 and 1913 reflected on their interwar reading as one of those practices that shaped their sense of self. One of them referred to 'anomaly', while the names of Carpenter, Ellis, Hall and Plato were often mentioned; not once, however, was reference made to Freud.[6]

If, as we have seen in the case of Wildeblood, Freudian ideas have not entirely displaced Ellis's focus on the congenital disposition of the invert, they have at least come to supplement Ellis's ideas, and in some quarters to exert more authority. Yet few scholars have traced the manner by which Freud's account of the aetiology of homosexuality came to enjoy the credibility it has, a process that took place in Britain in the 1920s and 1930s. Two of Ellis's biographers are not helpful in this matter: both assume the 'natural' superiority of Freudian logic and are consequently harsh on Ellis. Phyllis Grosskurth, for example, argued that Ellis lacked Freud's 'creative genius' and merely recorded the manifestations of sexual behaviour without any epistemological framework through which to interpret them. 'As a pioneer', she wrote, Ellis 'ploughed the fields in the valley, but the great conquistador Freud surveyed the shattered detritus of the nineteenth century from a summit only he could ascend.'[7]

Despite such assertions, it was not at all 'natural' that psychoanalytic accounts of same-sex desire should come to acquire the status they have. Indeed, it is a phenomenon that needs to be explained, rather than assumed, particularly given the general reluctance of learned homosexuals in interwar Britain to adopt a Freudian subject position. In part, Freud's status in official discourses of homosexuality in the 1950s owes much to the efforts of Freud and his followers to discredit Ellis's work. Ernest Jones, Freud's anointed disciple in Britain, for example, often dismissed Ellis and his supporters. Although he wrote a kind review of 'anomaly's' book, claiming that it might disseminate 'tolerance for these unfortunate victims of maldevelopment', he complained that its author was 'inadequately informed on the scientific subject of cause and cure' and possessed 'no knowledge of the important contributions that psycho-analysis has made on both these points'.[8] Additionally, Freud's post-war status owes much to the work of those interwar criminologists who adopted psychoanalytic thinking in their own campaigns for penal reform, who were sent convicted homosexuals for treatment, and who managed to convince the state of the social benefits to be derived from taking their ideas seriously.

Ellis and Freud

Before turning to the work of interwar criminologists, it might be helpful to summarize, briefly, the major ideas of Freud and Ellis pertaining to homosexuality. Freud once claimed that the nature of inversion was such that it could be explained neither by the hypothesis that it was an innate condition, nor by the hypothesis that it was an acquired tendency.[9] Despite this assertion, each writer staked his claim to an understanding of the subject that was largely dependent on its mapping in terms of this opposition. Ellis held that homosexuality was a 'congenital anomaly' and he looked to the emerging science of endocrinology to explain this anomaly in hormonal terms, or what he referred to as an unco-ordination of the 'internal secretions'. In the 1915 edition of *Sexual Inversion*, he admitted that environmental factors external to an individual's biological make-up might excite the 'latent condition', although he insisted that such factors required 'a favourable organic predisposition' upon which to act.[10] It followed that Ellis had little sympathy for those who claimed to be able to 'cure' what for him was always an inborn condition.

Like the work of Ellis, that of Freud displayed a number of ambiguities, inconsistencies and uncertainties. Interested in the psychic mechanisms that determined sexual object choice, he opposed the work of sexologists who believed that homosexuals needed to be demarcated as a special category of person. It is 'possible to doubt the very existence of such a thing as innate inversion', he argued, claiming that every person was capable of making a homosexual object choice.[11] For Freud, homosexual and heterosexual object choices were simply two of the possible outcomes of each individual's psychic development and he rarely judged one to be superior to the other, despite his tendency to cast homosexuality as an inhibition of 'normal' psychosexual progress. As Diana Fuss has suggested, implicit in Freud's work is the notion that homosexuality is a regressive phenomenon, a 'falling back' into an earlier stage of development.[12] British criminologists often drew such conclusions from Freud, arguing that homosexuality was the result of 'arrested development' and hence treatable by therapeutic means. Freud was less sanguine about this, claiming that it was often futile to attempt to alter a well-established object choice, a point he reiterated in a letter he wrote in 1935 to an American mother of a homosexual son. In that letter Freud also told his correspondent that if she did not believe him she should 'read the books of Havelock Ellis'.[13] Despite this tribute to Ellis, however, it should be clear that in terms of their beliefs about homosexuality Freud and Ellis differed from each other in profound respects.

Freud's understanding of the aetiology of homosexuality came to supplement that advanced by Ellis. But the transition was a slow one, much more so than was the case in the United States. Although, prior to World War I, psychoanalytic ideas had been disseminated in learned circles in Britain, those who attempted to popularize Freud were cautious in discussing his work on sexuality.[14] Moreover, while Ernest Jones published the first book in English on psychoanalysis in 1912, he suggested that an awareness of Freud's importance in Britain only developed during the five years after the war.[15] Even then hostility remained. Reluctant to deal with sexual matters, the medical press had been hostile to the work of Ellis, although by 1910 it viewed him as an acceptable face of sexology, a home-grown product in a field dominated by foreigners. Such was not the case with Freud, who was seldom mentioned in the medical press throughout the 1920s. In a discussion of 'sexual perversion' in the *Lancet* in 1918, for example, Freud's name was conspicuous by its absence. One doctor tried to distinguish between perversions that were suitable for psychological treatment and those that were not. In so doing, he anticipated subsequent criminological debates, although he did not enlist Freud to legitimate his call for treatment in the way criminologists would.[16] Freud was also largely absent in the work of the British Society for the Study of Sex Psychology. Established in 1913 to urge various sex reforms, the organization at first looked promising to those who advocated Freudian ideas (Jones became a member in 1916). But interest in psychoanalysis waned and the society remained more indebted to the ideas of Hirschfeld, Ellis and Carpenter.[17]

Such reformers often felt they were better served in their work by Ellis than by Freud. For them, the congenital invert, as mapped by Ellis, could be imagined as an incurable object of pity, against whom penal sanctions should be removed. But the person whose homosexual condition resulted from 'arrested development' – whose status appeared to be acquired, rather than innate – was, in the hands of many of Freud's followers, suitable for treatment. While British Freudians were not as enthusiastic as many of their American counterparts about the prospects of 'curing' the homosexual, much of their interwar work broke with Freud in two important respects. First, while Freud believed that biological determinants remained a factor in the aetiology of homosexuality, his British followers were more environmentally disposed. When Freud first met Jones in 1908, he was struck by his would-be disciple's rejection of biology: he viewed Jones as a fanatic, later writing, 'to his mind [. . .] I am a reactionary'.[18] Second, and following from this, British Freudians were more willing to stress the benefits to be derived from therapeutic intervention in attempting to alter the object choice of their homosexual patients than was Freud. Jones, for example, once criticized Freud for his tolerant attitude to his famous lesbian patient, suggesting that much was to be gained if the path to heterosexual gratification was opened.[19]

Nowhere were these differences more evident than in the work of Thomas Ross, who argued that all homosexuals should be 'investigated psychologically' and helped to rise above those impediments 'which forbade the development of normal adult love'.[20] Ross claimed he could 'cure' his homosexual patients and demonstrated this through the case of a 47-year-old man he treated in 1925. This rather learned patient was familiar with Freudian thought: as Ross noted, by this time 'no widely-read person can hope to be in a state of virginity regarding it'.[21] Nevertheless, Ross's patient, like 'anomaly', insisted he was an invert, regarding his condition as innate, hereditary and inevitable. His doctor disagreed and urged him to consider a very different story about his desires, part of an effort to recast his patient as a Freudian subject. Through attempts to elicit repressed memories of enjoyable moments spent with women, Ross tried to convince him that he was 'not an obligatory homosexual', that he had merely been 'diverted from the heterosexual path'.[22] Soon thereafter, the patient began to fall in love with a woman: whatever virginity with regard to Freud he might have possessed when he began analysis was stolen from him during the course of treatment.

What is most significant about this study is not only its repudiation of Ellis's ideas, but the extent to which its promise of a cure depended on the manufacture of a new type of being, more susceptible to treatment than was Ellis's invert. While Ross's patient initially conceived of himself in Ellis-like terms, his self-understanding was reconfigured during analysis – or so his doctor liked to believe. In short, the work of those who championed Freudian ideas in the 1920s included, in part, an attempt to reconstruct the subjectivity of the individuals they studied, to refashion the congenital invert as a treatable homosexual. Nobody recognized this more than Ellis himself. He had argued that many inverts felt compelled to write a narrative of their own experience after reading those written by others, and in his work he published lengthy extracts from the stories he had accumulated with little editorial intervention. By contrast, he insisted that analysts dismissed all histories not obtained by their own methods, and he accused them of arranging the stories they were told according to their own, particular logic. While Ellis's work could offer a space in which homosexual desire might be articulated positively in the form of a self-affirming autobiographical narrative, it is not clear whether such self-affirmation was possible on the couch of Dr Ross, a couch on which the story of congenital inversion was rewritten as one of thwarted heterosexual desire.[23]

By the 1930s, psychoanalytic discourses of homosexuality had made considerable headway in Britain and for many students of the subject Ellis's work already seemed discredited. But this is not to suggest that Freudian work had become wholly ascendant. New discoveries in the field of endocrinology, for example, led to an interest in Ellis's so-called 'internal secretions', which were now deemed to be a precipitating factor in homosexuality. Such work was strenuously resisted by Freudians, leading to battles that pitted members of the medical and psychoanalytic communities against each other.[24] Some doctors attempted to create a composite of various strands of thought, and in 1938 Desmond Curran admitted his own debts to both Ellis and Freud. While he agreed with Ellis that the congenital invert should not be subjected to treatment, he encouraged those Freudians who felt that the homosexual whose deviation resulted from developmental abnormalities might benefit from therapy.[25] The treatable homosexual had joined the ranks of the untreatable invert, an uneasy alliance that was consolidated by the work of interwar criminologists.

Freudians, Criminologists and the 'Problem' of Homosexuality

In no area of public life did Freudian ideas garner as much support between the wars as in the fields of education and criminology. James Hadfield's *Psychology and Morals*, published in 1923, was an often-cited text that claimed social and moral problems to be rooted in individual behavioural disorders that were amenable to psychotherapeutic treatment. At the same time, Cyril Burt focused on the roots of juvenile delinquency in the maladapted child and saw psychoanalysis as a kind of practical re-education of delinquents. By the 1930s, as Nikolas Rose has argued, such thinking 'sought to establish itself by claiming its ability to deal with the problems posed for social apparatuses by dysfunctional conduct'.[26]

One of those so-called 'problems' was the growing number of 'sexual offenders', whose behaviour was now studied, and out of which emerged new taxonomies of deviant pleasures, indebted to the work of Freud. M. Hamblin Smith, chief medical officer of Birmingham Prison, discussed the application of psychoanalysis to the investigation and treatment of crime as early as 1922; five years later he suggested that, in the wake of Freud's findings, homosexual offenders required investigation by well-trained experts.[27] Initially, however, it was the study of delinquency in general, rather than a specific focus on homosexual inmates, that characterized the earliest work of psychoanalytically oriented criminologists. In fact, rarely did such individuals set out to apply their knowledge to imprisoned homosexuals; it was instead their desire to apply their ideas to inmates in general that led them to undertake studies through which they encountered the 'problem' of homosexuality.[28]

It was the work of William Norwood East that focused attention quite specifically on the homosexual inmate population for the first time. Chief medical inspector of prisons for England and Wales, East discussed how normal development might fail, leading to forms of aberrant behaviour that resulted in prosecution.[29] In his 1936 study, *Medical Aspects of Crime*, he offered an elaborate taxonomy of the sexual aberrations he had encountered, writing about homosexuality in detail. Echoing the confused thinking of the decade, not quite sure whether to view homosexual conduct as a result of Ellis's 'congenital inversion', Freud's 'premature arrest in sexual evolution', or, in the case of male prostitutes, just plain 'commercial cupidity', East was convinced that the result of such conduct was a form of anti-social behaviour that needed to be controlled.[30] In 1939, East and his colleague, W.H. de B. Hubert, a prison psychotherapist, published their influential *Report on the Psychological Treatment of Crime*. As in East's earlier work, they viewed homosexual behaviour to be the outcome of both constitutional and acquired factors. This debt to both Ellis and Freud is important to note, for it was the relative balance of these factors in the make-up of each offender that determined whether or not treatment was considered appropriate. Overall, they cautioned that therapeutic intervention was no panacea; but they also claimed that 'more socially useful tendencies' were easier to release in offenders whose behaviour was deemed to result from environmental factors – who had, for example, suffered disappointment in an earlier heterosexual relationship (like Ross's patient). For them, the purpose of psychiatric investigation was to determine which offenders could be mapped according to a Freudian grid and to focus their therapeutic energies accordingly.[31]

East and Hubert's report contains many case studies, the first such publication in Britain to include extensive data on homosexual inmates. Of the 406 prisoners studied to determine their suitability for treatment, 79 had been jailed for homosexual offences; of these, 52 were deemed treatable. In their description of these cases, they broke with the work of Ellis in one significant respect. While Ellis often discussed the invert in terms of gender inversion, tracing the operations of a 'feminine temperament' in men, and noting the 'masculinity or boyishness' of the female invert, East and Hubert claimed that their male prisoners could not be differentiated into stable masculine or feminine types.[32] In this respect, their work was resolutely Freudian, in so far as it held that same-sex object choice was not necessarily accompanied by gender inversion, a point Freud had made when he claimed that homosexual object choice in men was usually accompanied by the 'most complete mental masculinity'.[33] Nevertheless, East and Hubert remained at least partly indebted to Ellis's notion of congenital inversion, describing some prisoners whose condition was often experienced as innate and for whom treatment would thus be of little benefit.

East and Hubert divided their homosexual prisoners into the treatable and untreatable, on the basis of their assessment of each prisoner's profile. Case 42 was successfully treated because, while in his behaviour he was 'strongly homosexual', his fantasies were heterosexual and by stressing their importance his heterosexual drives could be 'released'; case 49 was deemed to have developed homosexual tendencies because of ties to his mother that had delayed his emotional development, ties that could now be severed; as for case 53, his 'homosexual trends' did not appear to be fixed and it was thus 'possible to remove some of the difficulties in the way of heterosexual development'.[34] In each of these instances, East and Hubert made use of Freud's understanding of the aetiology of homosexuality to legitimate therapeutic intervention. But this was not always possible: sometimes a prisoner refused to co-operate; sometimes, no matter how hard they tried, they could not discover any traits (the overbearing mother, the case of early seduction, and so on) they considered a necessary prerequisite for successful therapy. They nevertheless persisted in their search, and like Thomas Ross they attempted to instil a very different aetiological story in their subjects. Occasionally this worked, but usually such prisoners continued to insist they were congenital inverts. In these cases East and Hubert felt that intervention was hopeless. As they wrote of one 'intellectual type of man', the fact that he had 'by intellectual processes and rationalization built a stability upon [. . .] [his] personality weaknesses makes [. . .] treatment difficult'.[35]

Commissioned by the Home Office, East and Hubert's report echoed the findings of the Committee on Persistent Offenders, which heard evidence from Cyril Burt, Thomas Ross and Hamblin Smith, among others, and cautiously embraced the new work on the psychological treatment of crime.[36] Such work was often cited by doctors, magistrates and barristers who used it to legitimate their own calls for the treatment, rather than imprisonment, of homosexual offenders.[37] It also influenced the Home Office, which drafted legislation that would make it possible for prison authorities to adopt measures that were now being advocated by a number of medical and legal experts. Clause 19 of the 1938 Criminal Justice Bill permitted courts to sentence individuals for psychiatric treatment if they deemed it appropriate. Debate in the Commons was generally favourable to the Bill, despite some hostility to its Freudian enthusiasms. The outbreak of war led the government to shelve the Bill for the duration of the conflict, although a decade later most of its provisions were finally enacted.

Optimism regarding psychiatric treatment for homosexual offenders was widespread in the 1930s, even though in that decade few of the suggestions pertaining to treatment were implemented. But this did not stop doctors, magistrates and barristers from calling for institutions where homosexuals could be isolated and treated. Such ideas were indebted to Freud in so far as they developed from the notion that, as one barrister and medical officer put it, homosexuality was a mental disorder that arose 'from repressive influences in infancy and childhood which retard or distort the normal development of the sex instinct' – a state of arrested development that required therapeutic attention.[38] But not all criminologists or doctors held this view. And not all Freudians were prone to draw the conclusions from the aetiological premises put forward by Freud that Ross, and to a lesser extent East, did. Most notable in this respect was Dr Edward Glover, the eminent Freudian who established the Institute for the Scientific Treatment of Delinquency (ISTD) in 1932, an organization committed to the examination and treatment of various forms of anti-social conduct. Backed by a roster of luminaries, including Ellis, Freud and Jones, along with Alfred Adler, C.G. Jung, Bronislaw Malinowski, H.G. Wells and the Archbishop of York, the ISTD was examining 160 cases a year by the later 1930s, most referred by magistrates and probation officers, roughly one third of whom were sexual offenders.[39]

Work with homosexual patients convinced Glover that the prospects of therapeutic intervention were not promising, and in the 1950s he would argue that most problems experienced by homosexuals resulted from the social ostracism they faced. But this particular position only emerged gradually. Initially, Glover was more optimistic about the promise of psychoanalysis, although as early as 1939 he had written that the 'stronger the constitutional factor [in homosexuality] the less likely is resolution by psychotherapeutic means'.[40] While this statement might appear to link him with those who remained indebted to Ellis, it also suggests that Glover paid more attention to the nuances of Freud's thought than did his compatriots like Ross. Moreover, unlike Ross, neither Glover nor his co-workers felt compelled to coerce their patients into a Freudian subject position in order to find a condition amenable to treatment. John Bowlby, the famous post-war child psychiatrist, took many notes on the case of one homosexual he treated while employed by the ISTD in the 1930s. Documenting in detail the suffering experienced by this man, Bowlby wrote that he was only concerned 'to help him live happily'. Likewise, Kate Friedlander, after recounting several cases of homosexuality she had treated, concluded that the distress she encountered often resulted from the position in which the homosexual found himself in society. The nation's dominant moral sentiments, she wrote, 'should not be used as an excuse for inflicting irreparable damage on the lives of people because, through no fault of their own, they have not succeeded in developing socially accepted sexual desires'.[41]

As early as 1932, Glover began to ponder the meaning of normality and what constituted 'the normal' in psychoanalytic thought. He argued then that 'in the present state of Western civilization we have no grounds for assuming that normality and complete reality adaptation are identical'.[42] Twenty-five years later, in the influential written testimony he submitted to the Wolfenden Committee, he argued that psychological treatment should not be viewed as the answer to homosexuality, concluding, 'there is no answer to homosexuality save tolerance on the part of the intolerant anti-homosexual groups in the community'.[43] Freud, who had once been used to justify attempts to redirect homosexual behaviour, had now been appropriated as an advocate of reform, and it was Glover's argument, rather than those of Ross or East, that had the greatest influence on the members of the Wolfenden Committee.

After World War II, Freudian arguments came to play an important role in much of the public discussion of homosexuality in Britain, whether put forward by advocates of reform, like Glover, or by advocates of repressive treatment, like Clifford Allen. That they enjoyed such status is in part attributable to the work of a generation of interwar criminologists who had used Freud to further their own goals of reclaiming the delinquent. But many lesbians and gay men remained suspicious of Freud and continued to conceive of themselves through the experience and language of others, as documented and made available in print by writers like Ellis and Carpenter: as one lesbian wrote in 1963, 'I have felt very strongly that I was a male who had, by some horrible cosmic mistake, been put into a female body.'[44] Some, like Wildeblood, were willing to pander to Freudian enthusiasms on tactical grounds, hoping that time spent in a therapist's office would be more pleasant than time spent in prison. No doubt it was, although it often failed to effect the hoped-for changes. Trevor Thomas, director of the Leicester Art Gallery, was not imprisoned for his homosexual offences because the judge believed he would corrupt others; instead he was sentenced to see a psychoanalyst for a year to be 'cured'. The analyst gave up after six months.[45] The journalist Michael Davidson, shaped by his reading of Carpenter and Ellis in the 1920s, received a sentence of four months with hard labour for his offences in 1936. The sentencing magistrate, he noted, 'added in the tones of a headmaster announcing some special benefaction, that in prison I should receive "psychological treatment"'. Davidson recalled that the treatment consisted largely of his being told that, in order to avoid subsequent prosecution, he might consider choosing partners above the age of consent. This, he added, was not what the magistrate probably had in mind.[46]

Examples like these abound, although such treatments were comparatively rare in Britain. Despite the enthusiasm of doctors who believed they could effect a transformation in the object choice of their homosexual patients, and despite the cautious hopes of many criminologists, there was no wholesale embrace of such ideas in Britain to the extent that there was in the United States. In part, this was because American optimism about the possibility of transforming individual character – an optimism that shaped the unique American appropriation of Freud – was largely lacking in Britain. In part, it was because Britain, facing the Depression and then the harsh realities of austerity for a decade after the war, failed to devote scarce resources to the reclamation of the homosexual offender. But in part it was because of a continuing allegiance to the work of Ellis, even if that allegiance was more subdued than it had once been. When 'anomaly' characterized inversion as 'one of those strange things which happened when God was not looking', he appealed to a keen British distrust of theory, as had Ellis himself. Moreover, his was a claim the likes of which Edward Glover must have heard often from patients at the ISTD. And it was a claim that he – more attuned to the nuances of Freud's thought than were many of his compatriots – was willing to entertain as he began to turn his attention from the need to treat the homosexual offender to the need to understand the social milieu that deformed the very individuals who were sent to him for treatment.

Notes

For their comments on earlier drafts of this essay, I want to thank Lucy Bland, George Chauncey and John Vincent. I also want to acknowledge the support of the National Humanities Center, which provided me with a stimulating and happy environment in which this article was conceived and written.

   Place of publication is London, unless stated otherwise.

1 Gordon Westwood [Michael Schofield], *Society and the Homosexual* (Victor Gollancz, 1952); D.J. West, *Homosexuality* (Duckworth, 1955). For Glover's essays on homosexuality, see Edward Glover, *The Roots of Crime* (International Universities Press, New York, 1960), pp. 197–243. For William Norwood East, see East, *Sexual Offenders* (Delisle, 1955); East and W.H. de B. Hubert, *Report on the Psychological Treatment of Crime* (HMSO, 1939).

2 Peter Wildeblood, *Against the Law* (Weidenfeld and Nicolson, 1955), pp. 3–4, 16, 91; Chris Waters, 'Disorders of the Mind, Disorders of the Body Social: Peter Wildeblood and the Making of the Modern Homosexual, in *Moments of Modernity: Reconstructing Britain 1945–1964*, eds Becky Conekin, Frank Mort and Chris Waters (Rivers Oram, 1998).

3 Esther Newton, 'The Mythic Mannish Lesbian: Radclyffe Hall and the New Woman', *Signs*, 9 (1984), pp. 557–75.

4 Havelock Ellis, *Sexual Inversion* [1897], 3rd edn (1915), in his *Studies in the Psychology of Sex*, vol. 1, part 4 (Random House, New York, 1936), pp. 318, 322 (subsequent references, this edition); Paul Robinson, *The Modernization of Sex* (Harper and Row, New York, 1976), p. 6.

5 'Anomaly', *The Invert and his Social Adjustment* (Balliere, Tindall and Cox, 1927), p. 18.

6 Kevin Porter and Jeffrey Weeks, eds, *Between the Acts: Lives of Homosexual Men 1885–1967* (Routledge, 1991), pp. 3, 36, 52, 61, 76, 86, 110. For the relationship between discourse, experience and identity, see Lisa Duggan, 'The Trials of Alice Mitchell: Sensationalism, Sexology, and the Lesbian Subject in Turn-of-the-Century America', *Signs*, 18 (1993), pp. 791–814.

7 Phyllis Grosskurth, *Havelock Ellis: A Biography* (New York, Knopf, 1980), p. 360; see also pp. 216–17, 232, 291–3; Vincent Brome, *Havelock Ellis: Philosopher of Sex* (Routledge and Kegan Paul, 1979).

8 Ernest Jones (review), *International Journal of Psycho-Analysis*, 8 (1927), pp. 431–2.

9 Sigmund Freud, 'Three Essays on Sexuality' (1905), in *The Standard Edition of the Complete Psychological Works of Sigmund Freud*, ed. James Strachey (Hogarth Press, 1953), vol. 7, p. 140 (hereafter *SE*).

10 Ellis, *Sexual Inversion*, p. 324; see also pp. 303–4, 310–11, 316–17, 322–3, 327–33. For Ellis's ideas, see Brome, *Ellis*; Grosskurth, *Ellis*; Robinson, *Modernization of Sex*, ch. 1; Jeffrey Weeks and Sheila Rowbotham, *Socialism and the New Life: The Personal and Sexual Politics of Edward Carpenter and Havelock Ellis* (Pluto Press, 1977).

11 Freud, 'Three Essays', p. 140; see also pp. 145–6. For Freud's ideas on homosexuality, see Teresa de Lauretis, 'Freud, Sexuality, and Perversion', in *Discourses of Sexuality: From Aristotle to AIDS*, ed. Domna C. Stanton (University of Michigan Press, Ann Arbor, 1992), pp. 216–34; Kenneth Lewes, *The Psychoanalytic Theory of Male Sexuality* (Simon and Schuster, New York, 1988), ch. 2; Mandy Merck, 'The Train of Thought in Freud's "Case of Homosexuality in a Woman"', *m/f*, 11/12 (1986), pp. 35–46; Jeffrey Weeks, *Sexuality and Its Discontents: Meanings, Myths and Modern Sexualities* (Routledge and Kegan Paul, 1985), ch. 6.

12 Diana Fuss, *Identification Papers* (Routledge, 1995), pp. 57–9, 64, 77.

13 Sigmund Freud, 'The Psychogenesis of a Case of Homosexuality in a Woman' (1920), *SE*, vol. 18, p. 151; Freud, 'Letter to an American Mother', in *The Problem of Homosexuality in Modern Society*, ed. Hendrik M. Ruitenbeek (Dutton, New York, 1963), pp. 1–2; Henry Abelove, 'Freud, Male Homosexuality, and the Americans', in *The Lesbian and Gay Studies Reader*, eds Henry Abelove, Michèle Aina Barale and David Halperin (Routledge, 1993), pp. 381–5; Lewes, *Psychoanalytic Theory*, pp. 31–4.

14 Dean Rapp, 'The Early Discovery of Freud by the British General Educated Public, 1912–1919', *Social History of Medicine*, 3 (1990), pp. 217–43.

15 Ernest Jones, *Free Associations: Memories of a Psycho-Analyst* (Basic Books, New York, 1959), pp. 230, 240.

16 *Lancet*, 22 June 1918, pp. 884–5; 13 July 1918, p. 56.

17 Lesley A. Hall, '"Disinterested Enthusiasm for Sexual Misconduct": The British Society for the Study of Sex Psychology, 1913–47', *Journal of Contemporary History*, 30 (1995), pp. 665–86.

18 Quoted in Frank J. Sulloway, *Freud, Biologist of the Mind: Beyond the Psychoanalytic Legend* (Basic Books, New York, 1979), pp. 438–9.

19 Weeks, *Sexuality and Its Discontents*, p. 151; Ernest Jones, 'The Early Development of Female Sexuality' (1927), in his *Papers on Psycho-Analysis*, 5th edn (Beacon Press, Boston, 1961), pp. 438–51. For one of the earliest Freudians in Britain to advocate this position, see C. Stanford Read, 'Homosexuality', *Journal of Mental Science*, 67 (1921), pp. 8–12.

20 T.A. Ross, *An Introduction to Analytical Psychotherapy* (Edward Arnold, 1932), pp. 109, 118.

21 T.A. Ross and R.D. Gillespie, 'Progression and Regression in Two Homosexuals', *Journal of Neurology and Psychopathology*, 7 (1927), p. 315.

22 Ibid., p. 319.

23 Ellis, *Sexual Inversion*, pp. 89–91. For the narrative space sexologists provided for the affirmation of homosexual identities, see Harry Oosterhuis, 'Richard von Krafft-Ebing's "Step-Children of Nature": Psychiatry and the Making of Homosexual Identity', in *Science and Homosexualities*, ed. Vernon Rosario (Routledge, 1997), esp. pp. 83–4.

24 See, for example, the work of Clifford Allen: 'Adrenal Dysfunction and its Relation to Sexuality', in *The Adrenal Cortex and Intersexuality*, ed. L.R. Broster (Chapman and Hall, 1938), pp. 55–131; *The Sexual Perversions and Abnormalities: A Study in the Psychology of Paraphilia* (Oxford University Press, 1940), esp. pp. 79–84.

25 Desmond Curran, 'Homosexuality', *Practitioner*, 141 (1938), pp. 280–7. For discussion of similar complexities in American thought in the 1930s, see Jennifer Terry, 'Anxious Slippages Between "Us" and "Them": A Brief History of the Scientific Search for Homosexual Bodies', in *Deviant Bodies: Critical Perspectives on Difference in Science and Popular Culture*, eds Jennifer Terry and Jacqueline Urla (Indiana University Press, Bloomington, 1995), pp. 129–69.

26 Nikolas Rose, *The Psychological Complex: Psychology, Politics and Society in England 1869–1939* (RKP 1985), p. 5.

27 M. Hamblin Smith, *The Psychology of the Criminal*, 2nd edn (Methuen, 1933 [1922]), esp. pp. v, 126; Smith, 'Psychology and the Law', *Howard Journal*, 2 (1927), pp. 144–5.

28 See, for example, Grace W. Pailthorpe, *Studies in the Psychology of Delinquency* (HMSO, 1932); Hermann Mannheim, *Social Aspects of Crime in England Between the Wars* (George Allen and Unwin, 1940).

29 W. Norwood East, 'The Interpretation of Some Sexual Offences', *Journal of Mental Science*, 71 (1925), pp. 410–24.

30 W. Norwood East, *Medical Aspects of Crime* (J. and A. Churchill, 1936), pp. 315, 323, 341–4.

31 East and Hubert, *Report*, pp. 21, 84–7, 91, 153; see also East, 'The Modern Psychiatric Approach to Crime', *Journal of Mental Science*, 85 (1939), esp. pp. 663–5.

32 East and Hubert, *Report*, p. 86; Ellis, *Sexual Inversion*, pp. 201, 244–5, 250, 288, 290. At times Ellis argued that inverts could be gender conformists, although he was more prone than Freud to equate homosexuality and gender inversion.

33 Freud, 'Three Essays', p. 142. Freud was less sure about whether or not this was the case with lesbians.

34 East and Hubert, *Report*, pp. 92–3, 99–100, 103.
35 Ibid., p. 95.
36 *Report of the Departmental Committee on Persistent Offenders*, cmd. 4090 (1932), esp. pp. 43–6.
37 See J.R. Rees, 'Prognosis in the Sexual Neuroses', *Lancet*, 20 April 1935, pp. 948-9; J.L. Moir, 'Some Medical Aspects of Crime [. . .] ', *Medico-Legal Review*, 8 (1940), pp. 111–32; Claud Mullins, *Crime and Psychology* (1943), esp. pp. 38–40, 48–9.
38 William A. Brend, *Sacrifice to Attis: A Study of Sex and Civilisation* (William Heinemann, 1936), p. 43.
39 Edward Glover, *The Diagnosis and Treatment of Delinquency: Being a Clinical Report on the Work of the Institute During the Five Years 1937–1941* (ISTD, 1944), p. 5; Denis Carroll, 'Observations on the Psychiatric Handling of Delinquents', *Medico-Legal Review*, 8 (1940), pp. 182–98.
40 Edward Glover, *Psycho-Analysis* (John Bale Medical Publications, 1939), p. 124.
41 Bowlby Papers, PP/BOW/Box 13/c.2/2, 23 September 1935 (Wellcome Institute for the History of Medicine); Kate Friedlander, *The Psycho-Analytical Approach to Juvenile Delinquency* (Kegan Paul, Trench, Trubner and Co., 1947), p. 232.
42 Edward Glover, 'Medico-Psychological Aspects of Normality', *British Journal of Psychology*, 23 (1932), pp. 161, 164.
43 Edward Glover, ed., *The Problem of Homosexuality* (ISTD, 1957), p. 21.
44 A Lesbian, 'My Kind of Loving', *Twentieth Century*, 171 (1963), p. 147.
45 Porter and Weeks, *Between the Acts*, pp. 66–7.
46 Michael Davidson, *The World, the Flesh and Myself* (Gay Men's Press, 1985 [1962]), pp. 130–1, 168–70, 176–7.

Part IV

Cultural Perversions

11 Trial by Sexology?: Maud Allan, *Salome* and the 'Cult of the Clitoris' Case

Lucy Bland

'Few trials in modern times have excited such intense interest, or have been productive of such sensational allegations and disclosures' (*News of the World*, 2 June 1918). The trial to which the *News of the World* was referring was a libel case which was reported extensively in all the British newspapers during its six-day duration from late May to June 1918. The war was still under way, indeed Germany was thought to be winning, yet the public's attention turned to the Old Bailey, where hundreds queued for hours in an attempt to get a seat. 'Not since the days of Crippen has any trial so excited the public', declared the *Sunday Pictorial*.[1] Although the trial was famous in its time, few today have heard of its existence. Yet it marked a watershed: it was the first British trial in which the defendant drew on sexology as a key element of his defence. It was also one of the first in which lesbianism was at issue. How important was sexology's contribution to the final verdict? What representations of lesbianism did the trial convey? And what impact did the trial have on the wider culture, including the effect of the introduction of sexological ideas? To answer these questions it is necessary first to examine this extraordinary trial.

The accusation of libel was brought by the well-known dancer Maud Allan against the Independent MP Noel Pemberton-Billing, for his implication of lesbianism. In February of that year a paragraph headed 'The Cult of the Clitoris' had appeared in his paper the *Vigilante*: 'To be a member of Maud Allen's [sic] private performance in Oscar Wilde's *Salome* one has to apply to Miss Valetta of 9 Duke St., Adelphi. If Scotland Yard were to seize the list of these members I have no doubt they would secure the names of several thousand of the first 47,000.'[2]

The 'first 47,000' had been referred to in an article that had appeared three weeks earlier in the *Vigilante*'s predecessor, the *Imperialist*. This had suggested that a 'Black Book' was held by the Germans naming 47,000 English men and women who were open to German blackmail because of their 'sexual perversions'. Included were: 'The names of Privy Councillors, youths of the chorus, wives of Cabinet ministers, dancing girls, even Cabinet Ministers themselves [. . .] In lesbian ecstasy the most sacred secrets of the state were betrayed.'[3] During the trial the names of Herbert Asquith, his wife Margot, Lord Haldane and even the presiding judge, Justice Darling, were among those mentioned as being in the book.[4]

Maud Allan had taken exception to the linking of her name with the heading 'Cult of the Clitoris'. What was implied here by the term 'clitoris'? From late eighteenth-century through into the early twentieth century, one of the most consistent medical characterizations of the anatomy of the lesbian was the claim of an unusually large clitoris. Not only was the clitoris associated with female sexual pleasure separate from reproductive potential, but lesbians were assumed to be masculinized, and the supposed enlarged clitoris was one signifier of this masculinity. In presenting lesbians' bodies as *less* sexually differentiated than the norm – more masculine – it was inferred that they were atavists – throwbacks to an earlier evolutionary stage and thereby 'degenerates'. It was held that progressive differentiation of the sexes was one of the hallmarks of evolutionary progress. An enlarged clitoris or the inference of deviant genitalia was also given as the signifier of black women's sexuality and of nymphomania.[5] Lesbians, black women and nymphomaniacs were all grouped together as possessors of a 'primitive' sexuality. By the late nineteenth century, a number of sexologists were questioning some of these assumptions. Havelock Ellis, for example, asserted: 'There is no connection between sexual inversion in women and an enlarged clitoris.'[6] He suggested that although the 'older literature'contained many examples of enlarged clitorises, they were probably cases of 'pseudohermaphroditism'. Many doctors, however, still held to the older belief.[7]

Who were Maud Allan and Noel Pemberton-Billing? Born Maud Durrant in Canada in 1873, the daughter of a shoemaker, Maud Allan moved with her family to San Francisco six years later. In 1895, two months after she had gone to Berlin to study classical piano, her brother Theo murdered two young women in a church. He was executed and became one of San Francisco's most notorious criminals. In 1901 Maud Allan abandoned the piano and took up dancing. In 1907 at Marienbad, in front of Edward VII, she performed a dance which she had devised called 'the Vision of Salome'. The following year she came to Britain and gave over two hundred and fifty performances of a series of dances, including the 'Vision of Salome', at the Palace Theatre.[8] Allan was not the only

Western woman to portray Salome on stage; the biblical character who had figured in many nineteenth-century novels and paintings was now the inspiration for dancers such as Loie Fuller, Ruth St Denis, Ida Rubenstein and Mata Hari.[9] Allan was patronised by high society, including royalty and the prime minister Herbert Asquith and his wife Margot. Flower-pot statuettes of Allan were sold in Bond Street gift shops, and a 'Maud Allan dinner dance' was held for society ladies who were asked to appear in Salome costume; the evening was to be 'undesecrated by any man',[10] a command no doubt disturbing to the women's husbands.

But if Allan was famous,[11] she was also infamous. Two days before her public debut in London, a titillating illustrated pamphlet was circulated by the theatre manager focusing solely on the 'Vision of Salome' dance: 'The pink pearls slip amorously about the throat and bosom as she moves [. . .] The desire that flames from her eyes and bursts in hot gusts from her scarlet mouth infects the act with the madness of passion.'[12] Even without such a preview, there would have been certain expectations, given that to the Westerner, Salome signified the orientalist myth of the exotic, erotic but deadly Eastern female.[13] The Manchester Watch Committee (a morality group) was quick to ban her from appearing in their home town, followed by Liverpool and Bournemouth, amongst others. The following year, in 1909, a pornographic story was published about a wealthy prostitute who dances 'the dance of emancipation' and has four male admirers all of whom she sexually satisfies in various exotic ways. It was no accident that the eponymous heroine is called Maudie.[14] And when Allan travelled to India in 1913 her reputation went before her: the Viceroy protested that her dancing would be detrimental to 'the prestige of the white woman in India'.[15]

Allan's infamy, however, stemmed not only from her eroticized dancing; there was also the rumour of her lesbianism, largely due to her close friendship with Margot Asquith. For several years gossip had cast Margot Asquith as part of a lesbian grouping. When Allan was on tour in the USA in 1910, the newspapers reported that her friendship with Margot Asquith was greatly straining the Asquith marriage.[16] From 1910 Allan lived in West Wing, a grand apartment overlooking Regent's Park, that was paid for by Margot Asquith for the next twenty years. By the late 1920s Allan had become the lover of Verna Aldrich, her secretary/companion. They lived together at West Wing for at least ten years on diminishing funds. Although Allan had male lovers, her longest relationship was with Aldrich. In 1941 Allan returned to the States and died fifteen years later.

Noel Pemberton-Billing had been an actor, had trained as a barrister, and had been an MP since 1916. The following year he had formed the Vigilante Society to promote 'purity in public life'. He and his colleagues were explicitly anti-semitic, claiming that the British war effort was being undermined by the 'hidden hand' of German sympathizers and German Jews operating in Britain. What Pemberton-Billing carefully concealed from the court was that his wife was half German. His assistant editor was a young Canadian called Captain Harold Spencer, who had been discharged from the British army for insanity, something else that did not unfortunately come out in the trial. It was he who had written the 'first 47,000' article. Shortly afterwards Pemberton-Billing had received a letter from the romance writer Marie Corelli, who had seen a notice in *The Sunday Times* advertising the forthcoming private production of *Salome* starring Allan. Corelli suggested: 'it would be well to secure the list of subscribers to this new "upholding" of the Wilde "cult" among the 47,000'.[17] Spencer then wrote the 'Cult of the Clitoris' paragraph, hoping to raise a libel case and thereby get publicity for their claims of German infiltration and corruption.

Before the Old Bailey trial there was a preliminary hearing at Bow Street Police Court in April. Travers Humphreys, one of the counsel representing Allan, explained the prosecution's case: 'I find words which I must read, although I see there are ladies in the court [. . .] The cult of the clitoris [. . .] the words themselves are the filthiest words it would be possible to imagine.'[18] (Indeed, none of the newspapers would print the heading, save the *Vigilante*.) 'The cult of the clitoris can only mean one thing, and that is that the lady whose name is coupled with it [. . .] approves of that which is sometimes described in [. . .] less gross language as lesbianism, and a more horrible libel to publish of any woman [. . .] it is impossible to find.'[19] Later, in his summing up, Ellis Hume-Williams, Allan's other counsel, suggested that to be branded a lesbian was worse than being deemed a traitor to your country.[20]

At the Old Bailey, Pemberton-Billing presented his plea of justification: the Libel Act 1843 decreed that for a criminal libel, the defendant needed to establish both the truth of the libel and its public benefit. This allowed the libeller to assemble diverse witnesses and present much incriminating evidence. There were clear parallels between what was permissible for Pemberton-Billing to do and say, and what had been permissible as evidence at the first Oscar Wilde trial in 1895, in which Wilde had brought a libel case against the Marquis of Queensberry for his accusation of 'posing as a somdomite [*sic*]'. (Another parallel was the presence of Travers Humphreys, who had acted for Oscar Wilde in 1895 as a junior counsel.) Pemberton-Billing's plea of justification declared that all the defamatory matter alleged in Allan's indictment was true, i.e. that, first, Allan was 'a lewd, unchaste and immoral woman' (which was taken at this point in the trial as equivalent to saying she was a lesbian), who, second, was about 'to give private performances of an obscene and indecent character', which third, were 'designed as to foster and encourage obscene and unnatural practices among women', and, finally, Allan associated herself with persons 'addicted to obscene and unnatural practices'.[21] Pemberton-Billing was thus stating that Allan was immoral, *Salome* was obscene, *Salome* was designed to encourage obscenity among women, and Allan associated with obscene persons. The defence of this criminal libel resulted, in effect, not in Pemberton-Billing being on trial, but Allan and *Salome*. It had similarly been the case in the libel trial instigated by Oscar Wilde.[22]

Allan was discredited in a number of ways. It was implied that she was a German sympathizer by virtue of having undertaken musical training in Berlin. Surely in many people's minds was the execution of Mata Hari the year before for German espionage,[23] another 'orientalist' dancer to whom Allan must inevitably have been compared. Allan's friendship with Margot Asquith furthered such suspicions, for the latter had well-known German sympathies. To Pemberton-Billing, the Asquiths would also have been seen as part of an aristocratic, decadent, 'old order'. More significantly, asking if Allan knew Margot Asquith was a means of suggesting lesbianism. 'Has she [Margot Asquith] ever been to your dressing room at the Palace Theatre?',[24] Pemberton-Billing demanded. Allan denied it. She was asked again; again she denied it. (A few days earlier, at the Front, Margot Asquith's sexuality had been discussed by certain English officers, according to Duff Cooper: 'One of my brother-officers [. . .] believed that Mrs Asquith was a "female bugger" that being as near as his limited vocabulary allowed him to get to Sapphist.')[25]

The chief way in which Allan was defamed, however, was through the defence's deployment of sexological terms. When she was first called to the witness box, Pemberton-Billing immediately homed in on her brother. Much to her horror, and the court's amazement, he handed her a book entitled *Celebrated Criminal Cases of America*, asking rhetorically whether her brother was executed for 'murdering two young girls and outraging them after death'. 'The vices referred to in that book are hereditary',[26] he asserted. When Captain Spencer entered the witness box, he likewise referred to Allan as 'a very unfortunate hereditary degenerate', and maintained that as a child in Canada, her brother's crime 'was one of the dreadful tales they use to frighten us with'.[27] Pemberton-Billing's chief medical witness, Dr Serrell Cooke, who had recently worked in the psychiatric wing of Paddington hospital, added scientific authority by describing the crime as 'sadism', and confirming that sadism was indeed hereditary:

> [I]t occurs in families which have an hereditary taint either of insanity or some other neuropathic condition [. . .] The person who has this disease or this condition is probably not aware of it until something or other happens to light the whole thing in them up.[28]

The term 'sadism' had been coined by the Austrian psychiatrist Richard von Krafft-Ebing; Dr Cooke declared that he had made a special study of Krafft-Ebing's work. Krafft-Ebing's *Psychopathia Sexualis*, written in 1886, had been translated into English in 1892. Krafft-Ebing distinguished four main sexual perversions: sadism, masochism, fetishism and what he called 'contrary sexual instinct'. Under the fourth heading he subsumed various different behaviours and identities which were later reclassified by others as hermaphroditism, bisexuality, transvestism, transsexuality, etc., but he largely concentrated on homosexuality, which he saw as either acquired, brought on by certain conditions or behaviour, or congenital, and a sign of hereditary degeneracy.[29] By 1901 he was arguing that homosexuality was always inborn and not pathological *per se*.[30] He said little specifically about lesbianism and did not link it to sadism. He believed that in many cases perversion was neither a crime nor a sin, and that punishment was inappropriate.[31]

One outcome of the exchanges between Pemberton-Billing and his various witnesses in the court-room was that Allan was declared a sadist by virtue of her brother apparently being one. Her alleged sadism was reinforced by Dr Cooke's assertion that any woman acting such a part as Salome would, by definition, have to be a sadist herself. But she was discredited still further through being deemed to have inappropriate sexological knowledge. Pemberton-Billing asked her if she was acquainted with the term 'clitoris'. She answered: 'Yes, but not particularly.' He then informed the court that out of twenty-four people to whom he had shown the libel, only one, a barrister, knew what it meant. Dr Cooke said that he had shown it to fifty or sixty friends of his and none of them had known what it meant. (One hopes they were not doctors.) When Pemberton-Billing called Captain Spencer as a witness, he was asked about the 'Cult of the Clitoris' title. He replied that he had tried to find a title 'that would only be understood by those whom it should be understood by'. Spencer had telephoned a village doctor and was given the term 'clitoris' and told that it 'was a superficial organ that, when unduly excited or overdeveloped, possessed the most dreadful influence on any woman, that she would do the most extraordinary things'. He added 'An exaggerated clitoris might drive a woman to an elephant.' Salome he saw as 'a child suffering from an enlarged and diseased clitoris'.[32] 'Of course, clitoris is a Greek word', announced Dr Cooke, 'it is a medical term [. . .] nobody but a medical man or people interested in that kind of thing, would understand the term.'[33] Another medical witness, Dr J.H. Clarke, when asked whether there was any other term which might have done, replied: 'I cannot think of another [. . .] except [. . .] "lesbianism" and that word would be equally well known to the initiated and equally unintelligible to the uninitiated.'[34] This distinction between the initiated and the uninitiated was not as clear cut as Clarke imagined, for it ignored the recent publication, in March, of Marie Stopes's best-seller *Married Love*. Within a fortnight, the book had sold over 2,000 copies. The thousands of people who had read the book might well have recognized the term 'clitoris', for it is graphically described and presented as a key factor in women's sexual arousal.[35]

Pemberton-Billing asked Allan about her knowledge of other terms; she admitted to having read medical books and having heard of sadism and incest. She had not heard of masochism, or of Krafft-Ebing or Iwan Bloch. Sexological writings were assumed to be the preserve of experts; Krafft-Ebing was himself explicit on this point. In the preface to the first edition of *Psychopathia Sexualis* he wrote: 'In order that unqualified persons should not become readers, the author saw himself compelled to choose a title understood only by the learned.' The book was addressed to 'the physician and the jurist'.[36] Allan may not have admitted to having heard of Krafft-Ebing, but knowing the word 'sadism' was enough to condemn her, for it was he who had coined the term. And to know about the clitoris implied knowledge of women's sexuality autonomous from men. Non-experts such as Allan would only have such knowledge, the defence adamantly claimed, if they were compelled by their perverse proclivities to seek it out.

If Allan was on trial, so too was *Salome*. Oscar Wilde's play *Salome* was written in 1891, first in French. It was to have been performed in Britain by Sarah Bernhardt, but at the last minute it was banned by the Lord Chamberlain, ostensibly on grounds of blasphemy. There were, however, private British productions of the play in 1905 and 1906. The play involves the young Salome, besotted with the imprisoned John the Baptist (called Jokanaan in Wilde's version), who rebuffs her advances. She dances the 'dance of the seven veils' before Herod, her stepfather and uncle, on condition that he gives her anything she requests. Her request is the head of Jokanaan.[37] During the Old Bailey trial *Salome* followed Allan in being reviled through German associations. Pemberton-Billing quoted from Robert Ross's preface to *Salome* as to the play's great success in Germany. As Lord Alfred Douglas, Wilde's former lover, expressed it, it appealed to a certain German way of thinking. To the *Morning Post*, reporting on the trial: 'the play has its place in the minor literature of disease; but [. . .] these perversions of sexual passion have no home in the healthy mind of England.'[38]

Like Allan, however, *Salome* was principally discredited through the deployment of sexological terms. According to Dr Cooke, there was not only sadism in the play, but masochism, fetishism and incest as well. Cooke declared that the writing of *Salome* was only possible because of Oscar Wilde's knowledge of sexual perversion: 'The probability is that he had von Krafft-Ebing's book *Psychopathia Sexualis* in front of him all the time.'[39] Douglas confirmed this. *Salome*, he said, was founded on the writings of Krafft-Ebing. Wilde, Douglas suddenly declared, 'was the greatest force for evil in Europe in the last 350 years'.[40]

In his plea of justification Pemberton-Billing had suggested that *Salome* was designed to encourage obscenity in women. But in the trial, it was not this which is focused on (after all, the play is clearly *not* about sexual relations between women) but how the play might encourage general sexual perversion among women *and men*. If *Salome*'s writing was made possible by knowledge of Krafft-Ebing, its viewing was also claimed to be affected by such knowledge. There was much debate about the effects on people of witnessing or reading the play. Dr Cooke, who claimed to have made a detailed medical synopsis of *Salome* with the help of Krafft-Ebing's work, declared that 'healthy minded people' would not understand it, and would simply be disgusted. According to Cooke, if members of the public had read Krafft-Ebing, however, they *would* understand it, and if 'they had it in them' (if sexual perversion was lying dormant), they would *become* full-blown perverts. There were unfortunately inherited sexually perverse tendencies in many people, but these might lie unobserved until 'lit up'. (He was keen on repeating this imagery of sexual perversity as akin to hell-fire – a representation closer to evangelical rhetoric than his usual scientific discourse.)

Sexology may have been used to defame both Allan and *Salome*, but it in turn was defamed during the trial. Like Allan and *Salome*, sexology was deemed to be essentially German. (Krafft-Ebing was wrongly assumed to be German and the writings of non-German sexologists were ignored.) Justice Darling implied in his summing up that these sexological terms, as the preserve of the Germans, were possibly nothing but fabrication:

> You may think that the doctors [. . .] have discovered more than really exists. It is so easy to sit down [. . .] particularly easy for the Germans, and this thing seems to have started with the German Krafft-Ebing, [. . .] and make a list; to take a vice and split it up and say 'there is this and that characteristic' [. . .] people may be too clever by half.[41]

The *Sunday Pictorial*, commenting on the trial, asserted that:

> The Wilde cult started in Germany [. . .] the young Weininger [. . .] the scientific sex-dictionary of Kraft-Ebbing [*sic*] – these were the popular founts of inspiration and out of the orgy there arose nude schools of dancing.[42]

Krafft-Ebing's work was also undermined by the suggestion that it was basically pornography. Pemberton-Billing asked Douglas: 'Is it scientific?' He replied: 'I believe it is supposed to be, but [. . .] [i]t is pornographic;

that is the view that is taken by the medical authorities in England, so I am told.'[43] (Indeed, in 1902 the *British Medical Journal*'s review of the tenth edition of *Psychopathia Sexualis* had been very hostile, calling the book 'repulsive'.[44]) Pemberton-Billing did not take issue with Douglas's description, despite the fact that Allan's vilification had largely rested on the claim that Krafft-Ebing's work *was* scientific.

What defence did Allan manage to mount against the various attacks launched on her and *Salome*? Many of the accusations were difficult to counter. She knew the Asquiths; she had trained in Germany; she knew certain sexological terms. Her brother was indeed a murderer and no one attempted to question the 'scientific' assertion that sadism was hereditary. Her counsel did not appear aware of the *selective* use being made of sexology. Allan did try to counter Pemberton-Billing's claim that *Salome* was riddled with perversion: 'You could say "Mary had a little lamb" and read that in a good many ways',[45] she quipped. But the *double entendre* of 'having' a little lamb would probably have worked against her, since it again conveyed her 'inappropriate' sexual knowledge. Ironically perhaps, the main way in which *Salome* was defended against the accusation of sadism was in orientalist terms ('ironically' because one might have expected *Salome* to have been condemned in such terms). To Allan, 'Salome lived in the Eastern world at a time when our rules were not in vogue, and when to see his head in front of her was nothing.'[46] Or as Jack Grein, the play's producer replied, when asked by Pemberton-Billing 'would you think biting by a girl child of the lips of the severed head of a man an act of sadism?': 'No [. . .] I consider that an Eastern characteristic.'[47]

Towards the end of the trial Pemberton-Billing suddenly denied that he had called Allan a lesbian at all. (This was in fact a lie, since at the very beginning he had stated that the defamatory matters in the indictment were true, and the indictment claimed that the paragraph meant that Allan was a lesbian and consorted with lesbians.) Pemberton-Billing announced:

> There was no occasion for anyone to suggest that word [clitoris] refers to the sexual actions of woman and woman or man and woman [. . .] Captain Spencer said 'Cult of the Clitoris' meant 'a society of people who worship sexual excitement in all forms of inversion and perversion [. . .] they have a common patois, a common secret, a common guilt.'

He carried on: 'The word "clitoris" was calculated to be understood only by those people who [. . .] would refer to these things [. . .] Miss Allan knows immediately what it means.'[48] He was being contradictory and disingenuous: when he spoke of 'what it [the clitoris] means', he must have been implying lesbianism or nymphomania (the latter effectively being Spencer's given definition), yet he simultaneously claimed that 'the sexual actions of woman and woman or man and woman' were precisely *not* what 'that word' referred to. He was also conveniently overlooking the fact that one of his chief witnesses, Mrs Villiers Stuart, had said that *she* had immediately understood the libel when she had read it, and assumed the average person would have too.[49] But the jury seemed oblivious to the contradictions and gave Pemberton-Billing a verdict of 'not guilty'. He had withdrawn the accusation of lesbianism, but Allan had been labelled a sadist and one who consorted with others of her kind, namely non-patriotic, non-British, sexual perverts.

In court, the reaction to the verdict was loud cheering ('pandemonium', according to many papers) and crowds of thousands awaited Pemberton-Billing outside. As for Allan, theatre managers and her once adoring public now shunned her.[50] All the press editorials, however, condemned the verdict, and indeed the entire trial proceedings – 'a most lamentable affair' was one typical response; 'like a madhouse' was another.[51] To both the *Sunday Pictorial* and the *Daily News* the trial was reminiscent of *Alice in Wonderland*.

Returning to the three questions posed at the outset, first, how important was sexology to the final verdict? Part of the reason for Pemberton-Billing's success must surely have been his presentation of a scapegoat for Britain's seeming inability to win the war. The deployment of sexology, however – or rather, the *selective and opportunistic* deployment – undoubtedly played an important part, hitherto ignored by previous analyses of the trial. Above all, referencing sexological terms in a 'knowledgeable' fashion clearly lent scientific credibility. Not only were several sexological terms wielded as weapons in an attack on Allan and *Salome*, but the prosecution counsel – and the judge – were revealed to be ignorant amateurs compared to the defendant and his witnesses. The judge had to ask the meaning of sadism, masochism and fetishism, and when Spencer used the word 'orgasm', it was the prosecution counsel's turn to appear foolish.'Some unnatural vice?' inquired Hume-Williams; 'No, it is a function of the body', Spencer informed him.[52] Ironically, the fact that the defence witnesses themselves knew these terms should have rendered them suspect, for knowledgeable non-experts were supposedly perverts. Allan's 'inappropriate' knowledge was part of her undoing. But the prosecution never commented on this contradiction, or on the defence's apparent concession to the reduction of *Psychopathia Sexualis* to pornography, or indeed on the castigation of sexology as 'German'. Why no comment? As far as the defence witnesses' 'knowledge' was concerned, the prosecution was on dodgy ground: a woman's knowledge of sexual terms carried different implications from a man's knowledge, for ignorant women were innocent, while women with sexual knowledge were, by definition, 'tainted'.

Second, what representations of lesbianism did the trial convey? There were already rumours that Allan was a lesbian. Implying this was a trigger to ensure a libel case, which was, of course, Pemberton-Billing's intention. He was able to imply lesbianism through reference to the clitoris – a long-standing bodily signifier of lesbianism. But to sustain the accusation of lesbianism became difficult, and this, I would suggest, was why he suddenly denied that he had accused Allan of being a lesbian at all. The difficulty was threefold: there was no common understanding of what constituted lesbianism; most sexological texts did not actually lend themselves to an attack on lesbianism; it was hard to sustain an accusation of lesbianism via a condemnation of Oscar Wilde's *Salome*. In relation to male homosexuality there was now an identified sexual type – above all personified by the figure of Oscar Wilde. As Lord Alfred Douglas explained to the court: "To say that a man is an Oscar Wilde is to say – well, that he is a pervert.'[53] The stereotype of the male homosexual was of an effeminate, immoral, decadent, aesthetic, white and probably upper-class man.[54] Male homosexuality was now read not only via appearance and behaviour, but also via sexual object choice. The 1885 Criminal Law Amendment Act had aided that shift away from a focus on the criminal *acts* of sodomy to the obscene *relations* between men; the trials of Oscar Wilde had crystallized this new formulation. As yet, however, there was no equivalent sexual type in relation to the lesbian. Further, most sexological texts did not in fact aid a condemnation of lesbianism. Not only did Krafft-Ebing's text barely mention the subject, but he was explicitly against its criminalization. Havelock Ellis's *Sexual Inversion* of 1897 called for greater toleration of what he saw as a congenital 'anomaly', while Edward Carpenter's *The Intermediate Sex* of 1908 presented 'uranians', female as well as male, as frequently superior. The Swiss sexologist August Forel, however, was much more negative, claiming that nearly all inverts (of both sexes) were 'psychopaths' and 'neurotics', and some female inverts were nymphomaniacs.[55] (He was never mentioned by Pemberton-Billing or his witnesses, who may well not have heard of him.)

Pemberton-Billing also faced the difficulty of establishing lesbianism via an attack on *Salome*. He was forced to subsume lesbianism's specificity and to imply that it was an aspect of the sexual perversions which were more easily identifiable in *Salome* – sadism, masochism, fetishism, namely the other perversions listed by Krafft-Ebing. The fact that the clitoris also carried the inference of wider sexual deviancy – nymphomania, 'primitive' sexuality, hypersexuality – facilitated this reduction. If a representation of lesbianism was conveyed at all, it was one in which the perpetrator was sadistic, masochistic, fetishistic and nymphomaniac. And the continual references to the Germanic nature of sexual perversions added an extra dimension: sexual perverts, including lesbians, were also traitorous lovers of all things German.

Finally, what impact did the trial have on the wider culture, including the introduction of sexological terms? Certainly the trial was widely debated, if *The Times* is to be believed:

> No lawsuit of modern times has attracted such universal and painful interest. [. . .] Not only in London, but even more in the provincial towns and countryside, the daily reports have been read and discussed with almost as deep anxiety as the news of the war itself.[56]

What was the nature of this 'deep anxiety' ? To *The Times*, concern with public morality was clearly to the fore. The trial's verdict was 'an honest British repugnance for the whole Salome business'.[57] But there were other anxieties at large. Olga Loewenthal, an Austrian Jew, a lesbian and a well-known singer, was, according to her friend Lady Diana Manners: 'in a bad anxiety about the Billing case. I told her I knew her name was bound to come out; she stands I honestly believe but a very small chance of being overlooked, as she comes under "alien", "vice" and "house of ill repute".'[58] (I am unable to explain the latter intriguing reference.) The trial was widely discussed at the Front as well. Duff Cooper, a young officer, wrote to his future wife Diana Manners: 'No one here speaks or thinks of anything but the Billing case.' But from his account, it was not 'deep anxiety' that they were feeling: 'He [Pemberton-Billing] has kept the army amused for several days and provided a topic of conversation to officers who can never find one.[59] As for the various sexological terms bandied around in court, however, they were not widely reported in the newspapers. On the first day of the trial, the judge requested that 'in the interests of public decency the press will report as little as possible [of the disagreeable details]'.[60] The *Vigilante* (available by private subscription) and *The Times* were the only papers to mention the word 'lesbian'. 'Sadism' was named only in the *Vigilante*, the *Manchester Guardian*, and the *Daily Sketch*; 'Krafft-Ebing' only in the *Vigilante*, the *Times*, the *Manchester Guardian* and the *Westminster Gazette*. The *News of the World* mentioned 'homosexualists' (*sic*), while *The Times* quoted the word 'sodomitic'. Otherwise the newspapers generally wrote darkly of unspecified 'sexual perversions', 'a certain vice', or the favoured term 'moral pervert' (a combination of the older language of morality and the new language of sexology). The sexological information conveyed was thus fragmentary, even garbled.

For those not present at the Old Bailey, what sense was made of these hints of sexual deviancy? Diana Manners, who was nursing at Guy's Hospital in London, reflected on precisely this question to Duff Cooper: 'The nurses are just the same as your subalterns – they ask me all the time about the case and are totally ignorant of any significations. They have a dim vision of Sodom and Gomorrah, which is built for them by the word "vice". But even that is hazy.'[61] Diana and Duff may have understood what the libel was about, but others of the upper class were seemingly less clear. Diana informed Duff that 'Lord Albermarle is said to have walked into the Turf [Club] and said "I've never heard of this Greek chap Clitoris they are all talking of".'[62]

To the majority of the population, I suspect, the clitoris was neither a Greek chap nor a bodily part, but an unknown quantity. The new element introduced by the trial, however, was the sexological term 'sexual perversion'. These perversions – unspecified, yet thereby all the more sinister – were not simply 'vices' (the older moral term referring to vicious *acts*), but constitutive of genetic make-up and personal inclination. They were also essentially non-British, indeed *German* in essence, and their perpetrators were traitors. Xenophobia joined ranks with homophobia.

The drama of the trial drew on pre-existing assumptions concerning Maud Allan. The fact that she was a dancer, especially one who performed erotic 'oriental' dances, already cast her as sexually suspect, an appellation reinforced by her friendship with Margot Asquith. Pemberton-Billing and his witnesses deployed certain sexological terms in order to undermine Allan's credibility still further. They were not able to establish her lesbianism, but they claimed to have proved her sadism by virtue of her brother's crime (and thus her supposed hereditary disposition) and her wish to play the part of the 'sadistic' Salome. Her general sexual perversion was demonstrated by her dangerous knowledge of 'inappropriate' terms. Most sexologists would not have intended or desired their writings to have been used to police or silence, yet the defence's selective deployment of sexology had precisely this effect. Olga Loewenthal was unlikely to have been alone in fearing the consequences of the 'Billing' affair, for the 'cult of the clitoris' case sent out a message equating sexual conformity, heterosexuality and virility with Englishness and patriotism, versus sexual perversion, homosexuality, lesbianism, decadence, foreignness and treachery.

Notes

Many thanks to Laura Doan, Helen Crowley and Dave Phillips for their invaluable comments.
 1 *Sunday Pictorial,* 9 June 1918.
 2 *Vigilante,* 16 February 1918.
 3 *Imperialist,* 26 January 1918.
 4 Exposure of the 'Black Book' was part of another sub-plot to the trial, namely that Pemberton-Billing was working with others in an attempt to overthrow the coalition government, particularly its proposed peace talks. See Michael Kettle, *Salome's Last Veil* (Granada Publishing, London, 1977).

5 See Sander Gilman, 'Black Bodies, White Bodies: towards an Iconography of Female Sexuality in Late Nineteenth-Century Art, Medicine and Literature', in James Donald and Ali Rattansi (eds), *'Race', Culture and Difference* (Sage, London, 1992); Thomas Laqueur, 'Amor Veneris', in Michel Feher (ed.), *Fragments for a History of the Human Body*, part 3 (Zone, New York, 1989).

6 Havelock Ellis, *Sexual Inversion* (Watford University Press, Watford, 1897), p. 98.

7 See Margaret Gibson, 'Clitoral Corruption: Body Metaphors and American Doctors' Construction of Female Homosexuality, 1870–1900', in Vernon Rosario (ed.), *Science and Homosexualities* (Routledge, London, 1997).

8 Much of my information on Maud Allan comes from Felix Cherniavsky, *The Salome Dancer: The Life and Times of Maud Allan* (McClelland and Stewart, Toronto, 1991).

9 See Joanna de Groot, '"Sex" and "Race": The Construction of Language and Image in the Nineteenth Century', in Susan Mendus and Jane Rendall (eds), *Sexuality and Subordination* (Routledge, London, 1989); Bram Dijkstra, *Idols of Perversity* (Oxford University Press, Oxford, 1986), ch. XI; Amy Koritz, 'Salome: Exotic Woman and the Transcendent Dance', in Antony Harrison and Beverley Taylor (eds), *Gender and Discourse in Victorian Literature and Art* (North Illinois University Press, Urbana, IL, 1992); Elaine Showalter, *Sexual Anarchy: Gender and Culture at the Fin de Siècle* (Bloomsbury, London, 1991), ch. 8; Julie Wheelwright, *The Fatal Lover: Mata Hari and the Myth of Women in Espionage* (Collins & Brown, London, 1992).

10 Cherniavsky, *The Salome Dancer*, p. 174; *New York Times*, 8 August 1908, quoted in Ibid., p. 176.

11 Allan's fame briefly exceeded that of Isadora Duncan, to whom she was endlessly compared.

12 Quoted in *Pall Mall Gazette*, 11 March 1908.

13 See Rana Kabbani, *Europe's Myths of Orient* (Pandora, London, 1988); Reina Lewis, *Gendering Orientalism* (Routledge, London, 1996).

14 Author of 'Nemesis Hunt', *Maudie* ('Chetty' Club, London,1909).

15 Quoted in Cherniavsky, *The Salome Dancer*, p. 202.

16 Ibid., pp. 176, 193.

17 Kettle, *Salome's Last Veil*, p. 17.

18 *Vigilante*, 6 April 1918.

19 Ibid.

20 Kettle, *Salome's Last Veil*, p. 245. Unfortunately, the transcripts of the trial no longer exist. Michael Kettle, however, was able to read them in the 1970s, and a large part of them is reproduced verbatim in his book. I have thus relied heavily on *Salome's Last Veil*, in addition to reading the extensive press coverage of the trial. Other commentaries on the trial include Regenia Gagnier, *Idylls of the Marketplace: Oscar Wilde and the Victorian Public* (Scolar Press, Aldershot, 1987), appendix A; Jennifer Travis, 'Clits in Court: Salome, Sodomy and the Lesbian Sadist', in Carla Jay (ed.), *Lesbian Erotics* (New York University Press, New York, 1995); Philip Hoare, *Wilde's Last Stand: Decadence, Conspiracy and the First World War* (Duckworth, London, 1997). The trial is briefly mentioned in Pat Barker's wonderful novel *The Eye in the Door*

(Penguin, London, 1994).

21 *The Times*, 30 May 1918.

22 See H. Montgomery Hyde (ed.), *The Trials of Oscar Wilde* (William Hodge, London, 1948).

23 See Wheelwright, *The Fatal Lover.*

24 *The Times*, 30 May 1918.

25 Artemis Cooper (ed.), *A Durable Fire: The letters of Duff and Diana Cooper, 1913–1950* (Collins, London, 1983).

26 *The Times*, 30 May 1918.

27 *The Times*, 1 June 1918.

28 Kettle, *Salome's Last Veil*, p. 151.

29 Richard von Krafft-Ebing, *Psychopathia Sexualis* (F.A. Davis, Philadelphia, 1892).

30 Gert Hekma, 'A Female Soul in a Male Body', in Gilbert Herdt (ed.), *Third Sex, Third Gender* (Zone Books, New York, 1994).

31 For a good discussion of Krafft-Ebing, see Harry Oosterhuis, 'Richard von Krafft-Ebing's "Step-Children Of Nature": Psychiatry and the Making of Homosexual Identity', in Rosario (ed.), *Science and Homosexualities.*

32 Kettle, *Salome's Last Veil*, pp. 105, 144, 117.

33 Ibid., p. 159.

34 Ibid., p. 195.

35 Marie Stopes, *Married Love* (A.C. Fifield, London, 1918).

36 Krafft-Ebing, *Psychopathia Sexualis*, p.v.

37 For an interesting discussion of the play see Gagnier, *Idylls of the Market-place*; Peter Horne, 'Sodomy to Salome', in Mica Nava and Alan O'Shea (eds), *Modern Times* (Routledge, London, 1996).

38 *Morning Post*, 6 June, 1918.

39 Kettle, *Salome's Last Veil*, p. 152.

40 *The Times*, 3 June, 1918.

41 Kettle, *Salome's Last Veil*, p. 262.

42 *Sunday Pictorial*, 9 June 1918.

43 Kettle, *Salome's Last Veil*, p. 173.

44 Roy Porter and Lesley Hall, *The Facts of Life: The Creation of Sexual Knowledge in Britain, 1650–1950* (Yale University Press, New Haven and London, 1995), p. 163.

45 Kettle, *Salome's Last Veil,* p. 77.

46 Ibid., p. 74.

47 Ibid., p. 199.

48 Ibid., p. 229.

49 *Manchester Guardian*, 31 May 1918, and many of the other daily news-papers.

50 Cherniavsky, *The Salome Dancer*, p. 247.

51 *Evening News*, 5 June 1918; *Westminster Gazette,* 5 June 1918.

52 Kettle, *Salome's Last Veil*, p. 119.

53 *The Times*, 3 June 1918.

54 See Alan Sinfield, *The Wilde Century* (Cassell, London, 1994).

55 August Forel, *The Sexual Question* (1906; New Age Press, London, 1908).

56 *The Times*, 5 June 1918.
57 Ibid.
58 31 May 1918, in Cooper (ed.), *A Durable Fire*, p. 66.
59 3 June 1918, in ibid., p. 67 ; 6 June 1918, in ibid., p. 71.
60 *Manchester Guardian*, 30 May 1918.
61 31 May 1918, in Cooper (ed.), *A Durable Fire*, p. 66.
62 5 June 1918, in ibid., p. 70.

12 'Acts of Female Indecency': Sexology's Intervention in Legislating Lesbianism

Laura Doan

> [T]hose who have had to engage either in medical or in legal practice know that every now and again one comes across these horrors, and I believe that the time has come when [. . .] on account of its civil and sociological effects, this horrid grossness of homosexual immorality should [. . .] be grappled with.
>
> Frederick A. Macquisten, MP

Some feminist historians who enter the contentious and politically charged debate over sexology's role in constructing lesbianism in the late nineteenth and early twentieth centuries conclude that sexual science became a kind of weapon deployed against women, particularly feminists, to retaliate against their newfound economic and political freedom. Sheila Jeffreys, for instance, writes: "The significance of the sexological construction of the lesbian must be seen in its historical context of the backlash against feminism, alarm at spinsters and celibacy, and of the importance of passionate friendships to women in this period."[1] Following Jeffreys's lead, Margaret Jackson claims that the "sexological model of sexuality" was heterosexist and "anti-feminist": "the morbidification of lesbianism was undoubtedly a key factor in undermining feminism [. . .] in essence no more than the re-packaging, in scientific form, of the patriarchal model of sexuality which feminists were struggling to deconstruct."[2] Lillian Faderman is also highly suspicious of what she terms the sexologists' conscious or unconscious "hidden agenda," which aimed to "discourage feminism and maintain traditional sex roles by connecting the women's movement to sexual abnormality."[3] Without question, the scholarly preoccupation with the harmful effects of sexology has enhanced our understanding of the wider ideological stakes operating during this period, but this negative critique has also inhibited a strategic shift toward investigating how – or even if – sexological models of female homosexuality entered the public domain in the early decades of the century. Sexology, one presumes, must have been a powerfully incisive and devastating ideological force to undermine feminism, stigmatize lesbianism, and successfully connect the two.

In order to trace how and if such sexological constructions seeped outside of medical circles, and became in effect a tool of socio-political control, I propose to examine two historical moments, in 1920 and 1921, when the subject of criminalizing same-sex relations between women first entered legal discourse in England through the official record of parliamentary proceedings. I believe the realm of law is one effective starting point for exploring how sexology as ideology began to permeate public culture, since from the outset the designated readership of sexological literature included professionals in the medical and legal fields. According to Jackson, "Very few members of the general public had direct access [to these works] [. . .] since both sales and borrowing from libraries were restricted to people such as doctors, lawyers, and scientific researchers."4 Richard von Krafft-Ebing's important book *Psychopathia Sexualis* was "written for lawyers and doctors discussing sexual crimes in court," and Havelock Ellis, in his foreword to *Studies in the Psychology of Sex*, specified that copies of his work be sold "only to professional readers."5

By 1920, over two decades had passed since the initial publication of most of the influential sexological material on female sexual inversion, and thirty-five years had lapsed since the Labouchère Amendment had criminalized acts of gross indecency between men. Surely, in the immediate post-war era in England, we might reasonably assume that magistrates, lawyers, police and parliamentarians with privileged access to sexological literature could appropriate its medical epistemologies and taxonomies to devise regulatory legislation. Sexology's reservoir of case histories, its strategies of identification and classification noting the habits, behaviors and physical appearance of sexual inverts, would enable legal experts to challenge and deflect skeptics or sexual progressives who rejected the need for a clause or law to control the alleged threat female sexual deviants posed to civilized society, especially to the institutions of marriage and family. In its methodical delineation of abnormal behavior, sexological literature could demonstrate, with the ostensible force of scientific objectivity, the imperative for such a law and its implementation. By reading the minutes of parliamentary hearings and debates against sexological writings on female sexual inversion we will see whether some current assumptions and conclusions about how "scientific" knowledge disseminated into the public sphere attribute to sexology an exaggerated and extraordinary efficacy that it may in fact never have had.

On October 21, 1920, Cecil Maurice Chapman, a Metropolitan Police magistrate, was invited to comment further on the particulars contained in a note passed to Lord Muir Mackenzie, the chairman of the Joint Select Committee on the Criminal Law Amendment Bill (hereafter abbreviated as CLA Bill). The chairman remarked: "I notice in the note that you gave me [. . .] that you desire to suggest that the clause [concerning age of consent] should be extended so as to cover cases of gross indecency between women."[6] In the brief discussion that took place before the Joint Select Committee, and later in the debate on the "Acts of indecency by females" clause put before both Houses of Parliament in the late summer of 1921, competing and contradictory constructions of sexual activities between females would circulate uneasily. Whatever Chapman's motivations for introducing the note, it was soon clear that his interest was precise and narrow: his overarching concern was to protect all minors from adult sexual abuse, rather than to criminalize lesbianism as such. By calling for the extension of Clause 1 ("Consent ought not to be a defence to a charge of indecent assault on anybody up to the age of 16") to cover acts specifically between women and girls, Chapman intended to inscribe in law a long-standing feminist concern: the protection of young girls. This position was strongly supported by most feminist groups and social purity advocates (the sponsors of the CLA Bill), for whom the corruption of minors was a major issue. The Women's Freedom League (whose members included Chapman's own wife) set up a "Watch Committee" to monitor court proceedings and "concentrated particularly on cases of sexual abuse of children," especially young girls who could be preyed upon by anyone older, male or female.[7] Such groups recognized that, as Chapman put it to the committee, "it is very well known to the police, and it is very well known to many people who are students of criminology that women as well as men corrupt girls."

Chapman's interest in the protection of young girls explains the curious choice of cases he presented to the committee – each involving women and girls. He first mentions "a Home which was started for the reformation of girls where the police had to interfere because of the girls being corrupted by the woman controller of the Home." That same-sex institutions were frequently a breeding ground for sexual activities between females was documented by Krafft-Ebing, who explained that such sexual meetings were "practiced now-a-days in the harem, in female prisons, brothels and young ladies' seminaries."[8] In *The Sexual Question* August Forel concurs with Krafft-Ebing by specifying that "[a]ll these things take place chiefly in brothels or with prostitutes, in barracks, boarding-schools, convents, and other isolated places where [. . .] women live alone and separated from the other sex."[9] Ellis also opens his chapter on "Sexual Inversion in Women" with the assertion: "It has been found, under certain conditions, to abound among women in colleges and convents and prisons, as well as under the ordinary conditions of society."[10] According to Chapman's testimony, however, young girls were also vulnerable outside of same-sex environments. Thus he notes: "I have had very serious cases in my experience in which women have been in the habit of getting girls to their flats and houses in London, and I remember a case that took place at Bournemouth, where girls were practically being treated as if they were prostitutes." This image of the older woman as sexual predator is reminiscent of Forel's claim to "have known several women *of this kind*, who held veritable orgies and induced a whole series of young girls to become their lovers."[11] The phrase "of this kind" is highly significant, for Forel refers specifically to "feminine sexual inversion," and goes on to suggest that "[w]hen a woman invert wishes to seduce a normal girl, it is easy for her to do so." The idea that homosexual women prey on young girls surfaces also in the work of the Berlin sexologist Albert Moll, who undoubtedly contributed to an exaggerated concern for the welfare of young girls when he asserted that "many women inflicted with sexual inversion practice masturbation. [. . .] Those who masturbate themselves think of young girls during the act. [. . .] There seem to be women of homosexual tendencies who desire young immature girls."[12]

Chapman's primary concern for the welfare of girls was fueled by his experiences as a magistrate, but he may have also been influenced by the work of sexologists such as Forel, Moll and others, including the feminist and sexual progressive Stella Browne. As an early member of the radical British Society for the Study of Sex Psychology (BSSSP), Chapman may have heard Browne's 1917 paper where in several of the case histories she observed intimacy between women and young girls: two were devoted to children; one was involved with a girl "ten years her junior," and another was "professionally associated with children and young girls and [showed] her innate homosexual tendency by excess of petting and spoiling."[13] Browne's cases might seem to evoke the image of the predatory lesbian, but nowhere in the paper does it suggest that these activities were themselves ethically questionable. Browne and other progressive sexologists clearly differentiate between women who prey on young girls and the true or congenital sexual invert. Krafft-Ebing argues emphatically that while there are cases of teachers as "seducers" of "daughters of the high classes of society," these kinds of "sexual acts between persons of the same sex do not *necessarily* constitute antipathic sexual instinct. The latter exists only when the physical and psychical secondary sexual characteristics of the same sex exert an attracting influence over the individual and provoke in him or her the impulse to sexual acts."[14] In other words, women who engage in such practices may not be themselves inverted, but simply take advantage of the available supply. That such activities are extremely rare is underscored by the fact that in an entire chapter on female inversion, Ellis mentions only one case where a young girl was "indecently assaulted" by a woman and this case, he writes reassuringly, happened "some forty years ago."[15] Ellis generally dismisses some kinds of erotic attachment, such as those between girls and their school teachers, as a "spurious kind of homosexuality, the often precocious play of the normal instinct."[16] These attachments, he maintains, need not be of concern, for whether it occurs between girls, between schoolmistresses or between a girl and a schoolmistress, it is only if the individual is "congenitally predisposed" that her activity will persist, while "in the majority it will be forgotten as quickly as possible."[17] This notion that some women simply go through a phase would surface in the 1921 debate, where one member in the Lords reminds his peers that same-sex relations are disagreeable but inevitable: "we all know of the sort of romantic, almost hysterical friendships that are made between young women at certain periods of their lives."[18]

The cases Chapman presented to the Joint Select Committee were neither harmless nor a phase, but clear-cut incidents of sexual abuse. Yet Chapman scrupulously avoids using negative terms, such as "evil" or "vice," except when reporting what a police inspector had told him. On the other hand, although undoubtedly familiar with the clinical language for inversion, Chapman neither utters the words lesbian, female homosexuality or sexual inversion nor even implies that his cases involve female sexual inverts. In fact, he not only fails to invoke the proper medical terminology, but goes so far as to devise a method to raise the topic without public speech by passing a note to the chairman. I believe that Chapman refrains from sexological language precisely because he is well informed about sexological ideas – as a BSSSP member, which included Edward Carpenter, Ellis and Browne among others, Chapman would have been exposed to the notion of inversion as a category and perhaps shared their view that sexual activities between consenting adults should not be subject to legislation. Of all the participants in the parliamentary hearing, Chapman alone, it would seem, recognized that the acts he sought to criminalize – sexual relations between women and girls – had no *necessary* relationship to female sexual inversion. Just as both men and women have the potential to corrupt minors, so too do both heterosexuals and homosexuals. Such an understanding of inversion, however, is highly nuanced and the magistrate's subtle, even strategic, distinctions are clearly lost on most of the committee members.

Chapman's reticence, indeed his persistent invocation of the word "it" to encompass any manner of female indecency, has disastrous consequences, as it causes confusion among the committee members which, ultimately, results in the collision of contradictory constructions of sexual activities between females. This is evident from the moment Muir Mackenzie intones the phrase "gross indecency between women," and the subsequent lack of specificity leads to some farcical and scientifically vague discussions. For example, in the exchange between the Earl of Malmesbury (who did not support the clause when it came to the House of Lords in August of 1921), Lady Astor (who was noticeably silent during Chapman's testimony and later in the House of Commons debate) and Chapman, Malmesbury first asks Chapman whether it is "notorious that the particular vice to which you allude is extraordinarily common?" Chapman replies, "I think it is fairly common," but, when pressed by Astor, rephrases the answer to "I should not say that it was very frequent." Yet Lord Wemyss exclaims a few moments later that "One has always heard that it is on the increase as long as one remembers," while Muir Mackenzie notes "It has been known for centuries." No one queries how something that is not named could possibly be increasing because everyone has some – perhaps different – idea of what is being discussed. Because, as Chapman explains, "People were a little shy of raising it because not many knew that such a thing existed or could take place," committee members tiptoe tactfully around the topic and, consequently, the word "it" appears some twenty-four times in the short discussion. Each speaker seems convinced that particular people have particular knowledge, but no one is positive about what anyone else means by "it."

Such a parliamentary exchange reminds one of what Michel Foucault, in his analysis of what he terms the "repressive hypothesis," calls the myth about Victorian sexuality: where ostensibly "[o]n the subject of sex, silence became the rule."[19] In actuality, Foucault argues, "new rules of propriety screened out some words: there was a policing of statements. [. . .] Areas were thus established, if not of utter silence, at least of tact or discretion."[20] Yet both the magistrate's and the Joint Select Committee's reluctance to name the "particular offence" seems to have been confined only to the actual room – for the testimony itself reveals ample evidence of correspondence and numerous conversations on the subject occurring behind the scenes. Thus Chapman reports on conversations he had with people at the reform institution ("people told me [. . .] what the girls had to submit to"), with officials in Paris ("I was told it was a frequent occurrence"), and with various policemen in England ("I can only say what the police tell me" and "an Inspector said that the evil which was brought to my attention was very much on the increase lately"). That such discussions were by no means rare exposes unequivocally the existence of public secrets – in the formal setting of a parliamentary hearing, a silence of sorts ("it") co-exists alongside terse, cryptic references. As Foucault notes: "What is peculiar to modern societies [. . .] is not that they consigned sex to a shadow existence, but that they dedicated themselves to speaking of it *ad infinitum*, while exploiting it as *the* secret."[21] The refusal or simple inability to name the act or to distinguish between non-consensual, cross-generational sexual relations and same-sex relations between consenting adults demonstrates persuasively that sexological labels and distinctions had, at this stage, minimal impact outside of sexology itself. Consequently, by the end of Chapman's testimony, there is a subtle slip from his concern regarding sexual acts between women and girls to a discussion of the criminalization of sexual acts between women. Chapman's failure to clarify the nature of the sexual behavior results in a startling shift: his limited request to extend Clause 1 (concerning the defilement of girls 13 to 16 years of age) to include both sexes culminates instead in the committee's proposal to extend the Labouchère Amendment (criminalizing acts between men) to women, thereby criminalizing lesbianism.

This sort of confusion about what is under discussion or what should be criminalized dissolves when the question goes before Parliament during the debate on the CLA Bill, yet the delicate circumspection about discussing sexual inversion remains. With the support of some fifty-eight national women's organizations, this "agreed" bill (meaning that the introduction of any contentious or hostile clause would sink the entire bill) sought to strengthen further the laws to protect children from sexual abuse and would have removed a major loophole in the law that allowed men to claim "reasonable cause to believe" that a minor was over the age of consent. Among those opposed to the bill, dubbed by the feminist press as the "obstructionists," were three lawyers, Frederick A. Macquisten, Howard Gritten and Sir Ernest Wild, who, late in the evening of August 4, 1921, called for the introduction of a new (and contentious) clause, the "Acts of indecency by females," that read: "Any act of gross indecency between female persons shall be a misdemeanour and punishable in the same manner as any such act committed by male persons under section eleven [the Labouchère Amendment] of the Criminal Law Amendment Act, 1885." Macquisten opened the debate by announcing that the topic under consideration could not be discussed frankly in the Commons: "One cannot in a public assembly go into the details; it is more a matter for medical science and for neurologists. But all lawyers who have had criminal and divorce practice know that there is in modern social life an undercurrent of dreadful degradation, unchecked and uninterfered with."[22] When the Lords took up the clause, Malmesbury apologizes for even initiating "a discussion upon what must be, to all of us, a most disgusting and polluting subject," and the Earl of Desart notes that it is "very disagreeable talking of these things."[23] In an earlier pre-sexological age, one wonders if the whispers were also preceded by loud apologies, for such matters could not be discussed by "decent" people. Obviously none of the well-mannered gentlemen intends to abandon the "disgusting" subject, and so the apology becomes the formal mechanism to break into the hitherto unknown territory.

The parliamentarians' next crucial order of business was to gauge the boundaries of intelligibility; in other words, to speculate on who knew what. Two constituencies, according to the various speakers, have a degree of familiarity with the "gross practices": medical men (especially neurologists and physicians who work in asylums) and legal men (in particular criminologists, lawyers and police). As noted above, Macquisten indicates that "those who have had to engage either in medical or in legal practice know that every now and again one comes across these horrors." For this reason, one assumes, most of those who voted in favor of the clause were "leaders of the Bar who happen to be Members of the House."[24] Yet Macquisten exclaims: "to many members of this House the mere idea of the suggestion of such a thing is entirely novel; they have never heard of it." Colonel Wedgwood quickly asserts that the intention of the clause would have to be explained to members of the Labour party who, by their lack of a public school education, would not have encountered the "Lesbian vice": "For their benefit, I will tell them that the ordinary boy who goes to a public school learns at that public school from the classics which he reads about what is known as Lesbian vice." Thus, knowledge of such practices, demarcated by profession and class, can be exploited, as Foucault argues, as "*the* secret." Equally interesting is the assumption that the very group most affected by the proposed clause, women, are largely ignorant of such practices. The Lord Chancellor, for example, refutes the suggestion that the practice is well known and states that "the overwhelming majority of the women of this country have never heard of this at all [. . .] I would be bold enough to say that of every thousand women, taken as a whole, 999 have never even heard a *whisper* of these practices" (emphasis mine). Ironically, the knowledge of "such practices" circulated in some circles precisely in the form of whispers, which generates discourse as effectively as medical science.

Of all the members, only Sir Ernest Wild refers to specific sexologists in his speech, when he relates how in preparation for the parliamentary discussion of the clause (as a co-sponsor he researched the topic prior to the debate) he had consulted "one of the greatest of our nerve specialists." This unnamed "expert" affirms in his letter to Wild that sexological literature is indispensable in understanding the full spectrum of female sexual "malpractices":

It would be difficult to recite the various forms of malpractices between women, as it would be impossible to recite them in the House. If you wish for these it would be best to obtain a copy of Kfraft-

Ebing [*sic*] "Psychopathia Sexualis," or Havelock Ellis's work on sexual malpractices. My own feeling is simply to refer to the Lesbian love practices between women, which are common knowledge.

Curiously, according to the logic of the nerve specialist, it is sexology itself which is unspeakable and ordinary "Lesbian love practices" which are common knowledge. One wonders why Wild chooses to share with his colleagues the information that it would be wholly inappropriate for sexological knowledge to circulate beyond the confines of medical discourse. In a sense, Wild announces to the House that a whole range of sexual activities between females exists that cannot or should not be specified. In presenting a portion of the letter to the House that mentions two leading sexologists by name, Wild steals the prestige of scientific knowledge, its veneer so to speak, to legitimize his own political agenda. Wild thus speaks with the authority of science but cleverly distances himself from any of the arguments of these same sexologists, who, as "congenitalists," argue that since true sexual inversion is congenital it should not be subject to legislation. His eagerness to cite these men by name does not signal an acceptance of their conclusions, which explains why Wild's descriptive language is at loggerheads with sexology: lesbianism, for Wild, is "a beastly subject," "a vice" and "a very real evil." Wild fails to grasp, or chooses to ignore, sexology's principal achievement in shifting the terms of the debate from morality to modern medical discourse.

What we see here is the formation of an incipient understanding of how "scientific" objectivity could be deployed to work productively on behalf of a law to control sexual deviance. For men like Wild, sexology's real appeal is simply its guise of scientific authority. The use of sexology to call for the legislation of lesbianism thus represents not merely a selective use of its findings, but the virtual turning of sexology against itself. Consider, for example, Macquisten's vaguely oxymoronic phrase, "homosexual immorality," which marries a scientific term with a moral imperative. Inasmuch as the word "homosexual" operates as an adjective, the weight of the phrase leans more heavily toward immorality – demarcating simply one form over others, though the threat homosexuality poses to "feminine morality" strikes at the heart of civilization. That the preferred term for the "very real evil" is vice, which appears literally dozens of times throughout the debates, suggests again that the central tenets of sexology have been either rejected or unassimilated. This is evident in Desart's question: "How many people does one suppose are really so vile, so unbalanced, so neurotic, so decadent as to do this?" This laundry list of attributes, which slips between psychology, popular belief and cultural anxiety, reflects a real confusion and conflation about the subject matter.

A skilled lawyer, Wild cites a number of cases to support his argument in favor of the clause, some reminiscent of Chapman's earlier testimony. First, Wild recounts how the nerve specialist told him "that no week passes that some unfortunate girl does not confess to him [the specialist] that she owes the breakdown of her nerves to the fact that she has been tampered with by a member of her own sex." Wild also produces a report from the Central Criminal Court "in which a witness stated on oath that this practice had taken place between her and an elder woman," and that any "chief officers of police" would confirm that the case was not unusual. Finally, he reports that asylum doctors "assure me that the asylums are largely peopled by nymphomaniacs and people who indulge in this vice." (Macquisten also relates how "there is much victimization of young women by their own sex.") In conflating lesbianism and sexual relations between women and girls, Wild proves merely that the latter practices exist, with greater or lesser frequency, for it is inconsequential whether or not such cases are the result of congenital sexual inversion.

Wild ostensibly builds his case on behalf of the criminalization of lesbianism upon the convergence of medical and legal opinions; however, careful scrutiny of his "evidence" reveals that his batch of "experts" never specifically endorses his agenda, for the savvy politician would have most certainly cited them if they had. One presumes that his medico-legal "experts" were familiar with the dominant position among sexologists that homosexual acts between consenting adults should be exempt from the law. Such a position would have been in concert with the leading advanced views of the age, as articulated by sexologists such as Forel, who writes: "So long as homosexual love does not affect minors nor insane persons, it is comparatively innocent. [. . .] Legal protection of the two sexes against sexual abuses of all kinds should be extended at least to the age of seventeen or eighteen."[25] Just as in the 1920 parliamentary hearing, the question of whether female homosexuality was increasing was both at the forefront of the parliamentary debate and likewise lacked consensus. Macquisten asserted that "these horrors" occur "every now and again," while Wild claims doctors say "this is a very prevalent practice," only to contradict himself later by stating, "I will not say the vice is rampant in society [but] there are people in society who are guilty of it." Opponents of the clause such as Desart retorted: "You may say there are a number of them, but it would be, at most, an extremely small minority." The fixation on the frequency of same-sex relations between women suggests that, swirling beneath the legal body's determination that the "vice" should be halted before it spreads too far, is a growing anxiety, as feminist historians affirm, about female emancipation and increased sexual sophistication. For supporters of the clause such as Wild, female homosexuality was just one indication of the decline of civilization which "saps the fundamental institutions of society." Wild elaborates on this point by claiming that the vice "stops childbirth, because it is a well-known fact that any woman who indulges in this vice will have nothing whatever to do with the other sex. [. . .] [This] vice [. . .] must tend to cause our race to decline." This idea is echoed by Macquisten who argues that "it's best to stamp out an evil which is capable of sapping the highest and the best in civilization." Chapman's earlier concern for the welfare of young girls pales in comparison with a lesbian threat that strikes out at a vulnerable society, indeed the survival of the race itself.

Jeffrey Weeks speculates that the writer responsible for establishing this "well-known" fact was Arabella Kenealy in her book *Feminism and Sex Extinction*.[26] For Kenealy, the women's movement "de-sexed and masculinized" women, and although masculinized women had always been considered "abnormal" in previous years, lately it "has become a serious Cult." Such a woman "is incapable of parenthood," and thus feminism leads to "Race-suicide."[27] Before the war, in 1909, the eugenist couple William and Catherine Whetham warned that the "interests of active public life [. . .] exert such a fascination on the minds of [unmarried] [. . .] women that they become unwilling to accept the necessary and wholesome restrictions and responsibilities of normal marriage and motherhood. Woe to the nation whose best women refuse their natural and most glorious burden!"[28] The feminism under attack in this passage is responsible for the decline of female morality and for the increase in lesbianism. In fact, several sexologists, including Carpenter, Forel and Magnus Hirschfeld, believed there was a strong lesbian presence in the women's movement, as Ellis notes: "[Iwan] Bloch and others believe that the woman movement has helped to develop homosexuality."[29] Ellis himself was perhaps the "most concerned," as Lucy Bland observes, for he believed the "Women's Movement was encouraging [. . .] not true inversion but its 'spurious imitation'."[30] Female homosexuality thus becomes a significant threat to civilization and the future of the race. Pervading the parliamentary discussion is this new "fact" of modern life: same-sex relations between females signalled the decline of civilization and the undermining of the institution of marriage. In fact, both Macquisten and Wild describe particular cases known to them where marriages had been wrecked because the wife had been lured and corrupted by another woman. Wild cites a marriage where the "wife had been taken from [the husband] by a young woman," and Macquisten tells of a home ruined "by the wiles of one abandoned female." Fortunately, in the latter case, the wife shortly thereafter became involved with a man and thus the husband could establish grounds for divorce. In both cases, though especially in the latter, it is unclear whether the activities constitute clinically defined female inversion or consensual same-sex relations between women, and again, legislators are uninterested in the distinction.

From opponents of the clause we find a greater sympathy, if not a particularly clear-cut understanding, for the position of groups like the BSSSP, who in 1914 published an English translation of a 1903 German pamphlet on *The Social Problem of Sexual Inversion* which argued that since "God, or Nature, has brought into being not only normal men and women but uranians [. . .] it is really too ridiculous to imagine that the process of nature can be abolished, or even appreciably restrained, by pen and paper enactments."[31] Obviously, those opposed to criminalizing lesbianism were somewhat at a disadvantage inasmuch as the very reason for the discussion – to insert a clause into the Criminal Law Amendment Bill – already plunged the subject into a criminal context with a moral tone. But as Wedgwood explains, "you cannot make people moral by act of Parliament." Lieutenant-Colonel Moore-Brabazon, who concedes the need for a certain "moral courage" to join the discussion, also urges his fellow members to remember "that on this subject we are not dealing with crime at all. We are dealing with abnormalities of the brain [. . .] [and must] decide whether it is wise to deal with mental cases in the Law Courts." He then continues, with an interesting twist on Kenealy's "race-suicide" argument, by pointing out that "these cases are self-exterminating [. . .] they have the merit of exterminating themselves, and consequently they do not spread or do very much harm to society at large." Here Moore-Brabazon maintains that the very inability of such women to bear children is positive, as the failure to procreate prevents the spread of lesbianism – a point also voiced by Malmesbury: "I believe that all these unfortunate specimens of humanity exterminate themselves by the usual process." This argument had been made some years earlier by Forel when he queried, "What is the use of prosecuting inverts?":

> It is comparatively innocent for it produces no offspring and consequently dies out by means of selection. [. . .] It is a fortunate thing for society that [. . .] [they] are contented with their mutual sexual intercourse, the result of which is sterile and therefore does no harm to posterity.[32]

The feminist press branded the men who successfully derailed the CLA Bill "obstructionists," whose aim was to prevent at any cost the passage of a bill that would eliminate the favored loophole, "reasonable cause to believe." When the "acts of female indecency" clause returned to the Commons from the Lords, the "obstructionists" protested that wrecking the bill had never been their intention for, like the bill's many supporters, they too were motivated solely by a concern for the protection of the young, male and female alike. A thorough analysis of the political aims of both sides of the debate falls beyond the scope of this chapter, but it is unlikely the "obstructionists" were sympathetic to the larger bill.[33] On the contrary, these men were so intent on achieving their political aims that they devised a clause that would create maximum embarrassment to the women's movement. Despite the obstructionists' dire warnings of the threat and danger of the female sexual invert, no law against "gross indecency between females" ever passed. The obstructionists, however, "won" – for not only did the CLA Bill fail, but the feminists were successfully smeared with the unsavory label of inversion, a happy by-product.

In the end, lesbianism was not the primary target, and sexology was not the effective strategic weapon its detractors claim. Rather than a tool of control in the service of patriarchal hegemony, sexology served multiple functions and conflicting political agendas, for men of law who sought to protect children or preserve a legal loophole were just as inclined to rely on sexological notions as on hearsay and rumor, gleaned in the backrooms of police stations or in reports from unnamed sources. In the attempt to impose regulatory legislation of same-sex relations between women, sexology could be abused whether one's political agenda was conservative or liberal, homophobic or homogenic, or even feminist. Historians invested in the negative critique of sexology presume – incorrectly – that it drifted into the public domain in a more or less pure state, and that sexologists were complicit with anti-feminists and homophobes who launched a backlash against both feminists and lesbians. On the contrary, far from avidly consuming sexology, legislators would exploit its nuanced findings in ways that many sexologists would not have sanctioned. Whether articulated as an "it" or as a perversion of sexological language, as with "homosexual vice," female sexual inversion as a coherent sexological construction did not exist within 1920s' legal discourse. The invocation of the medical labels never signified necessarily the unmediated acquisition of the relevant medical knowledge. Words like lesbian or invert could refer to *any* sort of sexual act between females, without regard to the fine distinctions advanced by Ellis, whose designation "congenital sexual inversion" was intended to remove any stigma of sin, mental illness or physical disease. In legal discursive practices at this time we see that sexology would all too often be read against itself, its ideological force diluted through misinterpretation and simplification, its medical taxonomies ignored or glossed. Feminist historians who view sexology as a weapon are therefore both right and wrong; that is, they are correct in their conclusions, but wrong in their method, for we must always be cautious, as George Chauncey, puts it, not to attribute "inordinate power to ideology as an autonomous social force."[34] Sexual science obliquely facilitated legislation by lending its veneer of prestige; however, the full explanatory power of sexology's case histories, its epistemologies and taxonomies, became, in the hands of the would-be oppressors, misused, adulterated and impure.

Notes

1 Sheila Jeffreys, "Women and Sexuality," in *Women's History: Britain, 1850–1945*, ed. June Purvis (UCL Press, London, 1995), pp. 193–216, esp. 205.

2 Margaret Jackson, *The Real Facts of Life: Feminism and the Politics of Sexuality c. 1850–1940* (Taylor and Francis, London, 1994), pp. 121, 108.

3 Lillian Faderman, *Odd Girls and Twilight Lovers: A History of Lesbian Life in Twentieth-Century America* (Columbia University Press, New York, 1991), p. 48.

4 Jackson, *The Real Facts of Life*, p. 159.

5 Harry Oosterhuis, "Richard von Krafft-Ebing's 'Step-Children of Nature': Psychiatry and the Making of Homosexual Identity," in *Science and Homosexualities*, ed. Vernon A. Rosario (Routledge, London, 1997), pp. 67–88, esp. 70; Havelock Ellis, 1902, *Studies in the Psychology of Sex, Complete in Two Volumes* (Random House, New York, 1942), p. xxii.

6 Report by the Joint Select Committee of the House of Lords and the House of Commons, *Minutes of Evidence Taken Before the Joint Select Committee on the Criminal Law Amendment Bill* (HMSO, London, 1920), 936, para. 1479. Subsequent references to this parliamentary exchange can be found in paras 1479–1502.

7 Jackson, *The Real Facts of Life*, p. 42.

8 Richard von Krafft-Ebing, *Psychopathia Sexualis, with Especial Reference to the Antipathic Sexual Instinct. A Medico-Forensic Study* [1886] (Stein and Day, New York, 1965), pp. 262, 263.

9 August Forel, *The Sexual Question: A Scientific, Psychological, Hygienic and Sociological Study for the Cultured Classes* (Heinemann, London, 1906), p. 274–5.

10 The choice of the word "abound" is strategic, for his purpose here is to establish that inversion is as common in women as in men. Havelock Ellis, *Studies in the Psychology of Sex*, 7 vols (F.A. Davis, Philadelphia, 1928), *Vol. II: Sexual Inversion*, p. 195.

11 Forel, *The Sexual Question*, p. 252. Emphasis added.

12 Albert Moll, *Perversions of the Sex Instinct: A Study of Sexual Inversion* [1891] (Julian Press, Newark, 1931), pp. 231, 233.

13 In this paper, published six years later, Browne advocates an acceptance of female sexual inversion well ahead of her time: "Let us recognize this force [female sexual inversion], as frankly as we recognize and reverence the love between men and women." F.W. Stella Browne, 'Studies in Feminine Inversion', *Journal of Sexology and Psychoanalysis* (1923), pp. 51–8, esp. 55.

14 Krafft-Ebing, *Psychopathia Sexualis*, p. 262. Emphasis added.

15 Ellis, *Sexual Inversion*, p. 214.

16 Ibid., pp. 216–17.
17 Ibid., p. 216.
18 *Hansard* (1921) Official Reports, 5th Series, Parliamentary Debates, House of Lords Vol. 14. All citations of this debate on 15 August, 1921, 565–77.
19 Michel Foucault, *The History of Sexuality*, 1976, 3 vols (Penguin, Harmondsworth, 1990), *Vol. 1: An Introduction*, p. 3.
20 Ibid., pp. 17–18.
21 Ibid., p. 35.
22 *Hansard* (1921) Official Reports, 5th Series, Parliamentary Debates, House of Commons Vol. 145. All citations of this debate on 4 August, 1921, 1799-1806.
23 Lords debate, 15 August, 1921, p. 568.
24 *Hansard* (1921) Official Reports, 5th Series, Parliamentary Debates, House of Commons Vol. 146. 17 August, 1921, p. 1596.
25 Forel, *The Sexual Question*, p. 247.
26 Jeffrey Weeks, *Coming Out: Homosexual Politics in Britain from the Nineteenth Century to the Present* (Quartet Books, London, 1977), p. 106.
27 Arabella Kenealy, *Feminism and Sex Extinction* (T. Fisher Unwin, London, 1920), pp. 246, 253, 263.
28 W.C.D. Whetham and C.D. Whetham, *The Family and the Nation: A Study in Natural Inheritance and Social Responsibility* (Longmans, Green and Co., London, 1909), p. 199.
29 Ellis, *Sexual Inversion*, p. 262.
30 Lucy Bland, *Banishing the Beast: English Feminism and Sexual Morality 1885–1914* (Penguin, London, 1995), p. 264.
31 Scientific Humanitarian Committee, *The Social Problem of Sexual Inversion*, in *We Are Everywhere: A Historical Sourcebook of Gay and Lesbian Politics*, eds Mark Blasius and Shane Phelan (Routledge, London, 1997), p. 140.
32 Ibid., pp. 247, 404.
33 See my forthcoming *Fashioning Sapphism: The Origins of a Modern English Lesbian Culture* (Columbia University Press, New York). It is important to mention that the tenor of the debate in the Lords, where the clause was rejected, is entirely different, as the Lords generally refer to the sexual activities between women as this "particular subject." Twice the topic is called "disgusting" and once "polluting," but overall references to the subject are quite restrained in comparison to the discourse of the House of Commons.
34 George Chauncey, "From Sexual Inversion to Homosexuality: Medicine and the Changing Conceptualization of Female Deviance," *Salmagundi*, 58–9 (1983), pp. 114–46, esp. 115.

13 'Sex Is An Accident': Feminism, Science and the Radical Sexual Theory of *Urania*, 1915–40

Alison Oram

The aim of this chapter is to argue that the development of new and radical ideas about sex, gender and sexuality in the interwar years was not the prerogative of the traditional sexologists alone. Historians usually identify key individual male figures such as Havelock Ellis, Sigmund Freud and Edward Carpenter as responsible for shifting ideas about sexuality towards a 'modern' scientific set of discourses, and this process as augmented by the popularizing work of several important but typically secondary female figures such as Marie Stopes and Stella Browne. This classic approach highlighting key individuals and texts obscures the activities of other groups who were also developing ideas about sex, sexuality and gender during and after World War I. One particularly interesting and important example is the journal *Urania*, published between 1915 and 1940. I have previously argued that sexological ideas about women were not as hegemonic by the interwar period as is often assumed by historians, and that feminists in this period deployed a range of discursive responses to sexology.[1] As well as these somewhat defensive positions, there were also distinctly radical attempts such as that made by *Urania* to develop ideas about sex which effectively, if indirectly, critiqued sexology on very different scientific and epistemological grounds. *Urania*, it will be demonstrated, created an alternative feminist position on sex, sexuality and gender which was textually separate and theoretically distinct from, yet parallel to, mainstream sexology.

Urania was a privately circulated magazine, produced by a small group of feminist women and men, and published six (later three) times a year between 1915 and c.1940. Its contents consisted mainly of reprinted selections from books and the international press, with some occasional editorial comment. *Urania*'s stated aim was 'the abolition of the "manly" and the "womanly"', i.e. all distinctions of sex and gender. Every issue carried its declaration against the false distinction of sex:

> *Urania* denotes the company of those who are firmly determined to ignore the dual organization of humanity in all its manifestations. They are convinced that this duality has resulted in the formation of two warped and imperfect types. They are further convinced that in order to get rid of this state of things no measures of 'emancipation' or 'equality' will suffice, which do not begin by a complete refusal to recognize or tolerate the duality itself.

Urania attacked the social construction of gender (masculinity and femininity), advocating independence for women and sweetness for men. It carried reports of women's success in new fields of endeavour to illustrate the fact that women's intellectual competence was equal to men's, while the many press stories of women's courage and strength showed that physical power and bravery were not possessed by men alone. *Urania* regularly reprinted examples of both male/female and female/male cross-dressing from newspapers around the world, including transvestism, mistaken sex, passing for the other sex, and same-sex marriage. These demonstrated the mutability and fluidity of gender distinctions; gender identity was a sham, a masquerade, and a creation of society. But the continuum the paper suggested between cross-dressing and spontaneous transsexualism (physical change of sex), also often reported in the late 1930s, was more radical still in its refusal of the essentialist construction of the body itself. The sexed biological body was no more stable than the social category of gender. (In late twentieth-century terms we could see *Urania* as attempting to build a feminist theory of radical transgender. This was not simply about moving from one embodied sex to the other, but, more radically, about abolishing the physical boundaries between masculinity and femininity altogether.)[2]

This exploration of astonishingly new territory was accompanied by a continuing hostility towards marriage and heterosexual sex, even for the purposes of procreation, in the pages of *Urania*. Yet at the same time, the journal published a steady stream of material that delighted in the appeal of love relationships between women. Its politics had developed directly out of the complex and powerful debates among turn-of-the-century feminists about women's nature, the exploitation of women by male sexuality, and the joys of comradeship between women in the battle for women's suffrage.[3] This strength of purpose and idealism continued within feminism in different ways after World War I. In the publication of *Urania* over many years the evolution of these ideals formed a significant contrast to mainstream feminism and to the development of sexological discourses.

The Legacy of Turn-of-the-Century Feminism

Five people were listed as contacts in each edition of *Urania*, all of whom had their political roots in Edwardian suffrage feminism and related interests including pacifism, theosophy and animal rights, through which they had met before or during World War I. The driving force behind *Urania*, who supplied most of the reprinted articles and wrote nearly all the editorial material, was the person who signed him/herself T. Baty or Irene Clyde. In their detailed scholarly work on Clyde's published books, Daphne Patai and Angela Ingram have shown that – living out his transgendered persona in print – Irene Clyde was the pseudonym often used by Thomas Baty (1869–1954), a highly educated and internationally respected legal scholar.[4] Baty, who lived in Japan from 1916, was a pacifist and a vegetarian and described himself as a feminist. He extolled the virtues and attractions of femininity, writing in 'An Autobiographical Sketch' that he 'adored Beauty and Sweetness; considered ladies had both, as well as Persistence and Tenacity. Therefore, longed passionately to be a lady.'[5] Clearly Baty saw himself as what we might now term a transgendered person, and developed his gender theories at length in his fiction and non-fiction published as Irene Clyde, as well as in *Urania*.[6] Before the launch of *Urania* these ideas had been floated within a group he founded around 1912 called the Aëthnic Union.[7] The other key people associated with *Urania* were the prominent feminists Eva Gore-Booth and Esther Roper, central figures in the suffrage movement in Manchester who had met in 1896 and lived together in a life-long, loving partnership.[8] Eva, a poet and a mystic as well as a practical political campaigner, was a particularly inspirational figure for *Urania*. Lines of her poetry were quoted under the title piece in most issues after her death in 1926, and her aphorism 'Sex is an accident' was referred to more than once as summing up the philosophy of *Urania*.[9] Two other people were listed as contacts: Dorothy Cornish, a Montessorian and long-term friend of Baty's, and Jessey Wade (1860–1952), an animal rights campaigner.[10] We can surmise that *Urania*'s readership was found among similar networks: the journal was privately published and sent free to anyone expressing an interest in its ideals. It referred to and sometimes printed correspondence with 'friends', including, in 1919, the prominent feminist writer Mona Caird, and claimed a circulation of between 200 and 250 throughout its period of publication.[11]

The feminists who published *Urania* throughout the interwar years had formed their political ideas a generation earlier, from the 1890s through to the 1910s, a fertile period of feminist debates about sex and sexuality, as Lucy Bland has shown. These feminist ideas included the condemnation of masculinist heterosexuality as oppressive to women, the idealization of feminine qualities as higher, more admirable and more spiritual than masculine ones, the repudiation of marriage in favour of spinsterhood, and the celebration of female romantic friendship.[12] Many late-nineteenth century feminists (some personally known to Roper and Gore-Booth), such as Elizabeth Wolstenholme Elmy and Frances Swiney, had condemned men's sexual exploitation of women in marriage and argued for the transmutation of physical sexuality into 'psychic love'.[13] Arguments against marriage and heterosexuality continued to be developed and sharpened into the 1900s by feminists including Christabel Pankhurst and Cicely Hamilton, in her book *Marriage as a Trade* (1909). *Urania*'s continual emphasis on the virtue of celibacy and its stress on transcending the physical body to enable development of the spiritual self also had significant links with feminist readings of theosophy in the same period.[14]

Earlier feminists had assumed a biologically essentialist basis to their celebration of feminine traits, but *Urania*'s editors stressed that gender was socially constructed. Arguing that legislative equality was insufficient on its own, *Urania* declared that the emancipation of women could only be achieved if the duality of gender were overcome: 'If the world is to see sweetness and independence combined in the same individual, *all* recognition of that duality must be given up. [. . .] There are no "men" or "women" in Urania.'[15] However, out of the whole range of human qualities which should be available to both sexes, *Urania* emphasized those typically gendered as feminine as being most desirable. 'Our propaganda is a passionate call for the union of a fearless and spirited independence with delicacy, charm and affection.'[16] The education of boys which led to war and violence was strongly condemned: 'So long as the male arrogant and torture-tolerant spirit is inculcated in schools, so long will channels be found for its exhibition in life.'[17]

An integral part of *Urania*'s feminist perspective was its strong rejection of both marriage and heterosexual sex. Marriage, it was claimed, inhibited individual development and spirituality, especially of women, since it enforced gender differentiation. Heterosexuality was a means of dominating women, and heterosexual desire was socially conditioned into people:

> When we see the whole force of its environment being concentrated on each child that comes into the world, to instil into it a consciousness of sexual desire, the only rational conclusion is that without this tremendous pressure, the desire would hardly exist.[18]

'Irene Clyde' wrote in a review of Winifred Holtby's book *Women*: 'to obtain real equality one must throw sex overboard'.[19] As a reward for freeing oneself from 'sex' – understood as both gender differentiation and heterosexuality – *Urania* put forward an ecstatic utopian mysticism:

> It is impossible to express the sense of emancipated exhilaration which floods the soul when it has discarded the idea of sex. [. . .] We are set free: the infinitely Lovely, the infinitely Valiant, is no longer the object of mad and hopeless worship, – so far as we can conceive it, we can proudly take it into our own being, and become one with its splendour. [. . .] What is the union of bodies compared with that? The pale, barren and watery delusion of a moment [. . .] We have only to refuse to wear the shackles of sex.[20]

Love between women was also a key theme for *Urania*. The journal consistently published a variety of 'lesbian-like' features, including love poetry between women, accounts of well-known romantic friendships such as that of the Ladies of Llangollen, scholarly articles on Sappho's poetry, many stories of cross-dressed female husbands, including the contemporary case of 'Colonel Barker', and reports of the trials of the lesbian novel *The Well of Loneliness*.[21] It also printed homoerotic descriptions of the admiration of younger women for older women and stories of women's attraction to androgynous figures. In 1919 an extract from the Irish poet Katherine Tynan's autobiography was published, describing her passionate attachment to an older girl at convent school:

> what was it that turned the January morning to June and made the chilly dark rose-coloured and shining? In the dark corridor on the way to mass, as we passed the warm kitchen, delightful on a cold winter morning, she came behind me and kissed me. Oh, delight! Oh, ecstasy! *Was there anything in more mature passions quite as good?*[22]

Urania's celebration of passion between women echoes the loving relationships engaged in by many turn-of-the-century feminists, including Roper and Gore-Booth themselves. These were experienced as a powerful and elevating form of love and commitment, comparable and indeed superior to heterosexual marriage.[23] But *Urania* had moved on from suffrage feminism, since it directly promoted the naturalness and desirability of love between women in contrast to the negative relationship of marriage and heterosexuality. This was quite extraordinary in the context of interwar feminism, where discussion of same-sex love was almost entirely avoided.[24]

Urania's approach also diverged from earlier feminist thinking in its rejection of motherhood alongside marital sexuality (earlier feminists such as Swiney and Elmy had idealized women's key role as mothers), and in its lack of interest in legislative change regarding male sexual exploitation of women. Its interest in cross-dressing and ideas about transgender stand out as very original (and virtually unthinkable) in the context of pre-World War I feminist debates on sexuality. Baty had originally floated some of these ideas in the Aëthnic Union and in the *Freewoman*, a magazine that between 1911 and 1912 published a variety of perspectives on sexuality and feminism, including explorations of sexological writing.[25] In developing these sets of ideas further between the wars, and arguing against the virtues of sexual expression and gender differentiation, *Urania* took a remarkably different line to most other contemporary feminist groups. Mainstream interwar feminism increasingly accentuated gender difference in its attempts to elevate the status of women, arguing for benefits for mothers and family allowances. Following the influence of sexology, some groups and individuals also championed birth control and women's (hetero)sexual pleasure. In this context, *Urania*'s project was innovative and extremely radical.

Urania and Sexology

Urania's sponsors had some contact with those feminists in the *Freewoman* circles who, before World War I, were interested in sexology. Such interest was located in radical fringe groups; sexology was not respectable or widely debated and certainly not taken on by the medical profession until after the war.[26] But given that *Urania* was published in the interwar years when sexological ideas were entering the mainstream, it is extraordinary that the journal never directly referred to the work of the sexologists. By comparing some key ideas in *Urania* with the sexological writing of Otto Weininger, Edward Carpenter and Havelock Ellis, we can see that there were some apparently common starting points (especially with Weininger and Carpenter's work), but that in important respects *Urania* took its feminist ideas along original and diverging tracks. Although using a different starting point (gender as opposed to sexuality), *Urania* was engaged with just the same sorts of themes as the sexologists: the social meaning of scientific research on sex and gender difference, how to improve relations between women and men, the place of sexuality in human life, same-sex relationships, and transgender behaviours such as cross-dressing and transsexuality. But *Urania*'s project was fundamentally different; it aimed to *resist* exactly those categories of sex and sexuality which the sexologists were busy establishing. Through its own feminist theorizing of sex and gender, *Urania* mounted a powerful, though indirect, critique of mainstream sexology.

Urania's discussions about the similarities of the sexes challenged the dominant stress on absolute gender difference, but did echo some early twentieth-century sexual theorists, including the Austrian philosopher Otto Weininger. There is no direct reference to Weininger in the extant published writings of the Aëthnic Union or *Urania*, but his infamous book *Sex and Character* was widely read in the feminist circles within which the editors of *Urania* moved.[27] In the first part of the book, published in England in 1906, Weininger argued that despite the contrasting nature of masculinity and femininity, there was frequently a considerable overlap or mixture of male and female characteristics within the physical and mental constitution of the human organism. Many people were in some ways in an intermediate condition between male and female:

> The fact is that males and females are like two substances combined in different proportions, but with either element never wholly missing. [. . .] Living beings cannot be described bluntly as of one sex or the other. The real world from the point of view of sex may be regarded as swaying between two points, no actual individual being at either point, but somewhere between the two.[28]

However, although the starting point was similar, the intended trajectory of these ideas was in very different directions for Weininger and *Urania*. After observing this overlap between the sexes, Weininger went on in his book to deplore it, arguing that the aim should be to encourage the ideal and opposing types of pure male and female, and he developed his theories along misogynist and anti-semitic lines.[29] In contrast, *Urania* celebrated the lack of sexual difference wherever examples were found.

The British socialist writer Edward Carpenter extended this idea of the blending of sex and gender in more progressive directions (although not as far as *Urania* was to go later). His project, like *Urania*'s, was utopian, politically charged, and allied with feminism. Roper and Gore-Booth are likely to have come into contact with Carpenter's work from their concurrent years in the northern labour movement and feminist circles.[30] Drawing on the ideas of Weininger and others, Carpenter wrote in his work on the 'intermediate sex' that the two sexes should not be seen as completely isolated, but as two poles of the human race, with a large number of people in the middle who shared some emotional characteristics of both sexes.[31] Carpenter thus suggested a continuum of gender difference, with a group in the middle, the intermediate sex, who had 'a union or balance of the feminine and masculine qualities'.[32] These urnings or uranians were 'on the dividing line between the sexes [. . .] while belonging distinctly to one sex as far as their bodies are concerned they may be said to belong *mentally* and *emotionally* to the other'.[33] They were characterised in particular by the tendency to form love relationships with one of their own sex. (On the face of it, *Urania*'s title appears to link back to the term urnings or uranian, but its meaning was not discussed in the extant issues of the journal.)[34] Liz Stanley has shown that many women found Carpenter's ideas about the intermediate sex helpful in locating their own love relationships.[35] Carpenter described the emotions of love and friendship as closely related, and not confined to the conventional pattern of love between people of the opposite sex, and friendship between those of the same sex. Although uranians were characterized by their same-sex attachments, Carpenter was at pains to stress that 'It would be a great mistake to suppose that their attachments are necessarily sexual, or connected with sexual acts. On the contrary [. . .] they are often purely emotional in their character.'[36] Such relationships had an important place in society; emotionally supportive comrade unions would enable individuals to do progressive work (for the liberation of women, for example) unhampered by conventional family ties.[37] These ideas have considerable echoes in the idealization of love between women found in *Urania*, which was represented as a natural and powerful attraction, though not necessarily a sexual force.

Though writers in *Urania* never referred to Carpenter, it is interesting to compare his ideas on sex and gender with those later developed by the journal. The characteristics of Carpenter's intermediate types were apparently identical to *Urania*'s ideal human qualities. He described men with 'a rather gentle, emotional disposition', who were intuitive and instinctive in their perceptions, with artistic feeling and inborn refinement.[38] The uranian woman had 'a temperament active, brave, originative, somewhat decisive, not too emotional; fond of outdoor life, of games and sports, of science, politics or even business [. . .] making an excellent and generous leader'. She was often to be found working in the public world, perhaps for women's advancement.[39] These are extremely similar to the new types of women and men discovered and applauded in the pages of *Urania*. But *Urania* was prepared to see a much more extensive breaking down of gender distinctions. Thomas Baty/Irene Clyde wrote in favour of men adopting ladylike and peaceful qualities, for example, while Carpenter described the more extreme and exaggerated intermediate types as unattractive and undesirable.[40] Furthermore, while Carpenter believed gender distinctions has been over-emphasized by society, he did refer to Nature as the determining force which created the actual mixture of femininity and masculinity in people, and the intermediate sex.[41] As discussed above, *Urania* took a more radical approach, suggesting that gender was entirely socially constructed, that the 'natural' situation would be one where qualities were not associated with gender, and that biological sex was not strongly fixed in the body either. While both conceptualized the phenomenon of gender confusion as a positive social development, Carpenter's model was one of a relatively fixed group of people on the dividing line between the sexes, whose function in the wider social order was to reconcile and interpret the two sexes (i.e. the rest of humanity) to each other.[42] *Urania*'s route towards the vision of a harmonious and feminist world was to undo the fixity of gender (and thus the harm caused by exaggerated masculine and feminine types), and enable all people, not just one group, to move into the fluid space of being without gender constraints.

Sexology and Science

Carpenter's ideas had become much less influential in the period after World War I when *Urania* was being published. Instead, the more scientifically based work of Havelock Ellis was being popularized. *Urania* gradually came to acknowledge the contemporary power of scientific discourses around sexuality. An article in 1937 looked back upon 'the disquieting phenomena' which had marked the period since the turn of the century. These included 'the growing sexuality apparent during the reign of King Edward the Seventh; and [. . .] the increasing tendency to worship the biologist'.[43] *Urania*'s ideas were completely contrary to those underpinning Ellis's model of sex, gender and sexuality, and the journal powerfully indicted the ideas of mainstream sexology – its codification of gender and normalizing of heterosexuality – and the scientific basis upon which they were built. There were also significant textual differences between *Urania*'s presentation of ideas and that of the sexologists. Mainstream sexology circulated (in the first instance) through single-authored books, and ostensibly set out organized arguments supported by scientific research, giving 'sexual science' considerable authority. In contrast, *Urania* explored its arguments indirectly, through a bricolage of reprints: selected passages from biographies and autobiographies, poetry, book reviews, essays and newspaper reports. While editorial material was published from time to time, *Urania* shifted considerable responsibility for drawing conclusions to its readers.

Ellis worked from the premise that there were clear physical differences between men and women that were biologically determined through evolution and therefore not susceptible to alteration. These essential sex-specific characteristics were described in his early book *Man and Woman* (1894). In so far as he did acknowledge some stages between the complete male and the complete female, he explained this 'intersexuality' as an inborn (and therefore fixed) phenomenon, brought about by hormonal abnormality.[44] In its view of the world, *Urania* proposed the exact opposite – that sexual difference was unnecessary and undesirable, and that sex was mutable in every physical body. The journal at times challenged sexological beliefs on their own terrain of scientific authority. In

1924, for example, *Urania* described a lecture to the Royal Institution in which a scientist drew attention to sex changes in frogs, newts, fish and birds, some occurring naturally and some under experimental conditions.[45]

In the 1920s *Urania* relied on stories of cross-dressing and mistaken identity to support its arguments for gender flux. But from the mid-1930s, the journal also drew attention to a number of case studies of spontaneous physical sex changes. Typical stories along these lines were those of young women (or men) gradually, or suddenly, developing the physical characteristics of the opposite sex:

> 'Sex Is An Accident'. Two Yarmouth 'sisters', Marjorie and Daisy Ferrow of Middlegate Street, are no longer 'girls' but 'boys'. After leaving home for a period they have returned in trousers, smoking pipes and with the names of Mark and David. Marjorie, now 17, won a scholarship to a central school, but had to leave at 13 when her voice deepened and masculine characteristics began to appear. Later, she tried to study at Yarmouth Art School, but so many embarrassing incidents occurred that she left. Eventually she entered the London Hospital for treatment.[46]

Rather than be governed by biology, it might be possible to use science in a more proactive way to *create* the brave new world of post-gender. This approach was especially apparent in the late 1930s' editions of *Urania*, which enthusiastically (and uncritically) lauded the beginnings of medically assisted sex-change operations. The 'Authentic Change of Sex' of a Czech athlete was reported as a front-page news story in 1936, and the following editorial article delightedly commented that this was 'a clinching corroboration of our main thesis: that sex is an accident'.[47] The subsequent issue claimed 'Another Extraordinary Triumph' in describing the (female-to-male) sex change of the British athlete Mary Weston, including an operation at the Charing Cross Hospital.[48]

For sexologists like Ellis, the biological basis of sexual difference led directly to the inevitability of the 'sexual impulse', explained scientifically as involving the chromosomes, glands and endocrine system.[49] Human sexual courtship was a biological process mirrored throughout the animal world, involving innate sex-differentiated behaviour, the male taking the active part and wooing the passive but responsive female.[50] Following the growing influence of these sexological ideas during the 1920s, *Urania* increasingly criticized what it termed 'materialism', (i.e. biological determinism) a growing trend that worked against its cause. In 1930, an anonymous editor (probably Clyde/Baty) wrote in an article entitled 'The Slimy Enemy' that tradition and convention were not the only barriers to *Urania*'s ideal of abolishing sex distinctions. 'A far more serious and sub-

tle enemy has to be overcome. And that is pseudo-scientific Determinism
– in other words, Materialism. The spirit is conceived of as a function of
the body, and its character and energies as determined by the nature of the
bodily frame.' This led to the:

> fallacy of supposing that girls naturally are inclined by some inex-
> plicable alchemy to admire boys and *vice versa*. [. . .] Another as-
> pect of the same pseudo-scientific Determinism is seen in the *furore*
> with which the emancipated modern girl interprets her freedom as
> freedom to enslave herself to men. [. . .] But the physiological evangel
> is loudly preached, and the duty of faithful obedience to the laws of
> bodily existence bids fair to eclipse all instincts of the spirit.[51]

This condemnation of 'Determinism' can be read as a powerful attack on
sexological discourses of the Ellis type. *Urania* believed people could deliberately develop feelings and behaviours that were beneficial and morally correct, and the journal picked up on other examples of scientific
research to challenge the idea of sexual drives and innately gendered behaviour. In a long article entitled 'Instinct A Myth' in 1931, a series of
extracts was reprinted to argue that what were assumed to be animal
instincts were socially learned behaviour patterns:

> Dr Zing Yang Kuo shows that the supposed mouse-catching 'in-
> stinct' of kittens is in the main, not a mysterious kittenish anti-mouse
> urge at all; but an implanted taste imparted to the kitten by exam-
> ple. Just in the same way, the supposed mysterious mannish or wom-
> anish 'sexual instinct' is nothing but an implanted taste fostered by
> universal inculcation.[52]

To a Darwinian scientist like Ellis, the purpose of sexual drives was ultimately to foster the success of reproduction. Sexual intercourse was a
good and healthy function for women and men alike: Ellis weighed up the
disadvantages of celibacy and recommended marriage as the most suitable solution. Since women's main biological function was motherhood,
he also recommended that every healthy woman should bear children.[53]
As discussed above, *Urania* argued that sexual intercourse caused spiritual harm by emphasizing gender difference and the dominance of men
over women, and attacked the positive modern view of it:

> Pursuing the idea which we developed in our last issue, namely, the
> absurdity of deducing the mental and moral characteristics of per-
> sons from their physical constitution, we proceed boldly to chal-
> lenge a prevalent superstition of the day, to the effect that Love –
> and not only Love, but Art, Music and all Loveliness, – spring from
> sexual intercourse. This repulsive by-product of materialism appeared

shyly as a hypothetical suggestion in the eighteen-eighties, gathered confidence with the turn of the century, and now faces the world with the brazen assurance of an accepted truth.[54]

Urania turned the tables by rejecting this idea as a superstition. Its constant faith in the superiority of the mind and spirit over the body and its broad epistemological approach enabled *Urania* to draw on both science and myth in suggesting the possibility of reproduction without sexual intercourse. Citing examples of parthenogenesis and virgin birth in myths and legends, and as characteristic of other species, the journal assumed this was another scientific breakthrough which could be expected in the future.[55] *Urania* built up its argument that sex, gender and sexuality were culturally constructed from a whole range of sources. The editors welcomed Margaret Mead's contemporary anthropological findings which showed that different systems of social and gender relations were possible.[56] The paper also drew on historical and religious stories and myths, such as 'Amazons in the Ancient East' to suggest the existence of an (often hidden) cultural knowledge and memory in many different societies that gender was not fixed, and especially that the feminine could be powerful.[57] Such ungendered societies were not entirely 'unthinkable'.

Another central theme for *Urania*, which has parallels with sexological writing but also important divergences from it, was the journal's celebration of love between women, which it put forward as a template for love and passion in an ideal society which had transcended sexual intercourse and gender identity. Contemporary sexologists, in contrast, disparaged the female partnerships common among feminists.[58] Ellis and his fellow sexologists emphasized the primary model of lesbianism as an inborn condition. The female invert was likely to display masculine characteristics, including an active masculine sexual drive.[59] Inversion was thus linked to a fixed and 'scientific' idea of gender, and more firmly associated with actual sexual activity, as opposed to romantic love.

Urania's editors were clear about rejecting mainstream sexologists' emphasis on gendered behaviour as an inevitable aspect of the construction of 'the invert'. In an unsigned review of *The Well of Loneliness*, the writer (likely to have been Baty/Clyde), endorsed a model of love between women which was based on an idealized attraction, and condemned invented sexuality:

> There will inevitably be spirits in each garb who prefer their own type to the other. Since it is generally agreed that the feminine type is the more attractive and agreeable [. . .] it follows that feminine attachments must be expected. That they do not find expression in the violent and brutally limited physical form styled by the world 'perversion' is equally natural.

The writer made it clear that the problem with the sexological model was that it explained same-sex love in terms of the binary opposition of masculine and feminine, which it was *Urania*'s aim to abolish:

> The real *crux* of all problems of so called 'perversion' is not faced by the author. It lies in this, that the moralist and the novelist, in depicting a case of homogeneous affection, are prone to slip into attributing the distinctive shortcomings of the other sex to one of the pair. The 'perverted' girl must be masculine. The 'perverted' youth must be feeble and vain. [. . .] Her heroine, though bold and splendid, is not rough or inconsiderate. But still Radclyffe Hall cannot refrain from depicting her as masculine in shape and tastes. She is a 'mannish girl' [. . .] [but] [t]he really difficult problem arises when neither of the pair is 'mannish' and both are disposed to each other in an enthusiasm of maidenliness.

The reviewer went on to condemn, at least implicitly, the sexological model that desire had to be based on inversion, and on the attraction of difference. 'We have been accustomed to hear a great deal of "the attraction of opposites". But it is largely nonsense. [. . .] There is no attraction for anybody in mannishness or effeminacy. It was a gratuitous concession to popular foolishness on Radclyffe Hall's part, to make her heroine a little mannish.'[60] 'Perversion', for *Urania*, meant the imposition of society's conceptualization of same-sex love in terms of fixed gender characteristics, rather than love between women itself.[61]

Conclusions

This chapter has argued that *Urania* was a hybrid form of theorizing about gender and sexuality, meshing feminist politics with scientific discourses to produce a distinct feminist sexual politics. The longevity and persistence of *Urania* are impressive. It was apparently the only journal of its kind, and is important in challenging assumptions about the history of sexuality, taking a line on sex, gender and sexuality which was significantly at odds with the dominant politics of feminism and sexology in the interwar years. *Urania* was not a response to mainstream sexology and did not directly engage with it. The theories, premises and assumptions introduced by writers such as Ellis, Freud, Weininger or Carpenter might have barely existed for all the direct attention paid to them by *Urania*. The ideas put forward in the journal remained distinct and separate from sexology – it was not a reverse discourse. Instead we can see it as a set of negotiations around a model of radical transgender and same-sex love which was independent of sexology.

Urania's ideas were a huge challenge to contemporary sexological orthodoxies (which were themselves represented as radical), and undermined their philosophical and scientific assumptions. The contemporary sex reform movement was engaged in prescribing sexual identities and categories, exploring but also establishing notions of masculinity, femininity, heterosexuality and inversion. Gender differences were represented as having a fixed relationship to sexual identities, and variations were generally pathologized. In this context, *Urania* was highly transgressive, aiming to explore and break down the boundaries of what were understood to be immutable categories and instead foreground the liminality of gender, sexuality and the body.

Urania also shows that feminist ideas about sexuality did not all shift towards sexological discourses after World War I. In *Urania* we can see some continuing links with late nineteenth-century and suffrage feminist debates. This feminist approach has moved on in celebrating passion between women fairly openly, albeit still generally seen as a spiritual love, rather than carnal passion. There is also a movement away from the pre-war glorification of womanhood towards the celebration of a more androgynous type. By the interwar years, mainstream feminism had been co-opted into working within notions of traditional femininity, and embracing gender difference. Only a few feminists (including Winifred Holtby, whom *Urania* referred to as a friend) questioned this approach. *Urania*'s aim was to merge the best gendered characteristics into a transgendered ideal that was nevertheless recognizably feminine. Thus *Urania* demonstrated a unique feminist theory of gender, transgender and sexuality – a radical new direction, though in an inhospitable political climate.

Notes

My warm thanks go to Joe Bristow for a number of stimulating conversations over the years about *Urania*, and for his comments on earlier manifestations of this chapter; to Anna Clark for her comments and suggestions; and to Lucy Bland and Laura Doan for being helpful and careful editors.

1 Alison Oram, 'Repressed and Thwarted, or Bearer of the New World? The Spinster in Interwar Feminist Discourses', *Women's History Review* 1:3 1992.
2 For current transgender debates see Sabrina Petra Ramet (ed.), *Gender Reversals and Gender Cultures: Anthropological and Historical Perspectives* (Routledge, London, 1996); Zachary I. Nataf, *Lesbians Talk Transgender* (Scarlet Press, London, 1996).
3 Lucy Bland, *Banishing the Beast: English Feminism and Sexual Morality 1885–*

1914 (Penguin, Harmondsworth, 1995). For a different interpretation see Sheila Jeffreys, *The Spinster and her Enemies: Feminism and Sexuality 1880–1930* (Pandora, London, 1985).

4 Daphne Patai and Angela Ingram, 'Fantasy and Identity: The Double Life of a Victorian Sexual Radical', in *Rediscovering Forgotten Radicals: British Women Writers 1889–1939*, eds Angela Ingram and Daphne Patai (University of North Carolina Press, Chapel Hill and London, 1993), pp. 265–302.

5 Thomas Baty, *Alone in Japan: The Reminiscences of an International Jurist Resident in Japan 1916–1954* (Maruzen, Tokyo, 1959), p. 185.

6 Irene Clyde, *Beatrice the Sixteenth* (George Bell, London, 1909), and *Eve's Sour Apples* (Eric Partridge, London, 1934).

7 T. Baty, 'The Aëthnic Union', *Freewoman*, 22 Feb. 1912, pp. 278–9; Patai and Ingram, 'Fantasy and Identity', p. 280. It is likely that Baty met Roper and Gore-Booth around this time; the latter were supporters of the Aëthnic Union. I am grateful to Lesley Hall for her suggestion that the three may also have met through their association with the Humanitarian League.

8 Esther Roper, 'Introduction', in *Poems of Eva Gore-Booth*, ed. Esther Roper. Also see: Gifford Lewis, *Eva Gore-Booth and Esther Roper: A Biography* (Pandora, London, 1988), and Jill Liddington and Jill Norris, *One Hand Tied Behind Us: The Rise of the Women's Suffrage Movement* (Virago, London, 1978).

9 The lines quoted were from her poem 'The Shepherd of Eternity'. An obituary, unattributed but probably by Thomas Baty, was published in *Urania* 57 and 58 (May–Aug. 1926).

10 For Cornish see Patai and Ingram, 'Fantasy and Identity', pp. 279, 289. I am very grateful to Hilda Kean for suggesting that the J. Wade in *Urania* might just be the animal rights activist Jessey Wade, confirmed when I found her book, *The "Animals' Friend" Cat Book* (G. Bell & Sons Ltd, London, 1917), advertised in *Urania*.

11 *Urania* 13, Jan.–Feb. 1919. This is the earliest issue of *Urania* available in the archive collections so far traced in Britain. For circulation see *Urania* 14, Mar.–Apr. 1919; 101 and 102, Sept.–Dec. 1933.

12 Bland, *Banishing the Beast*.

13 Jeffreys, *The Spinster*, ch. 2; Bland, *Banishing the Beast*, pp. 217–22; Frances Swiney, *Women and Natural Law* (C.W. Daniel, London, 1912). Elmy had worked with Esther Roper in the women's suffrage and labour movements in Manchester, while as late as 1933 *Urania* republished a positive 1907 review of one of Swiney's books.

14 Diana Burfield, 'Theosophy and Feminism: Some Explorations in Nineteenth Century Biography', in *Women's Religious Experience*, ed. Pat Holden (Croom Helm, London, 1983), pp. 27–56; Jeffreys, *The Spinster*, pp. 35–9, 44; Bland, *Banishing the Beast*, pp. 167–8.

15 Part of statement 'To Our Friends' in each issue.

16 *Urania* 121 and 122, Jan.–Apr. 1937.

17 *Urania* 95 and 96, Sept.–Dec. 1932.

18 From 'Suggestion', no author but probably Thomas Baty/Irene Clyde, *Urania* 101 and 102, Sept.–Dec. 1933.

19 *Urania* 115 and 116, Jan.–Apr. 1936.

20 'Enfranchisement', *Urania* 109 and 110, Jan.–Apr. 1935.

21 See, for example, *Urania* 57 and 58, May–Aug. 1926; 99 and 100, May–Aug. 1933; 121 and 122, Jan.–Apr. 1937.

22 'An Irish Schoolgirl', from Katherine Tynan, *Twenty-Five Years' Reminiscenses*, in *Urania* 14, Mar.–Apr. 1919. Emphasis in the original.

23 Bland, *Banishing the Beast*, pp. 291–3; Sandra Holton, *Suffrage Days: Stories from the Women's Suffrage Movement* (Routledge, London, 1996), pp. 202–4.

24 Oram, 'Repressed and Thwarted', pp. 418–19.

25 T. Baty, 'The Aëthnic Union', *Freewoman*, 22 Feb. 1912, pp. 278–9. Dora Marsden, the main editor of the *Freewoman*, was acquainted with Eva Gore-Booth and Esther Roper, according to her biographer: Les Garner, *A Brave and Beautiful Spirit: Dora Marsden 1882–1960* (Avebury, Aldershot, 1990), p. 26. Letters from some former Aëthnic Union members were published in *Urania* in the early 1920s, showing a continuing connection with these circles.

26 Roy Porter and Lesley Hall, *The Facts of Life: The Creation of Sexual Knowledge in Britain, 1650–1950* (Yale University Press, London, 1995), pp. 161–3, 167–8, 208–9. Jeffrey Weeks, *Sex, Politics and Society* (Longman, London, 1981), pp. 142, 166, 181–4.

27 Porter and Hall, *The Facts of Life*, p. 164; Joseph Bristow, *Sexuality* (Routledge, London, 1997), pp. 38–9. Weininger was discussed in the pages of *The Freewoman*: Garner, *Brave and Beautiful Spirit*, p. 145.

28 Otto Weininger, *Sex and Character* (William Heinemann, London, 1906), pp. 8–9; Porter and Hall, *The Facts of Life*, pp. 164–5. I am grateful to Lucy Bland and Joe Bristow for stressing the relevance of Weininger's ideas to my research on *Urania*.

29 For an extended discussion of Weininger, see Bristow, *Sexuality*, pp. 37–43.

30 Liddington and Norris suggest links through a mutual friend, Enid Stacey: *One Hand Tied Behind Us*, p. 130; Lewis, *Eva Gore-Booth*, pp. 100–2.

31 Edward Carpenter, *Love's Coming of Age* (Methuen, London, 1915, 2nd edn), pp. 114.

32 Ibid., p. 115.

33 Ibid., p. 117. Emphasis in the original.

34 The term 'urning' was originally coined by Ulrichs to describe homosexual men and women, and adapted by Edward Carpenter, who spoke of the intermediate sex as 'uranians': Jeffrey Weeks, *Coming Out* (Quarter, London, 1977), pp. 30, 47; Carpenter, *Love's Coming of Age*, pp. 116–18.

35 Liz Stanley, 'Romantic Friendship? Some Issues in Researching Lesbian History and Biography', *Women's History Review* 1:2, 1992. Also see Bland, *Banishing the Beast*, pp. 263, 291–3.

36 Carpenter, *Love's Coming of Age*, p. 123, also see pp. 115–17; Edward Carpenter, *The Intermediate Sex* [1909], reprinted in *Selected Writings Volume 1: Sex* (Gay Men's Press, London, 1984), p. 214.

37 Carpenter, *The Intermediate Sex*, pp. 216–19.

38 Carpenter, *Love's Coming of Age*, pp. 124, 129–30.

39 Ibid., pp. 132–3.

40 Ibid., pp. 126–8.
41 Ibid., p. 115.
42 Ibid., p. 134.
43 *Urania* 121 and 122, Jan.–Apr. 1937.
44 Havelock Ellis, *The Psychology of Sex* (William Heinemann, London, 1933), pp. 194–7, 208–10. This was an abridged version of Ellis's *Studies in the Psychology of Sex* (1897–1910).
45 *Urania* 47 and 48, Sept.–Dec. 1924, reprinted from the *Weekly Despatch*, 11 May 1924. Also see *Urania* 113 and 114, Sept.–Dec. 1935.
46 *Urania* 139 and 140, Jan.–Apr. 1940, reprinted from the *News Chronicle*, 26 Aug. 1939; also see *Urania* 109 and 110, Jan.–Apr. 1935; 113 and 114, Sept.–Dec. 1935; 121 and 122, Jan.–Apr. 1935, and others.
47 *Urania* 115 and 116, Jan.–Apr. 1936.
48 *Urania* 117 and 118, May–Aug. 1936; also see *Urania* 131 and 132, Sept.–Dec. 1938, etc.
49 Ellis, *Psychology of Sex*, pp. 7–24.
50 Ibid., pp. 26–31.
51 *Urania* 79 and 80, Jan.–Apr. 1930; also see *Urania* 93 and 94, May–Aug. 1932.
52 *Urania* 85 and 86, Jan.–Apr. 1931.
53 Ellis, *Psychology of Sex*, pp. 24, 221–8; Weeks, *Sex, Politics and Society*, pp. 126, 128, 149–50; Jeffreys, *The Spinster*, p. 130.
54 Irene Clyde, 'Love and Eroticism', *Urania* 81 and 82, May–Aug. 1930.
55 *Urania* 24, Nov.–Dec. 1920; *Urania* 97 and 98, Jan.–Apr, 1933; *Urania* 127 and 128, Jan.–Apr. 1938.
56 *Urania* 115 and 116, Jan.–Apr. 1936.
57 *Urania* 47 and 48, Sept.–Dec. 1924.
58 Havelock Ellis, *Sexual Inversion* (Random House, New York, 1933 [1897]), pp. 261–2.
59 Ibid., pp. 222–3, 244–5, 250–1, 255–6; Ellis, *Psychology of Sex*, pp. 197–9.
60 *Urania* 75 and 76, May–Aug. 1929.
61 Emily Hamer's teleological reading of *Urania* as a lesbian/gay paper means she finds it difficult to account for *Urania*'s equivocation about *The Well of Loneliness*. *Urania*'s review has to be seen in the context of the tension between its transgender politics and the gendered sexological idea of inversion that it condemned. Emily Hamer, *Britannia's Glory: A History of Twentieth-Century Lesbians* (Cassell, London, 1996), pp. 71–2.

Index